Dishonoured by Philosophers

Upamāna in Indian Epistemology

Dishonoured by Philosophers
Upamāna in Indian Epistemology

Uma Chattopadhyay

D.K. Printworld (P) Ltd.
New Delhi

Cataloging in Publication Data — DK
[Courtesy: D.K. Agencies (P) Ltd. <docinfo@dkagencies.com>]

Chattopadhyay, Uma, 1955-
Dishonoured by philosophers : upamāna in Indian epistemology / Uma Chattopadhyay.
p. cm.
Includes bibliographical references (p.).
Includes index.
ISBN 13: 9788124605202
ISBN 10: 8124605203

1. Upamāna. 2. Knowledge, Theory of. 3. Philosophy, Indic. I. Title.

DDC 121 22

ISBN 13: 978-81-246-0520-2
ISBN 10: 81-246-0520-3
First published in India in 2009

Published and printed by:
D.K. Printworld (P) Ltd.
Regd. Office: 'Srikunj', F-52, Bali Nagar
Ramesh Nagar Metro Station
New Delhi – 110 015
Phones: (011) 2545 3975; 2546 6019; *Fax*: (011) 2546 5926
E-mail: dkprintworld@vsnl.net
Website: www.dkprintworld.com

To

Three Revered Persons

who respectively
brought me to Philosophy,
opened the world of Logic to me,
and
taught me enjoying Philosophy and Darśana

Preface

THIS book mainly considers the challenge of establishing the independent status of *upamāna pramāṇa*. The author's intention is to show why and how the *upamāna pramāṇa* is dishonoured as well as honoured in Indian epistemology. The peculiar status of *upamāna* in Indian epistemology attracted me since my undergraduate classes. These became much more interesting when we were taught *Nyāyakusumāñjali* in our postgraduate classes. I was really surprised to see the two important points:

(A) Only the two schools of Indian tradition admit this source and all the others are against this.

(B) The two schools again are admitting the same for two purposes.

In my PhD programme I wanted to see the matter as closely as possible. I was fortunate to have my revered teacher Professor Pradyot Kumar Mukhopadhyay of Jadavpur University as my supervisor at this time. Though the research took a long time to be completed, I had the rare opportunity of prolonged interactions with him during this period. It was possible to study a considerable number of original texts in connection with my research under his able guidance. My indebtedness to him is boundless. I should also mention the unusual closeness I had during the time of research with two stalwart *paṇḍit*s of West Bengal in the twentieth century. They were the Late Pandit Narmada Tarkatirtha and Pandit Panchanan Shastri, both of whom had a deep academic expectation from my studies of original texts with them. Over and above all, I had the rare opportunity of meeting the legendary Professor Gopinath

Bhattacharya several times during his lifetime and immensely benefited from my interactions with him.

In this book I have done some revision and also given a consistent and limited shape of my research. Here, I have considered the views of both the Nyāya and Mīmāṁsā. Finally, I have defended the Nyāya position following the view of Udayanācārya. Udayanācārya in a sense is considered as the foremost philosopher in the Navya-Nyāya tradition. It would have been better if I could include the views of Gaṅgeśa Upādhyāya, the famous and the chief exponent of Navya-Nyāya tradition, but I could not. I have, of course, the desire to write on Gaṅgeśa in future.

The striking feature which I want to show all through this work is this. Some philosophers such as the Buddhists, Jainas and Sāṁkhyas or even those in the sister-system of Nyāya, the Vaiśeṣikas are against *upamāna*. But at the same time, barring a few, most of the Nyāya and Mīmāṁsā philosophers from the Sūtra-Bhāṣya texts to the recent literature are in favour of this and admits the independent status of the *upamāna*.

In course of developing the views of different philosophers many important issues are considered, such as the issue of language learning process in some particular cases or the metaphysical status of *śakti* (word-meaning relation) and similarity at least from the Buddhist standpoint. The question also is raised : Is *upamāna* an useful *pramāṇa*? The views of the Buddhist logicians are given much importance to have the deeper understanding of the issue. However, the book is neither a historical account of the views nor is a descriptive exposition of the theory of *upamāna*. This text is an analytical and not merely a textual study of the theme of *upamāna*. But on the basis of my close study in original Sanskrit, I have arranged and developed the thesis of *upamāna* in a logical and analytical way. Here by "Theories of *upamāna*" I understand the positive theories of *upamāna*. So I have given effort to elaborate the theories of

Mīmāṁsakas and the Naiyāyikas. The views of a number of internal and external critics of the positive theories of *upamāna* have also been considered. The different philosophical views relating to *upamāna* belong to different ages distributed over several centuries. Their style of thinking and writing are widely different.

I am happy to mention here that I found Jayanta most enjoyable. In Mīmāṁsā I found Prabhākara most difficult and Pattabhiram Shastri most easily intelligible. But contemporary to Pattabhiram Shastri, Pandit Badrinath Shukla, the great Naiyāyika, has written on *upamāna* (mostly unpublished) more extensively than Pattabhiram Shastri. This also was very much enjoyable to me. Excepting Kumārila, Mīmāṁsā philosophers in general have written far less extensively on *upamāna* than the Nyāya philosophers. This, and not my subjective bias, has helped me to defend the Nyāya position.

My desire for the present publication is long standing. While taking my viva-voce examination for the Ph.D degree years ago, it was Prof. Raghunath Ghosh, now Dean, Faculty of Arts, North Bengal University, who first suggested me to make my dissertation a book for larger audience. I am grateful to Professor Ghosh for this early suggestion. I was late in doing the same for some deep emotional reasons. For bringing me out from the crisis, Professor Arun Bandopadhyay, former Dean of Arts and currently Nurul Hasan Professor of History, University of Calcutta was mainly instrumental. He inspired me greatly for the new venture of publication of the book. His inspiration and co-operation is immeasurable.

Professor Suranjan Das, Vice-Chancellor, University of Calcutta took keen interest in the publication of this volume. I am deeply obliged to him for this expression of support.

My brother Dr. Chandan Kumar Goswami, Reader and Head, Department of Philosophy, Jogesh Chandra Choudhuri

College, Kolkata is another scholar who came forward to do immense help in preparing the manuscript for final publication. I pray to God for blessings for him and for his loving family. My esteemed colleague Professor Subir Ranjan Bhattacharya of the Department of Philosophy, University of Calcutta has always encouraged me to complete the book. I am grateful to him. My other beloved colleagues Dr Manidipa Sanyal, Dr Krishna Chatterjee, Dr Sarmistha Bakshi and Dr Aparna Banerjee have been very much positive in different ways. Dr Nini Chanda, our Head of the Department, helped me to concentrate on the matter by her good leadership for the Department. I am obliged to them all.

Some of my teachers of Jadavpur University influenced me in many ways during my study there and after. Special mention should be made of Professor Sukharanjan Saha, Professor Tapan Kumar Chakraborty, Professor Krishna Roy and Professor Sreelekha Dutta. I owe more to them than they know. I convey my regards.

My senior colleagues, Professor Indrani Sanyal, Professor Ratna Dutta Sharma and my friend Professor Madhumita Chattopadhyay of Jadavpur University have been constantly with me in all academic pursuits. Their silent co-operation is unforgettable. My friend Dr Gopa Gupta, Reader and Head of the Department of Philosophy, Bethune College, Kolkata is a real friend indeed. I have deep obligation to her in many ways.

Professor Nilima Misra, former Principal of Bethune College, Kolkata, Professor Puspa Misra, former Head of the Department of Philosophy and former Principal of the same College, Professor Gopa Dutta, former Principal of Lady Brabourne College, Kolkata and currently President of Higher Secondary Council, West Bengal, Dr Aditi Nag Chowdhury currently Reader and Head of the Department of Microbiology, Lady Brabourne College constantly encouraged me to continue an academically creative career. Another very silent person Sri Jagadindra Samajpati, an official of the Government of West Bengal, did a lot for me. I am obliged to every one of them.

Dr Manjushree Chowdhury, former Professor of Philosophy, Rabindra Bharati University and my sister Dr. Sarbani Banerjee, currently Reader in Philosophy in the same university have always inspired my academic activities. A loving bondage developed among us. Smt. Annapurna Bhattacharya, daughter of the late Pandit Panchanan Shastri, frequently came to me and inspired me throughout the years almost as the representative of Panditmasai. Our relationship has been so familial as to require no formal obligation. But I am personally indebted to her.

My father and the elder brother of my father, and my father-in-law and the elder brother of my father-in-law had great trust in me and my academic future. None of them is alive today. I feel blessed that I may fulfil their dream partially by the publication of my book. My mother-in-law till her death in 2006, gave me all-out support in academic matters. My ailing mother is still giving me sustenance in her own ways. My *praṇāma* to them both. Throughout the days of research and authorship, the distraction created by four of my young relatives — Mumna, Nannai, Munia and Buri — remained attractive. I acknowledge their loving concern.

Earlier versions of some of the chapters of this book have been already published in the *Journal of Asiatic Society* and *Jadavpur Journal of Philosophy*. I am grateful to both these institutions. My deep gratitude is to Mr. Susheel K. Mittal of D.K. Printworld. He has unusually taken so much interest and care for this publication. I am also grateful to my computer typists Sri Somen Mukhopadhyay and Mrs. Tapati Mitra.

I feel proud in stating that I am grateful to my loving undergraduate and postgraduate students. Their positive attitude always gave me a deep inspiration. My M.Phil. and

Ph.D. scholars are also with me in their own ways. My academic obligation to my students is boundless.

I am very much obliged to my domestic supporters, my sisters Manju and Shibani. They are always with me and with my ailing mother and with their prompt domestic works. I could not have completed my academic work but for their constant assistance.

My greatest pleasure is to declare that my non-demanding son Bapan (Manasij) was always with me in my pleasure and pain. His loving attitude is always my strength of life. Arun, my husband, though not able to do the household work, is uncompromising about any gap, lacuna, break, or insensitiveness regarding my academic commitment. Research and publication are two different things. Without Arun's encouragement it was impossible for me to do this publication.

Finally, without the aid of the many persons mentioned above, the book would not have been published. My gratitude does not imply their endorsement. The mistakes in this book, large or small, are my own.

Kolkata **Uma Chattopadhyay**
Aug. 5, 2009

Contents

PART FOUR
Some More Objections from Internal and External Critics

PART FIVE
Positive Views of Two Naiyāyikas

Introduction
Setting the debate

EPISTEMOLOGY or the theory of knowledge is a common concern both for the philosophers of the East and the West. Different issues relating to knowledge are raised in epistemology. Certain issues or problems are common to both these traditions while there are some other issues where these two traditions have their own uniqueness. Regarding the nature and criterion of knowledge, for example, both these traditions have taken interest. But debate concerning the number of *pramāṇa*s (valid cognitions or sources of valid cognitions) is a unique issue in Eastern, particularly in Indian philosophical literature. Philosophers of Indian traditions are not unanimous with regard to the number of basic valid cognitions (*pramā*) or with regard to the process of these valid cognitions (*pramāṇa*). Perception (*pratyakṣa*) and inference (*anumāna*) are generally admitted by all the different schools. Of course, the Cārvākas and some Buddhist philosophers are the exceptions. Though the debate between the Cārvākas and others with regard to the status of *anumāna* is very strong, the debate regarding the number of *pramāṇa*s generally concentrates with regard to the other *pramāṇa*s, viz. *upamāna* (knowledge by analogy), *śabda* (knowledge from sentences), *anupalabdhi* (non-cognition) or *arthāpatti* (postulation), etc. It is to note that perception and inference are very much useful both for our day-to-day life and also for natural sciences. But the important question is: in addition to these two why the different schools of Indian philosophical traditions have admitted the other different kinds of knowledge and their sources (*pramā* and *pramāṇa*)? Philosophers of this tradition have given their own reasons for accepting such independent irreducible knowledge and their sources. In establishing their thesis, they have always considered the possible objections against their positions. Accordingly, in the vast literature of Indian philosophy we find the philosophers belonging to a particular school always providing some new arguments which were not given by his predecessors in favour of this philosophical position.

In addition to perception and inference, *śabda* (authority) is admitted at least as a valid cognition by all the Vaidika schools of Indian tradition. Accordingly most of them in their own way have taken the challenge for proving that *śābda* is a *pramā* even though they are not unanimous in accepting independent status of *śabda pramāṇa* (source of valid congnition). With regard to the *arthāpatti* (postulation) or *anupalabdhi* (non-cognition), the picture is different. These two *pramāṇa*s (valid cognitions or the sources of these) are admitted only by the Mīmāṁsā schools in Indian tradition. Accordingly they have provided a vast literature to prove their position against all the other schools. They have considered the possible objections and answered accordingly from their own positions.

This is not the picture in relation to the admission of *upamāna* (knowledge by analogy). In Indian philosophical tradition, excepting Nyāya and Mīmāṁsā philosophers, all the schools are against this *pramāṇa*. Either they have discarded this altogether or they have reduced it to other *pramāṇa*. But at the same time this is also an important feature that this *pramāṇa* is admitted by the two stalwart realist schools of Nyāya and Mīmāṁsā. The two schools at the same time admit this in two different senses. Both of them though admit that *upamāna* is knowledge by analogy, they differ with regard to the object of knowledge by *upamāna*. Here another very interesting point is to note that normally we see that the controversy about a thing amongst the parties is concerned with some minor points. But with regard to this *upamāna*, the Naiyāyikas and the Mīmāṁsakas differ on some major points. In fact, major agreement between them, that they both admit *upamāna*, is deceptive. They admit *upamāna* completely in different senses. There is no other *pramāṇa* about which this is true.

The next interesting point about *upamāna* which attracted my attention is the following. Of the four *pramāṇa*s which the Naiyāyikas admit, *upamāna* is completely different from the other three. For the other three are the *vastu sādhaka* while *upamāna* is only *śakti grāhaka*. The critics are of the opinion that while other means for *śaktigraha* (knowledge of word meaning relation) is present, there is no necessity of *upamāna* and more than that there is no need for giving *upamāna* an independent status with the other *pramāṇa*s like *pratyakṣa*, etc.

This is also to note that though Mīmāṁsakas have admitted *upamāna*, they have not taken much interest in giving a definition of this *pramāṇa*. While giving the definition of *upamāna*, at best Śabarasvāmī, the very early Mīmāṁsā philosopher, is not giving the definition in the way the definition is generally offered. Much care is taken by him with regard to the other *pramāṇa*s. The Naiyāyikas, on the other hand, are very definite with regard to the definition of *upamāna*. The Nyāya *sūtrakāra* himself has given the definition of this *pramāṇa* in *Nyāya-Sūtra* itself. But the important feature of the Nyāya tradition is noteworthy. First, from within the system some philosophers are very much negative with regard to this *pramāṇa*. They have reduced this to inference, etc. Secondly, the philosophers while providing a vast literature in favour of the other *pramāṇa*s, the literature with regard to *upamāna pramāṇa* is very scanty. But it may also be noted that most of the great commentators of Gaṅgeśa ignored that part of *Tattvacintāmaṇi* (*Upamānacintāmaṇi*) which discussed very extensively and critically the positive theories of *upamāna* in Indian philosophy. Almost every text of Nyāya and Mīmāṁsā philosophy includes as a matter of rule discussion on *upamāna*. But the discussion of *upamāna* often seems to be short and oversimplified. In the classical period, up to the time of Jayanta and Vācaspati Miśra, among the Naiyāyikas, and Prabhākara and Kumārila among the Mīmāṁsakas, the discussion on *upamāna* used to be more serious. The two other great Naiyāyikas, Udayanācārya and Gaṅgeśa Upādhyāya, studied the problem very seriously and extensively. But the later commentators and writers of the Nyāya school did not show any great interest. So all these make us to think that the source, viz. *upamāna* is somehow very much ignored and disregarded or dishonoured not only by the philosophers other than Nyāya and Mīmāṁsā, but also by the Naiyāyikas and Mīmāṁsakas who admit this *pramāṇa* without being very respectful with regard to this *upamāna pramāṇa*.

In 1983 Sampurnananda University published Pragalvācārya's commentary on *Upamānacintāmaṇi* of Gaṅgeśa. On this occasion the editor wrote in his Foreword "it is quite interesting to note that Pragalva is the only great *ācārya* who is known to have commented on *upamāna* section of *Tattvacintāmaṇi*. . . . It is not known to posterity whether Mathurānātha has at all written a commentary on *upamāna khaṇḍa*. . . . It is likely that he has not thought it worthwhile to comment on *Upamānacintāmaṇi*. . . . It is a pity, however, that . . . a number of commentaries on *Tattvacintāmaṇi* have seen the light of day, but a well-written commentary on *upamāna* section could not be published and presented to the academic world (Pragalvācārya, 1983)." This comment clearly shows that the philosophers did not bother to show regard to *upamāna* which was admitted by Gautama in the original *sūtra*. In the Mīmāṁsā school also this topic has been nearly ignored. For example, many writers have not discussed whether the definition of *upamāna* given by Śabarasvāmī was his own or of Upavarṣa. Similarly it has not been resolved or seriously studied who is the Naiyāyika or Jaḍannaiyāyika whose views

Śabarasvāmī is believed to have refuted.

All these made the point clear that the status of *upamāna* is not very strong. It is neglected, ignored and dishonoured by the philosophers of Indian tradition not only by the opponents of Nyāya and Mīmāṁsā but also by many Nyāya and Mīmāṁsā philosophers themselves.

But at the same time we should look at the point that in the Nyāya tradition the Sūtrakāra Gautama admitted this with the other three *pramāṇa*s and the very stalwart Neo-Naiyāyika Gaṅgeśa Upādhyāya has written his monumental book *Tattvacintāmaṇi* where he devoted one full chapter on *upamāna,* named as *Upamānacintāmaṇi*. The position of these two stalwart philosophers made me think and accept this *upamāna* after a thorough analysis in a dialectical method. So though the issue relating to *upamāna* is very old, yet the attitude of dishonour and honour meted out to this *pramāṇa* made me think about its real status. At least when both Gautama and Gaṅgeśa on the one hand and Śabara and Pattabhirama Shastri or the recent scholar like Badrinath Shukla on the other have given importance to this *pramāṇa,* it shows that there is ample scope for research on the epistemological issue of *upamāna*. It will be like honouring the dishonoured.

In this text I have tried my best to consider different objections against *upamāna,* even the criticism of the Mīmāṁsakas against the Naiyāyikas. But finally I have tried to establish the Nyāya position and tried to show the usefulness of *upamāna*. I have taken the Nyāya position for very many reasons. One among the reasons is that excepting Kumārila, Mīmāṁsā philosophers in general have written far less extensively on *upamāna* than the Nyāya philosophers. The Nyāya theory of *upamāna* which I have finally defended is among the least explored areas of Indian philosophy. Considering everything, the Nyāya position appears to me more attractive and a very realistic one. My aim here is not to give a historical report on the very concept of *upamāna*. But I have tried to make an analytic study by the dialectical method about *upamāna*. So it is not merely a textual study. The nature of my work is such that I had to consult quite a number of original texts very closely. These works belong to different ages distributed over some fifteen centuries. The authors of these works are widely different in their views as well as style of thinking and writing.

Accordingly the views of a number of internal and external critics of the positive theories of *upamāna* have been considered. I could not make thoroughly the views of the schools like Sāṁkhya and Jaina, etc. But I have made reference to their characteristic tenets at the appropriate places.

Here the important point which I should mention is that if we want to have the complete picture of *upamāna* of the Nyāya tradition we should start from Gautama and should end with Gaṅgeśa or the philosophers who came after Gaṅgeśa. But as Gaṅgeśa himself is an institution and raised many important philosophical issues in relation to *upamāna*, here I am ending my discussion with the view of Udayanācārya.

As we are using the dialectical method, i.e. considering the views of all internal and external critics of Nyāya theory of *upamāna*, so our discussion on Udayana may make clear the Nyāya spirit regarding the acceptance of *upamāna pramāṇa*. In future if there is any scope for writing on Gaṅgeśa's *Upamānacintāmaṇi*, I would think myself blessed. The lesson that we get from Gaṅgeśa is this: instead of dishonour, the scholar should honour this *upamāna* which is not very similar with the other *pramāṇas*. At least there is ample scope of rethinking on the issue of *upamāna*.

I should now state in which ways I have made the discussion, and so briefly I have to sum up the arguments given in my different chapters. This book is divided into five parts, each part containing two chapters. The volume opens with an explanation of the classical Nyāya view of *upamāna* of Gautama and his followers like Vātsyāyana, Uddyotakara and Vācaspati Miśra. Here I have elaborated the nature of the knowledge of *upamiti* as understood in the classical Nyāya literature. Against the analysis of *upamāna* given by Vātsyāyana, Mīmāṁsakas could raise an objection. I gave a hint of it in the very first chapter. This enabled me to make easy and natural transition to the second chapter.

In the second chapter I have discussed the classical Mīmāṁsaka view of *upamāna* following Śabarasvāmī.

In chapter three, objections of Bauddhas and Vaiśeṣikas against the classical Mīmāṁsaka theory of *upamāna* have been considered. It has been shown from the Buddhist standpoint that the existence of similarity cannot be accepted. Here in this chapter it has also been explained from the Vaiśeṣika standpoint that *upamāna* is not at all needed for the knowledge of similarity.

Against these objections I have discussed the development of the Mīmāṁsā view in the Prābhākara tradition in chapter four. In this tradition similarity is held to be an independent category. So the admission of similarity removes the previous objection raised in chapter three. The Bhaṭṭas are the internal critics of Prābhākara so far as admission of similarity as a separate category is concerned. To give the complete picture of the Mīmāṁsā view of *upamāna,* I have considered the view of the Bhaṭṭa school. This chapter I have ended with the Neo-Mīmāṁsā view of Gāgābhaṭṭa.

In chapter five, I have presented the Bauddha and Vaiśeṣika criticisms either against the notion of meaning relation or against the notion of *upamāna* as a source of knowledge of this meaning relation. The Mīmāṁsā view so far appears to be superior to the Nyāya view of *upamāna*. For criticisms have been offered against the *śakti* relation and against *upamāna* as the source of knowledge of it. The Naiyāyikas admit *upamāna pramāṇa* to explain knowledge of meaning relation. But *upamāna* is understood differently by the Mīmāṁsakas. The Mīmāṁsā theory of *upamāna* cannot, however, explain the knowledge of denotation of words we know.

At this point I turned to the positive view of the Naiyāyikas in chapter six. I could show here that the Nyāya theory is indispensable, and cannot be replaced by the Mīmāṁsā theory. But answer has not been given to the objections which the Mīmāṁsaka philosophers raised and which we noted in chapter one.

In chapter seven I have considered the view of the internal critic of the Nyāya school. The famous internal critic is here Bhāsarvajña who has reduced *upamāna* to some other *pramāṇa*. The view of Bhāsarvajña can be named as *nyāya ekadeśī* view, which is very important from the Nyāya point of view. In the following chapter (chapter eight) I have considered some more objections against *upamāna* as such and Nyāya view of *upamāna* in particular. There I have also tried to give answer to such objections and dwelt on the unefulness of *upamāna*.

Considering all the possible objections against *upamāna* I come to present the positive view of the Naiyāyikas in chapters nine and ten. In chapter nine I have shown the view of Jayanatabhaṭṭa and in chapter ten I come to the conclusion by showing the view of Udayanācārya. The position of Jayanta and Udayana will make us understand how much the Naiyāyikas are logical in accepting a particular view on *upamāna*. At the end of the book I have also tried to re-open the question of the longstanding dishonour shown to this subtle theory of knowledge by analogy in Indian epistemology and thereby tried to remove some of the doubts raised about *upamāna*.

Part One

Classical Versions of Nyāya and Mīmāṁsā Theories of Upamāna

1

Nyāya Theory of Upamāna
Classical Version

THE subject of our study is *upamāna*. In the Indian philosophical literature the word *upamāna* is used in relation to and in contrast with the word *upamiti*. In the context of poetics or aesthetics (Alaṁkāra Śāstra) this word is a member of the pair *upamāna-upameya*. As an item of the said pair the *upamāna* stands for the thing (the moon) with which certain other thing is *upameya*. Two things are viewed as *upamāna* and *upameya* if they resemble each other. In the philosophical context certain knowledge of resemblance (and not one of the resembling thing) is called *upamāna*. In this context the word *upamāna* is taken as one of the words which carry the sense of *karaṇa* like the word *pramāṇa*. Accordingly the word *upamāna* means a *karaṇa* and a *pramāṇa* The word *pramāṇa* means *karaṇa* of *pramā*. So in its philosophical sense the word *upamāna* or the knowledge of resemblance is a *karaṇa* of a *pramā*. So there must be a corresponding *pramā*. This *pramā* or the class of such *pramā* is called *upamiti*. We shall later see that the existence of the knowledge of the kind called *upamiti* is controversial. Similarly the objective existence of resemblance is also disputed. But if there is no objective similarity then there is no objective basis of comparison. Nor is there any objective meaning of our statements of comparison.

The word *upamāna* is sometimes used in a broader sense. In this sense it can be understood to mean either *upamiti* or *upamiti-karaṇa* depending on the context. Standard grammar permits derivation of both these meanings. From the grammatical point of view the word *upamāna* is a complex expression. It is constituted by an *upasarga* (prefix), *dhātu-prakṛti* (a verbal root) and a *pratyaya* (suffix). Therefore the structural analysis of the word *upamāna* is *upa* + *mā* + *lyut*. The suffix may or may not add anything by way of meaning to the word *upamā* to which it is added to form the word *upamāna*. When it adds any meaning it adds the meaning *karaṇa* and then the word *upamāna* means *upamiti-karaṇa*.

I

In Indian tradition more than one school admit this *upamāna pramāṇa*. The author arranges the views of *upamāna* of these rival schools keeping the Nyāya view in the centre. The author will compare other views in terms of their nearness to or remoteness from the Nyāya view. In Indian philosophical literature the picture is this. *Upamāna* has been admitted mostly by the realist philosophers. The Advaita Vedāntins are the exceptions. But it is known that their theory of *pramāṇa* (including *upamāna*) mostly follow the Bhāṭṭa Mīmāṁsaka. In Indian philosophical tradition there are three major realist schools. They are Nyāya, Vaiśeṣika and Mīmāṁsā. Of these three schools the first and the third accept *upamāna* as a distinct *pramāṇa* while the Vaiśeṣika realist does not admit *upamāna* as a distinct source of valid cognition.

I propose to begin with the exposition of the classical versions of the theory of *upamāna* which we find in the Nyāya and Mīmāṁsā literature. In this chapter, I shall state the *prācīna* or classical Nyāya position. From there we can make a natural transition to the *prācīna* or classical Mīmāṁsā view. There is another reason why I want to begin with the Prācīna Nyāya account. Kaṇāda the Vaiśeṣika *sūtrakāra* is older than Gautama. But whereas in Gautama we find a fully developed and explicitly stated theory of *upamāna* we do not find this either in Kaṇāda or in Jaimini. Vaiśeṣika view is found in some detail in

Praśastapāda and Mīmāṁsā view in Śabara. Both of them flourished after Vātsyāyana and both of them criticized in some sense the sort of view the Naiyāyikas including Vātsyāyana held. Praśastapāda ends by reducing *upamāna* to *śabda* and (since he reduces *śabda* to *anumāna*) finally to *anumāna*. Śabara offers a new account of *upamāna* and argues that *upamāna* so considered is a separate *pramāṇa*. Thus Praśastapāda reduced *upamāna* to some other *pramāṇa*. Śabara revised the account of *upamāna* which is available in some other school, say Nyāya. In this way keeping the Nyāya view in the centre we can arrange all other views about *upamāna*.

But in presenting the initial version of the Nyāya theory of *upamāna* we face some difficulties. The reason is this. There is no single version of Nyāya theory of *upamānu*. The views or formulations of Gautama, Gaṅgeśa, Bhāsarvajña or Jayanta are somewhat different. It seems that the Nyāya theory of *upamāna* has been formulated, understood and interpreted somewhat differently by different Naiyāyikas over the ages. In the present chapter we shall first consider the classical version of this theory. But there seem to be more than one versions of this theory even in the classical period. For convenience of discussion we shall divide the history of Nyāya into three periods. I shall describe as Medieval Nyāya the views of Udayanācārya, though he also wrote a commentary on a sub-sub-commentary on Vātsyāyana who belonged to the classical period of Nyāya. So under the head *prācīnanyāya* or classical Nyāya I shall discuss the views of Gautama and of those who wrote commentary or sub-commentary on Gautama's *Nyāya Darśana* or *Nyāya-Sūtra*. So Viśvanātha's view as we find in his *Vṛtti*[1] will be discussed under

1. There is a controversy as to whether the author of *Vṛtti* and the author of *Bhāṣā Pariccheda* are one and the same Viśvanātha. There is also a controversy regarding the authorship of *Bhāṣā Pariccheda*. See Pandit Panchanan Shastri, 1377 (B), Introduction, pp. 1-2.

Prācīna Nyāya. Views of Gaṅgeśa and his followers will be discussed under Navya-Nyāya. The views of the author of *Bhāṣā Pariccheda* will be considered also as Navya-Nyāya view. We will consider as Prācīna Nyāya the views of both Bhāsarvajña and Jayanatabhaṭṭa.[2]

Before going to the detailed discussion of classical Nyāya, the very interesting feature is to note that the Naiyāyikas not only developed their theory of *pramāṇa, prameya,* etc. but they also developed very early a theory of theory. In his *Bhāṣya* Vātsyāyana clearly stated the nature and form of a philosophical theory. He said there that a scientific theoretical discussion of a topic consists in naming, defining and examining the thing under consideration.[3]

This conception of a theory is generally accepted by the theoreticians in Indian tradition. So the philosophers not only expound their theory, they expound their theory in a particular way. They first introduce a topic by verbally mentioning it. This is *uddeśa.*[4] Then they define the topic; and after that they examine the definition to test whether it is tenable. Accordingly in expounding the theory of *upamāna,* a Naiyāyika introduces and defines *upamāna* and then examines the definition given and also narrates all related matters.

---

2. This will be done following the normal practice of referring to Jayanta as jaḍannaiyāyika; and Bhāsarvajña preceded Jayanta. But according to Gopinath Kaviraj, both Bhāsarvajña and Jayanta belong to the medieval period of Nyāya. We have however revised this scheme slightly in this work which is not a historical treatise. We take Udayana to mark the beginning of the middle age, when the two different schools of old-Nyāya and old-Vaiśeṣika were combined into the syncretic school of Nyāya-Vaiśeṣika.

3. *trividhā ca asya śāstrasya pravṛttiḥ — uddeśaḥlakṣaṇaṁ parīkṣā ceti* — Vātsyāyana (1985), p. 83, under *sūtra* 1.1.2.

4. *nāmadheyena padārthamātrasya abhidhānam uddeśaḥ,* ibid., p. 84.

Now in his *sūtra* 1.1.3 Gautama first introduced *upamāna* by name.[5] From this aphorism it is clear that according to the Naiyāyikas *upamāna* is one of the four *pramāṇas*. Whether that *pramāṇa* is actually a *pramāṇa* or whether it is an independent *pramāṇa* is a point of controversy. Gautama will discuss all these later but here in 1.1.3 Gautama has included the name of *upamāna* in enumerating the *pramāṇas*. In *sūtra* 1.1.6 Gautama has given the definition of *upamāna*. How far the definition is acceptable and whether *upamāna* is really an independent *pramāṇa* have been considered in the *sūtras* 2.1.44–2.1.48 of *Nyāya-darśana* or Gautama's book of *Nyāya-Sūtra*. In that connection Gautama has stated critical examination of rival views and finally stated that *upamāna* actually is an independent *pramāṇa*.

The *sūtra* 1.1.6 as it stands is *prasiddha sādharmyāt-sādhyasādhanam upamānam*. It means in English, *upamānam* (analogy or knowledge by analogy) is the knowledge of the *sādhya* which results from *prasiddha* (known) similarity. Without the help of the commentaries and sub-commentaries the meaning of the *sūtra* cannot be understood clearly. Uddyotakara has shown that at least there are two ways in which the word *prasiddha* may be taken to be related to the other word *sādharmya*.[6]

Similarly Vācaspati Miśra has clearly indicated that it is the definition of *upamiti* and not of *upamiti-karaṇa*. So we should understand by the word *upamāna* here *upamiti*. From the statement of Vātsyāyana, it is clear what we are to understand by the word *sādhya*. In the light of all these clarifications the definition given in the *sūtra* 1.1.6 can be translated in this way. *Upamāna* is the knowledge (*sādhana*) of the relation a name has

5. *Nyāya-Sūtra* 1.1.3. Gautama (1985), p. 85.

6. *prasiddha sādharmyāt iti, prasiddhaṁ sādharmya yasya, prasiddhena vā sādharmya yasya, so ayam prasiddhasādharmyo gavayaḥ* — Uddyotakara, 1985, pp. 168-69.

(*samākhyā sambandha*) with its object, and this knowledge is caused by known similarity (*prasiddha sādharmyāt*).

From the above analysis it is clear that the definition given in this *sūtra* is the definition of *upamāna*; the word *upamāna* is *lakṣyapara*, i.e. it stands for the thing to be defined. But the word may mean both *upamiti* and the special cause of it (*upamāna pramāṇa*). So the question is this: Is it then a definition of *upamiti*- (knowledge by analogy, i.e. knowledge of *śakti* which results from the knowledge of *sādṛśya*)? Or is it the definition of *upamiti-karaṇa* that is special causal means of *upamiti*? Vācaspati Miśra suggests in his sub-sub-commentary *Tātparyaṭīkā* that it is the definition of *upamiti* or knowledge (*pramā*) which results from the third of the four *pramāṇa*s which the Naiyāyikas admit. Accordingly the whole *sūtra* actually becomes *prasiddhasādharmyāt sādhya sādhanam upamitiḥ*. Vācaspati Miśra tells us that if we are to get the definition of *upamiti-karaṇa* then we are to add to this *sūtra* the word *yataḥ*.[7] This word means "from where." Now according to Vācaspati Miśra the definition of *upamiti-karaṇa* is *yataḥ prasiddha sādharmyāt sādhya sādhanam upamānam* (i.e. *upamiti-karaṇam*). But one may think that the word *prasiddha-sādharmyāt* in the definition is an answer to the question "from where?". We will answer from *prasiddha sādharmya*, i.e. *prasiddha-sādharmyāt*. But if *prasiddha sādharmya* is the *pramāṇa* or special cause then the knowledge which results from it is *upamiti*. If it is said *yataḥ sādhya-sādhana* is *upamiti-karaṇa*, and *prasiddha-sādharmyāt sādhyasādhanam* then *prasiddhasādharmya* is *upamiti-karaṇa* and *sādhyasādhana* is *upamiti*.

---

7. *Upamānam upamitiḥ yata ityadhyāhāreṇa ca karaṇa lakṣaṇam*, Viśvanātha, 1985, p. 169. Viśvanātha has also considered this as a possible interpretation. But he thinks in the first place that the word *sādhana* in the *sūtra* 1.1.6 means the *karaṇa* (of *siddhi*) rather than *siddhi*. If this interpretation is accepted then there is no need to posit (*adhyāhāra*) the word *yataḥ*. Jayanta also thinks the same. Pt. Phanibhusan Tarkavagisa has noted this. Phanibhusan, 1989 (2nd impression), p. 188.

Vācaspati Miśra tells us here in this context that if the definition of *upamiti* is only *sādhyasādhanam* then the definition will be too wide. It will apply to the *sādhana* of perception or again to a jar which is *sādhana* of pleasure,[8] etc. An earthen jar (*ghaṭa*) is also *sādhyasādhana* or cause of something to be brought into existence. For it causes pleasure or perception of it (jar). Most of the things can be considered as *sādhana* in relation to something or other. But *upamāna* is not a *sādhana* of any or every *sādhya*; it is *sādhana* or *samākhyā jñāna*. As *sādhana* also it is different from other *sādhana*, for it causes its effect depending on known similarity. So Gautama has inserted the term *prasiddha sādharmyāt* in the *sūtra* 1.1.6 which states the definition of *upamāna*. Again if the definition were construed simply as *prasiddha sādharmya*, then the definition would have been over-inclusive; it would cover both *upamāna* or *upamānābhāsa*.[9]

A piece of cognition which appears to be *upamāna* but is not really so may result from known similarity. But in *upamānābhāsa* we cannot know the real object (the real *samākhyā-sambandha*). This *upamānābhāsa* is discarded by inserting the clause *sādhya-sādhanam* in the definitional statement. It is only *upamāna* (and not *upamānābhāsa*), which according to the Naiyāyikas knows the relation between a word or a name and the corresponding object. This relation is here *sādhya* in a particular sense of the term. So this much we understand from the original *sūtra* of Gautama that *upamāna* is a *pramāṇa* in respect to the knowledge of *sādhya* which results from known similarity. And to avoid the difficulty to over-inclusiveness Gautama has formulated the definition in a particular way. Finally *sādhya-sādhana* means knowledge of a thing as the meaning (*vācya*) of some word.[10]

---

8. *sādhyasādhanamityucyamāne pratyakṣādi-sādhane sukhādi-sādhane ghaṭe prasaṇgaḥ* — Vācaspati (1985), p. 169.

9. *prasiddhasādharmyamupamāna-ityucyamāna . . . tadābhāsanirākaraṇāya sādhyasādhanapadopādānam* — Ibid.

10. *bhāṣyakāreṇa hi saṁjñitayā gavayapratipattiḥ phalaṁ sādhyasādhana padavācyamuktā* — Ibid.

The word *upamānam* which, in the *sūtra*, means *upamiti* tells us what thing is being defined or is the *lakṣya*. The word *sādhanam* means *siddhi* or knowledge.[11] The word *sādhya* means *samākhyā-sambandha,* i.e. relation of a word to the object it names.[12] This is how the words of the *sūtra* 1.1.6 have been explained by Vātsyāyana, Uddyotakara and Vācaspati.[13]

But the problem arises when we want to understand the real nature of the *pramāṇa*. What is meant by *prasiddha sādharmya* or known similarity? With regard to the nature of *sādhya* or the object known by *upamāna* we do not face much difficulty. In the commentary of Vātsyāyana it has been stated explicitly that *pratipatti,* i.e. knowledge is about *samākhyā sambandha,* i.e. *upamāna pramāṇa* knows the relation of meaning, i.e. *samākhyā*.[14] And from the commentary it has also became clear what this *samākhyā sambandha* means. It means *saṁjñā-saṁjñi sambandha*. In English *saṁjñā* is name while *saṁjñi* is the object which corresponds to a name. Accordingly this becomes clear that *upamāna* is the *pramāṇa* for the knowledge of the relation between name and the corresponding object. But difficulty arises when we want to know the nature of this *pramāṇa* only from the *sūtra*. From the *sūtra* alone we do not fully understand this. Some Naiyāyikas, the followers of Gautama, clarified the nature of this *pramāṇa*.

In his commentary Vātsyāyana says *prajñātena sāmānyāt*

---

11. *sādhanam siddhiḥ* — Viśvanātha (1985), p. 169; see also Vācaspati (1985), p. 168.

12. *sādhya padena samākhyāsambandha ucyate* — Ibid., p. 357.

13. (a) *samākhyā sambandha pratipattirūpamānārthaḥ* — Ibid. (1985), p. 169.

    (b) *sādhyasādhanam iti. samākhyāsambandhapratipattirūpamānārthaḥ* — Uddyotakara (1985), p. 169.

14. Naiyāyikas like Jayanta or Udayana called it *samaya*. Professor Ujjalā Panse (Jha) has noted that this *samaya* is equivalent with notions like *Śakti* or *Vṛtti*, etc. Ujjalā Panse, 1992, p. 101.

prajñāpanasya prajñāpanam upamānamiti.[15] From this sentence we understand that here the word *upamāna* stands for the resulting knowledge, i.e. *upamiti*. The sentence is to be understood to mean that *upamiti* is the knowledge of the object (*prajñāpanīya*) on the basis of the knowledge of *sāmānya*. Here the word *sāmānya* stands for similarity (*prajñātena sāmānyāt*). So, as we have already said, *upamiti* is the knowledge of *sādhya* (*samākhyā sambandha*) caused by the knowledge of similarity.[16] But now the question is what is the nature of this knowledge by analogy?

II

Vātsyāyana says *yathā gaurevaṁ gavaya ityupamāne prayukte . . . saṁjñāsaṁjñi sambandhaṁ pratipadyata iti.*[17] In this passage the sentence *yathā gaurevaṁ gavayaḥ* or, to translate, "as the cow is so is the *gavaya*," i.e. "bison is like cow" has been said to be *upamāna*. This account of Vātsyāyana is important. For Śabara could not accept this account. Śabara states *upamānam api sādr̥śyam asannikr̥ṣte arthe buddhimutpādayati, yathā gavaya darśanaṁ go-smaraṇasya iti.* (S)[18] May be Vātsyāyana's analysis gave Śabara an excuse for offering a different account of *upamāna*. Kumārila has held this view in his *Ślokavārttika*.[19] This point we shall discuss now. But before that another point to note which will be discussed in the third section when again the classical version of Nyāya theory of *upamāna* will be considered. The important point to note is that in his commentary on 1.1.6 Vātsyāyana has said more clearly than Gautama that *upamāna* produces *upamiti* which is knowledge of the word-meaning relation. This view

---

15. Vātsyāyana (1985), p. 168.
16. Viśvanātha says *sādharmmyāt-sādr̥śyāt, tajjñānāt*, Viśvanātha (1985), p. 169.
17. Vātsyāyana (1985), pp. 169-70.
18. *Jaimini-Sūtra* 1.1.5.
19. *Ślokovārttika* (*kārikā* 2) *Upamāna Pariccheda*. Cf. Kumārila (1978), p. 308; see also Parthasarathi (1978), p. 308.

of *upamiti* makes Nyāya theory of *upamāna* different from Mīmāṁsā theory of *upamāna*. These are the important points about Vātsyāyana's exposition of Gautama's view of *upamāna*. To repeat, Vātsyāyana says in his commentary on 1.1.6 that (1) the sentence *gaurevaṁ gavayaḥ* is *upamāna* and (2) *upamiti* is the knowledge of the meaning relation which a name bears to the thing which corresponds to it. The Mīmāṁsakas do not accept (2); they have a different view of *upamiti*. But so far as *upamāna* is concerned they think that it consists in the knowledge of similarity. To clarify this point of the Mīmāṁsakas, Śabarasvāmī offered in his *Bhāṣya* on *Jaimini-Sūtra* 1.1.5, the following definition of *upamāna*, *upamānamapisādṛśyamasannikṛṣṭe arthe buddhimutpādayati, yathā gavaya darśanaṁ gosmaraṇasya iti*. In the second verse (*śloka*) of the chapter on *upamāna* (*Upamānapariccheda*) of his *Ślokavārttika*, Kumārila makes the remark : *etasaminnupamānatvaṁ prasiddham*. . . . Parthasarathi in his *Nyāyaratnākara*[20] has made the point clear. The point is this. Akṣapāda (Gautama) has already offered a definition of *upamāna*. Śabara therefore does not need to define it again. Kumārila in the said remark anticipated this objection. In the rest of his second *śloka* in question Kumārila offers an answer to this objection. He thereby offers on behalf of Śabarasvāmī a justification for offering a new definition of *upamāna*. Both the objection and the answer to it presuppose that the earlier definition of Akṣapāda made the statement of analogy itself to be *upamāna*. But we know that in the *sūtra* 1.1.6 Gautama did not include explicitly the statement of analogy as *upamāna*. It is Vātsyāyana who explicitly said that *upamāna* is the statement of the form *yathā gaurevaṁ gavayaḥ*; this is what we call the statement of analogy. Parthasarathi in his *Nyāyaratnākara* on the second verse of *Upamānapariccheda* of Kumārila's *Ślokavārttika* formulates Nyāya view in this way: *kīdṛśogavayaḥ ityevaṁ nāgarikeṇa pṛṣṭo vanyaḥ prasiddhenagavā sādharmyāt aprasiddhaṁ gavayaṁ yena vākyena*

20. Parthasarathi, 1978, p. 307.

bodhayati yathāgauriva gavaya. iti tadvākyam upamānamiti. Thus according to the Mīmāṁsakas the classical version of the Nyāya theory of *upamāna* contends that *upamāna* is a certain sentence. It is a sentence which states similarity or analogy of some unknown thing (*gavaya*) with some known thing (*go*). And Kumārila thinks that Śabarasvāmī found this account unacceptable. So he was led to offer a different account and definition of *upamāna*.

But why does Śabara think that the statement view of *upamāna* is unacceptable? The answer has been given by Kumārila in the remaining portion of the second verse referred to above: . . . *śābare punaḥ tasyāgamābahirbhāvāt anyathaiva upavarṇitam.*

Thus according to Kumārila statement view of *upamāna* reduces *upamiti* to *śabda*. The point of Śabara's defining *upamāna* independently (and in a way different from the way in which it has been defined in the classical version of Nyāya theory of *upamāna*) is to prevent such reduction. The Mīmāṁsakas (both *pūrva* and *uttara*) distinguish themselves from the philosophers of Cārvāka, Bauddha, Vaiśeṣika and Sāṁkhya schools by holding the view that the number of *pramāṇa*s is at least five or more. In other words they hold that *upamāna* is a separate (*svatantra*) *pramāṇa*. One of the things meant by them is that the knowledge by analogy (*upamiti* = *upamāna*) is a distinctive or irreducible kind of knowledge. It is different from *pratyakṣa* (perception), *anumiti* (inference), *śabda* (knowledge by verbal testimony) and the like. So according to the Mīmāṁsakas and whoever holds *upamāna* to be a *svatantra pramāṇa*, knowledge by analogy is distinct from *śābda*. A knowledge which is different from *śābda* cannot be produced by the cause which produces knowledge by verbal testimony (or *śābda*). On the other hand if a knowledge is produced by what the Naiyāyikas call the cause of the knowledge by analogy, then the resulting knowledge cannot be *śābda*. For the cause of knowledge by verbal testimony is admitted to be sentence or *vākya*, i.e. linguistic utterance of sentence. In the classical version of Nyāya theory of *upamāna*, certain *vākya* (*atideśa vākya*) or statement of analogy has been said to be *upamāna pramāṇa* or special cause (*karaṇa*) of *upamiti*. Śabara is believed to think therefore that on Nyāya account, or on this version of Nyāya theory of *upamāna* (*upamiti*), turns out to be *śabda-jñāna* as it is caused by a sentence. He therefore defines *upamāna* differently. According to him and his followers *upamiti* is a knowledge which has for its object similarity and is caused by the knowledge (perception) of similarity. *Sādṛśya-darśanotthaṁ jñānaṁ sādṛśya viṣayamupamānam.*[21] Thus according to Śabarasvāmī *upamāna* consists not in the sentence but in the knowledge of *sādṛśya*; *upamiti* is *sādṛśya darśanottham.*

We have so far seen, following Kumārila, what justification Śabara has for offering in his own way a definition of *upamāna* in terms of knowledge of similarity. The justification in brief is this. The account of *upamāna* which is found in the classical Nyāya fails to keep *upamāna* distinct from *śabda*. Because that account makes *upamāna* to consist in the statement (sentence) of analogy; and makes *upamiti* an effect of such statement. This way of justifying Śabara may be alternatively construed as objection against Nyāya definition of *upamāna*. For Nyāya definition of *upamāna* may be seen as too wide as it covers *śabda-jñāna*. Thus we find in the classical theory of *upamāna* (transition to which we have explained so far) of the Mīmāṁsakas (Mīmāṁsā), objections against the Nyāya theory. The objections are the following. (MO. 1) The Naiyāyikas (of the classical period) failed to keep *upamāna* distinct from *śabda*, i.e. they have reduced *upamāna* to *śabda*. (MO. 2) The classical Nyāya definition of *upamāna* is too wide; it covers *śabda*. In fact, these two objections are two sides of the same single objection or two ways of formulating the same objection. The objection or objections have been brought against the classical version of Nyāya theory on

---

21. Śālikanātha, 1961, p. 267.

the assumption that in this version of the Nyāya theory of *upamāna pramāṇa, atideśa vākya* has been said to be the *upamāna pramāṇa*. I am to explain later and answer the objections and examine the assumption. But before doing that I shall first complete in the next section, the explanation and exposition of the classical Nyāya theory of *upamāna* as we find it in the *Nyāya-Sūtra* 1.1.6 and in the commentary and sub-commentaries on it. Then we shall pass over to the exposition of the Mīmāṁsā theory of *upamāna*. I shall explain and examine the objections and the assumption of the Mīmāṁsakas later.

III

In this exposition of the classical version of the Nyāya theory of *upamāna* as noted above two important statements are found in Vātsyāyana. The first one, viz. *gaurevaṁ gavaya ityupamāne prayukte* made it possible for the old Mīmāṁsakas to raise the objection I have discussed.[22] According to these Mīmāṁsakas the (classical) Mīmāṁsā theory of *upamāna* differs from the (classical) Nyāya theory of *upamāna*. For, the Naiyāyikas hold certain *vākya* or linguistic utterance to be *upamāna*. According to the Mīmāṁsakas *upamāna* is the knowledge of similarity. Later we shall see that even if there had been a section of Naiyāyikas who held certain *vākya* to be *upamāna*, Jayanta or Vātsyāyana did not hold this view. The standard Nyāya view in the classical, medieval and modern period is that *upamāna* is knowledge of similarity. From this one should not conclude that the Nyāya theory of *upamāna* and Mīmāṁsā theory of *upamāna* are the same. For even if there is no difference between Mīmāṁsā and Nyāya about the nature of *upamāna* there still remains difference between them in respect of the nature of *upamiti*. The second of the two statements of Vātsyāyana as I have noted earlier states clearly that (according to the Naiyāyikas) *upamiti* is the knowledge of the meaning relation which names bear to

---

22. See page 19 above.

corresponding things. But according to the Mīmāṁsakas *upamiti* is the knowledge of similarity of certain kind. Thus for the Mīmāṁsakas both *upamāna* and *upamiti* are knowledge of similarity. One type of similarity (i.e. similarity with a known thing, say cow, which exists in a hitherto unknown thing like *gavaya*) is known in *upamāna*; another type of similarity (i.e. similarity as existing in a thing which is not being perceived now), is known in *upamiti*.

Now we see the importance of the second of the two statements of Vātsyāyana. Sentence (2) states one feature of the classical Nyāya theory of *upamāna* — the nature or content of *upamiti*. It is this feature which distinguishes the Nyāya theory of *upamāna* from the theory of *upamāna* of the only other school, viz. the Mīmāṁsā, which accepts *upamāna* as an independent *pramāṇa*.[23]

Another important thing which I find in Vātsyāyana's exposition of the classical Nyāya theory of *upamāna* is the following. Vātsyāyana not only says that the use of *upamāna* is that it gives us knowledge of meaning relation (*samākhyā sambandha pratipattiḥ upamānārthaḥ*), but he also gives illustration of (a) this *sambandha* and also of (b) the *atideśa vākya* (statement of analogy). In addition he cites (c) a concrete context where *upamāna* comes to man's help.

The standard example of statement of analogy is "as is cow so is bison" (*yathā gaurevaṁ gavayaḥ*).[24] One may wonder if we ever need to be told "as is cow so is bison." In other words one may suspect that the whole theory of *upamāna* has some kind of artificiality. In literature, particularly in verse, one may make

23. Advaita Vedāntins generally follow in matters like *pramāṇa* the Bhāṭṭa Mīmāṁsakas. As it is said *vyāvahāre bhaṭṭanaya*.

24. *Gavaya* is usually translated as bison. But I have been told that this is slightly inaccurate. Some authors have used the term "Bosgavaeus," Satish Chandra, 1978, p. 94.

use of *upamāna* as a literary device. In such context, statement, e.g. (her) face is like the moon does not claim to be a *pramāṇa*. And the sentence is not needed for the knowledge that the word "face" means moon. The objection of artificiality however does not seem to arise when we consider the other contexts which Vātsyāyana has mentioned. He mentions one very concrete and realistic context. A medical practitioner or a manufacturer of herbal drugs wants some medicinal herb called *mudgaparṇī* (to be brought for medical purpose). The person who is to bring the herb does not know which herb is called *mudgaparṇī*. He is then told *yathā mudgaḥ tathā mudgaparṇī*, i.e. *mudgaparṇī* resembles *mudga*. This other herb *mudga* is familiar. The man now goes to the forest. There he finds a herb which is similar to *mudga*. He remembers what he was told. And now he comes to know that this herb (which he finds to be similar to *mudga*) is called *mudgaparṇī*. He then collects this herb and brings it to his teacher or employer for medical use. Vātsyāyana says all these in the words *yathā mudgaḥ tathā mudgaparṇī . . . ityupamāne prayukte upamānāt saṁjñā-saṁjñī sambandhaṁ pratipadyamānastamoṣadhiṁ bhaiṣajyāya āharati*. It may now be said that there are many such familiar, concrete and realistic contexts where *upamāna pramāṇa* is used. And there are also other contexts which are equally concrete and realistic though may not be equally familiar. Context of *upamāna pramāṇa* where some one needs to be told *yathā gaurevaṁ gavayaḥ* is such a context. During some sacrificial rite (*yajña*) a *gavaya* is to be brought for some use in that rite. The person who is asked to bring a *gavaya* or bison does not know what animal is called *gavaya*. Then he is told *yathā gaurevaṁ gavayaḥ*. This enables him to identity some animal which resembles cow as the referent of the name *gavaya*. And he then brings the *gavaya* to be used in the rite.

So far we have discussed following Vātsyāyana different contexts of *upamāna pramāṇa* and different examples of statement of analogy. Vātsyāyana has also said *evam anya api upamānasya loke viṣaya bubhutsitavyaḥ*. This sentence is found to be difficult to explain. The sub-commentators are not even unanimous why Vātsyāyana said this. We can not discuss it here in detail. However it may be noted that according to Vācaspati Miśra Vātsyāyana said this to suggest that we can know the meaning relation from the knowledge of dissimilarity also. Where one knows meaning relation not from similarity (*sādharmya*) but from dissimilarity (*vaidharmya*) we have what is called *vaidharmyopamiti*. But there arises a question: how can Vātsyāyana mean this? For Gautama in his *sūtra* has explicitly used the term *sādharmya*. How can the *sūtra* 1.1.6 be interpreted in the *Bhāṣya* to refer to *vaidharmyopamiti* also? Vācaspati Miśra has given an answer. He says, *sādharmya grahaṇaṁ ca dharma mātropalakṣaṇam iti*. In other words the word *sādharmya* in the *sūtra* is used on its general connotation which includes dissimilarity or *vaidharmya* also.[25] Viśvanātha holds a different view. He thinks that Vātsyāyana wanted to indicate that *upamāna* can know other objects also. We can derive from *upamāna* a knowledge of the meaning relation; but we can also know that the herb which resembles *mudgaparṇī* acts as antidote of poison.[26]

The last and most important point which we find in Vātsyāyana's exposition of the *Nyāya-Sūtra* 1.1.6 is the following. He says *yathā gaurevaṁ gavaya ityupamāne prayukte . . . asya gavayaśabdaḥ saṁjñā iti saṁjñāsaṁji sambandhaṁ pratipadayata*. From the illustrations of *upamiti jñāna* he gives here, i.e. *asyagavayaśabdaḥ saṁjñā*, it is not clear what exactly is the form or content of the knowledge by analogy. What he said here may be understood

25. Vācaspati (1985), p. 172; see also Viśvanātha (1985), p. 170 and Phanibhusan Tarkavagisa (1989), vol. I, p. 18, See also Shivkumar (1980), p. 19.

26. *evam anyo api upamānasya viṣaya iti bhāṣyam. tathā ca mudgaparṇī sadṛśī oṣadhī biṣaṁhanti iti atideśa vākyārthe jñāte, mudgaparṇī sādṛśya jñāne jāte iyam oṣadhī biṣaharaṇī iti upamityā viṣayī kriyata ityādi*
— Viśvanātha (1985), pp. 170-71

differently. The words of Vātsyāyana here are *asya gavayaśabdaḥ saṁjñā*; these words mean "the word '*gavaya*' is the name of it." This again may mean either *sannikṛṣṭasya gavaya śabda saṁjñā*. Or the meaning may be *gavayatvaviśiṣṭasya gavaya śabda saṁjñā*. Nyāya position may be developed along both these lines.

If we accept the first meaning then the content of the knowledge called *upamiti* (i.e. the knowledge by analogy) will be the following. The word in question (say, the word *gavaya*) is the name of the thing (say *gavaya*) which now stands related to the sense organ (*sannikṛṣṭa*). The form of the knowledge will be "this word (*gavaya*) is the name of it." Now there remains a doubt about how should we understand the "it" which is the referent of the word in question. Should we take it as qualified by *sannikṛṣṭatva* or by *gosādṛśya* (similarity to cow) or by *gavayatva* (the property of being *gavaya*). The final Nyāya view is that the thing may be present to sense organ and it may be similar to cow. But it is the referent of the word *gavaya* only as having the property *gavayatva*. Or *gavayatva* is the *pravṛtti nimitta* or *śakyatāvacchedaka*. We shall see later that *gosādṛśya* is not *śakyatāvacchedaka* but is *upalakṣaṇa*. Accordingly the Nyāya view is that *gosādṛśya upalakṣita gavayatva viśiṣṭa prāṇī gavaya pada vācya*.

2

Mīmāṁsā Theory of Upamāna
Classical Version

THE Mīmāṁsā view of *upamāna* is already introduced as a response to the view of Vātsyāyana.[1] It appears, therefore, that the classical Mīmāṁsā view is not as old as classical Nyāya view. It has also been suggested that this classical version of the Mīmāṁsā view was formulated by Śabarasvāmī. For, the definition of *upamāna* which we quoted before occurs in Śabara's commentary. Not only that, Kumārila in his *Ślokavārttika* and Parthasarathi in his *Nyāyaratnākara* have given the impression that the classical definition of *upamāna* was given by Śabarasvāmī. But Pandit Ramakrishna Mishra in his *Yuktisnehaprapūraṇī* has said *ayaṁ ca go samaraṇasya ityanto bhāṣya granthaḥ upavarṣa sammata eva, bhāṣyakāreṇa likhitatvāt ṭīkākārādibhi bhāṣyatyena eva uccyate.*[2] In other words, according to Ramakrishna Mishra the definition of *upamāna* which we quoted from Śabara's *Bhāṣya* on *Jaimini-Sūtra* and which we took as Śabara's own view, is actually the view of Upavarṣa.

There had been three *vṛttis* (a type of commentary) on Jaimini's *Mīmāṁsā-Sūtra*. The *vṛttikāras* were (1) Bodhāyana (2) Upavarṣa and (3) Bhavadāsa. Subrahmanya Shastri in his introduction to *Prakaraṇa-Pañcikā* has written "Śabarasvāmī wrote his *Bhāṣya* on the *sūtras* of Jaimini to elaborate the ideas of Upavarṣa contained in his brief *vṛtti* adding here and there

1. See above, Chapter 1, p. 19.
2. Ramakrishna Mishra, 1913, p. 208.

his own ideas."[3] So what Ramakrishna Mishra said may be true. Of course, one should not gather this impression that Parthasarathi Mishra has explicitly said that the definition *upamānam api*, etc. is Śabara's own. Referring to the relevant *Bhāsya* text he has only said in his *Nyāyaratnākara* (p. 308) that *anyādṛśam lakṣaṇam bhāṣye varṇitam*, i.e. "a different definition has been stated in the *Bhāṣya*."

Whatever that may be, Śabara has noted this definition in his *Bhāṣya*. He has not given any other definition as his own. Therefore we can take this definition to be Śabara's also, not in the sense that he is the author of this definition but at least in the sense that he accepts it.

Let us now explain Śabara's definition of *upamāna*. The definition is this: *upamānam api sādṛśyam, asannikṛṣṭe arthe buddhim utpādayati yathā gavaya-darśanam go-smaraṇasya*.[4] We shall later explain how Kumārila Bhaṭṭa and Prabhākara Miśra interpreted this text and further developed Mīmāṁsā theory of *upamāna*. Here I shall try to explain the meaning of this text rather independently. And in this matter I shall follow what has been written by Parthasarathi in his *Śāstradīpikā*. Let us first reproduce the English translation of the *Bhāṣya* text following Ganganatha Jha. Jha has translated the *Bhāṣya* sentence in this way: "Analogy also is similarity and brings about the cognition of an object not in contact with the senses; as for example the sight of the *gavaya* reminds one of the cow."[5] This translation is almost literal. It

3. Subrahmanya Shastri, Introduction in Śālikanātha (1961), p. iv.
4. Śabara has written this while commenting on *Jaimini-Sūtra* 1.1.5. Jaimini himself has not said anything about *upamāna* in that *sūtra* directly. He has said there that *śabda-pramāṇa* (*śāstra*) is the only *pramāṇa* when the object is *dharma* (duty). This gave Śabara an occasion to discuss the nature of other *pramāṇa*s which do not help us in knowing duty. Anyway, Śabara seems to be the first Mīmāṁsaka who gave a definition of *upamāna* which is different from the definition given by Gautama. See Śabara, 1983, p. 12.
5. Jha, 1985, pp. 222-23.

does not remove the difficulty in understanding the *Bhāṣya* text.

Parthasarathi in his *Śāstradīpikā* re-writes the statement of Śabara in this way: *pūrva dr̥ṣṭe smaryamāṇārthe dr̥śyamānārtha sādr̥śya jñānaṁ upamānaṁ — yā asau asmābhirangane dr̥ṣṭa gauḥ sā 'nena gavayena sadr̥sīti.*[6] The purpose of re-writing in this way is to bring out the meaning Śabara intended to express. And that meaning has been captured by Ganganatha Jha's English translation of Kumārila's *Ślokavārttika.*[7] So regarding the translation we do not have much difficulty. But we face difficulty in understanding the relation between the words of Śabara's statement. Neither Parthasarathi nor Ganganatha Jha tells us how the words in the statement of Śabara are related. But we need to understand the statement of Śabara.

Śabarasvāmī's statement which I have stated earlier (S) about *upamāna* has two major parts (1) *upamānam api sādr̥śyam asannikr̥ṣṭe arthe buddhim utpādayati*; and (2) *yathā gavaya-darśanaṁ go-smaraṇasya*. The part (1) seems to be the definition of *upamāna* according to the Mīmāṁsakas. The part (2) is added as an illustration. Now in the part (1) there is a word *api*. But why has this word been added here? It has been added here because the context demands it. Before stating this definition of *upamāna* Śabara has given the definition of *śāstra* (roughly *śabda-pramāṇa*). His definition of *śāstra* is, *śāstraṁ śabda vijñānāt asannikr̥ṣṭe arthe vijñānam.*[8] It means *śāstra* (*āgama* or knowledge by testimony) is the knowledge of some object which is not in contact with the senses and which is produced from the knowledge of *śabda* (*śabda vijñānāt*). So we see that in this definition *Śāstra* has been defined as (partly) *asannikr̥ṣṭe arthe vijñānam*. Just after it (*śāstra*), Śabara defines (partly) *upamānam* as *asannikr̥ṣṭe arthe buddhi* (*vijñānam*). Both are the knowledge of

6. Parthasarathi Mishra, 1913, p. 208
7. Ibid., pp 222-23.
8. Śabara, 1883, p. 12.

asannikṛṣṭa artha; therefore after introducing *śāstra* while he introduced the other, i.e. *upamāna* he used the word *api* which means "also." Therefore the first part of Śabara's statement, i.e. (1), tells us that *upamānam api sādṛśyam* (and is also) *asannikṛṣṭe arthe buddhim utpādayati*. So the point of Śabarasvāmī is that like *śāstra, upamāna,* i.e. *sādṛśya* also causes knowledge in respect of some object which is (*asannikṛṣṭa*) not in contact with sense organ. Here the statement (1) has two parts : (a) *upamāna* in the sense of *upamiti-karaṇa* is *sādṛśyam* (*upamānamapi sādṛśyam*) and (b) *upamāna* in this sense causes *upamiti* which also is a knowledge in respect of a thing which is *asannikṛṣṭa* (*asannikṛṣṭe arthe buddhim utpādayati*). We will explain (a) when we will discuss Prabhākara's view.

Śabara offered his own definition of *upamāna* in response to classical Nyāya account of it, because he could not accept the classical Nyāya account. It follows that the account he has given here is different from the Nyāya account. But where is the difference?

It will appear that there is no difference in respect of (a) for in classical Nyāya also *upamāna* in the sense of *upamiti-karaṇa* has to do with *sādṛśya*. But if the difference is not in respect of (a) then it must be in respect of (b). Ramakrishna Mishra at least seems to think so. And at first glance this seems true if one considers Ramakrishna Mishra's description of the view of the Gautamīyāḥ. According to the Gautamīyāḥ or the Naiyāyikas, in *upamiti* one knows (in the standard case) *gavaya*. And *gavaya* is a *sannikṛṣṭa viṣaya,* i.e. an object in contact with sense organs. But *upamiti* according to Śabarasvāmī is *asannikṛṣṭe arthe buddhi* or knowledge in respect of a thing which is not in contact with sense organs. Ramakrishna Mishra in his *Yuktisnehaprapūraṇī* follows this line of explanation. He writes: *śrutātideśa vākyānāṁ ca vane gavaya-darśanāt ayaṁ sa gavaya iti go sādṛśya viśiṣṭa gavaya jñānaṁ tadupamānam iti gautamīyāḥ. tadapi asat . . . atideśa vākyārtha smaraṇa sahakṛta indriya janyatvāt ca savikalpaka pratyakṣam eva tat. ato yathā gavaya darśanaṁ go smaraṇasya iti udāharaṇāntaram āha bhāṣyakāraḥ.*[9] Thus according to Ramakrishna Mishra the followers of Gautama think that *upamiti* is perception. To distinguish Mīmāṁsā view from the view of the Gautamīyāḥ, Śabarasvāmī has defined *upamiti* as knowledge of *asannikṛṣṭa artha.*

To distinguish Mīmāṁsā view from the Nyāya view therefore part (1) or more accurately the part (1b), (i.e. *asannikṛṣṭe arthe buddhim utpādayati*) or Śabara's statement about *upamāna* is sufficient. Śabara had no need to include the part (2) in his statement (S) about *upamāna*. But this problem of redundancy of part (2) of *S* is created by Ramakrishna Mishra. This problem will vanish if we do not accept Ramakrishna's explanation, i.e. if we deny (1) that Nyāya-*upamiti* is perception (of *gavaya*) or (ii) if we deny that Mīmāṁsā-*upamiti* is distinguished from Nyāya-*upamiti* in this sense by (1b). According to Ramakrishna Mishra the Naiyāyikas take *upamiti* to be perception (of *gavaya*). And so Mīmāṁsā view can be distinguished by part (1) or (1b) of *S.*[10] Therefore part (2) of *S* is not necessary at all. So Ramakrishna Mishra must find an answer to the question what is the need of part (2), that is *yathā gavaya-darśanaṁ gosmaraṇasya.* It is not needed to distinguish Mīmāṁsā-*upamiti* from Nyāya-*upamiti.* But the suggestion is this: that it may still be necessary to distinguish two *pramāṇas* (*śāstra* and *upamāna*) within the Mīmāṁsā system itself. That is, it is necessary to distinguish *upamāna* (*pramāṇa* or *upamiti* according to Śabara) from *śāstra* (*pramāṇa* according to Śabara). Both in the case of *upamiti* and *śāstra* we have knowledge about *asannikṛṣṭa viṣaya*. How these two types of knowledge can be distinguished? Now one should remember that there are different types of *asannikṛṣṭa viṣaya*. For example *svarga* (heaven), *naraka* (hell), *śakti, sādṛśya* (similarity) all are non-sensuous or imperceptible things. But *sādṛśya*, as in

9. Ramakrishna, 1913, p. 208.

10. See above, and also p. 32.

the case of *gavaya-darśanam-go-smaraṇam*, is known in *upamiti*. However *svarga, naraka*, etc. can be known from *śāstra* only. This therefore is the answer to the question what is the need for part (2) of the statement *S*, i.e. *yathā gavaya-darśanaṁ go-smaraṇasya*. And this answer is consistent with Ramakrishna's explanation of Śabara's position. According to him Mīmāṁsā-*upamiti* is distinguished from Nyāya-*upamiti* by (1) or (1b). So far (2) of *S* is unnecessary. And this can be suggested that the Mīmaṁsā-*upamāna* is distinguished from *Śāstra-pramāṇa* of the Mīmāṁsakas by the part (2) of Śabara's statement *S*. Thus both the parts of *S* are necessary. No part is redundant. So far no objection may be raised against the way Śabara formulated the Mīmāṁsā position in response to some *prasiddha* or Nyāya view of *upamāna*.

So far we have tried to show the necessity of (2) by accepting at the same time Ramakrishna's explanation. But that explanation cannot really be accepted. For according to Ramakrishna's explanation *upamiti* in the Nyāya sense is perception (of *gavaya*). But this is not so. According to the Naiyāyikas *upamiti* is the knowledge of *śakti* or the relation of words to their meaning. This *śakti* is generally imperceptible. Therefore according to the Naiyāyikas *upamiti* is the knowledge of *asannikṛṣṭa viṣaya*. So we cannot say Mīmāṁsā-*upamiti* is different from Nyāya-*upamiti* because Mīmāṁsā-*upamiti* is knowledge of *asannikṛṣṭa viṣaya*. Nyāya-*upamiti* is also knowledge of *asannikṛṣṭa-viṣaya*. The question therefore remains how the *upamiti* of Mīmāṁsā is different from *upamiti* of Nyāya. Part (2) of *S* gives us a hint about the answer. The example of *asannikṛṣṭa viṣaya* which according to the Mīmāṁsakas we know in *upamiti* is the similarity in the cow which is at the moment remembered. But the *asannikṛṣṭa viṣaya* which we know in *upamiti* according to the Naiyāyikas is *śakti*. Therefore part (2) of *S* tells us that Mīmāṁsā-*upamiti* is different because the *asannikṛṣṭaviṣaya* it knows is different. And so Mīmāṁsā theory of *upamāna* is different from Nyāya theory of *upamāna*.

Between these two ways of showing the necessity of part (2) of *S* we prefer the second one. For the first line of explanation misrepresents the Nyāya view of *upamāna*. We may also consider the following fact. Neither Kumārila nor Parthasarathi said that according to the Naiyāyikas *upamiti* is perception. Nor did they suggest that to be the Nyāya view. Kumārila in his *Ślokavārttika* has suggested that Śabarasvāmī offered his own account of *upamāna* because he could not accept the familiar (*prasiddha*) account of *upamāna*. He also says that if the *prasiddha* account is accepted then *upamāna* cannot be distinguished from *āgama* or knowledge by verbal testimony. If this *prasiddha* account is the account of the Naiyāyikas or of the Gautama school (Gautamīya) then again Mīmāṁsā account cannot be distinguished from Nyāya account on the ground that Mīmāṁsā *upamāna* is the knowledge of *asannikr̥ṣṭa viṣaya*. For if the Nyāya account turns *upamāna* into *āgama* then there *upamāna* also will be knowledge of *asannikr̥ṣṭa viṣaya*.[11]

Two things are to be noted here. According to Gautama and his followers two types of *śabda* are *pramāṇa*. Some *laukika* or ordinary empirical statements are *śabda-pramāṇa*. And some *alaukika* scriptural sentences are also *śabda-pramāṇa*. Thus Gautama says in his *sūtra* 1.1.8, *sa dvibidho-dr̥ṣṭādr̥ṣṭārthatvāt*.[12] Vātsyāyana says in his commentary, *yasyeha dr̥śyate 'rthaḥ sa dr̥ṣṭārthaḥ. yasyāmutra pratīyate so 'dr̥ṣṭārthaḥ. evamr̥ṣilaukikavākyānāṁ vibhāga iti*.[13] From this it follows that some ordinary sentence or *laukika vākya* is also *pramāṇa*. Such *śabda-pramāṇa* is about objects which are (sensuously) experienced in this world. Therefore to say that *upamāna* is a case of *āgama* may not necessarily mean that

11. Ramakrishna Mishra has also noted this alternative. But he takes this *āgama* knowledge again as the knowledge of *gavaya*. For he says, on the Nyāya view, *upamāna* is knowledge of *gavaya* and *āptopadeśenaiva gavaya rūpa artha pratīteḥ*. Ramakrishna Mishra, 1913, p. 208.

12. Gautama, 1985 (*sūtra*, 1.1.8), p. 189.

13. Vātsyāyana (on *sūtra* 1.1.8), 1985, p. 179.

upamāna is *asannikṛṣṭa-viṣaye vijñānam.*

The second point is this. According to Kumārila and his followers, Śabara defined *upamāna* in terms of *asannikṛṣṭa viṣaya.* And he did so because he wanted to distinguish Mīmāṁsā-*upamāna* from Nyāya-*upamāna*. This Nyāya-*upamāna* is *āgama abahirbhūta,* i.e. not included in *āgama*. This means that *upamāna* is reducible to *śabda-pramāṇa*. But if so *upamāna* can be knowledge of *asannikṛṣṭa viṣaya* also. How then can one distinguish Mīmāṁsā-*upamāna* from Nyāya-*upamāna* on the ground that Mīmāṁsā-*upamāna* is *asannikṛṣṭa viṣaye jñānam*? We have said something towards answering this question before. We cannot discuss it any further here. For our purpose here we can only say that Śabara's major objection against the Naiyāyikas is that they have reduced *upamāna* to *śabda*. They failed to preserve the independence of *upamāna* as a *pramāṇa*. For according to them *upamāna* is the *atideśa vākya* itself. If a *vākya* or a sentence is *upamāna* then it is *śabda-pramāṇa*. And the knowledge that may be produced is *śabda*. Therefore the conclusion will be that the classical version of Mīmāṁsā brings the following objection against the classical version of the theory of *upamāna* of the Naiyāyikas. The Naiyāyikas defined *upamāna* in such a way that it becomes indistinguishable from *śabda-pramāṇa*.

So far the classical version of the theory of *upamāna* of the Indian Realists has been stated. The two important realists are Nyāya and Mīmāṁsā. To make the philosophical positions stronger the views of the opponent are to be considered. As it is known, *ekākini pratijñā hi pratijñātuṁ na sādhayet* (i.e. only the utterance of the position does not prove the position) and secondly it is also known to the philosophy students, *paramataḥ apratisiddhaṁ anumatam* (i.e. by discarding the position of the opponent by logic the position of the proponent is established), accordingly in the following chapter the objections against *upamāna* will be considered.

Part Two
Critical Development of the Mīmāṁsā and Nyāya Theory of Upamāna

3

Bauddha and Vaiśeṣika Objections against the Classical Mīmāṁsā View of Upamāna

I

IN the previous chapter I have considered the classical Mīmāṁsā view of *upamāna* as against the classical Nyāya view of *upamāna*. According to Śabarasvāmī, (1) classical Nyāya view of *upamāna* is not acceptable because it equates *upamāna* with *śabda-pramāṇa*. (2) Secondly *upamāna* in Śabara's sense of the term must be admitted for the knowledge of *sādṛśya*. On this account, first there is some existent thing which is *sādṛśya*. And secondly for the knowledge of this *sādṛśya* a distinct *pramāṇa* (which is not equivalent to *śabda-pramāṇa*) must be admitted. Against both these points of the Mīmāṁsakas, objections have been raised. The Bauddhas and the Vaiśeṣikas are the critics of the Mīmāṁsā view. They have rejected the view that there is such a thing or entity as *sādṛśya*. Accordingly they have also rejected the view that there is an independent *pramāṇa* for the knowledge of *sādṛśya*. The Vaiśeṣikas admit *sādṛśya*. But they do not admit it as an independent category. Similarly they do not admit *upamāna* as an independent *pramāṇa* for the knowledge of *sadṛśya* (or for any other thing). In earlier days Śabarasvāmī admitted *upamāna pramāṇa*. In later days the Mīmāṁsakas were divided into different traditions. In the Prābhākara tradition *sādṛśya* is admitted as an independent category. But in the Bhaṭṭa tradition Kumārila and his followers do not admit *sādṛśya* as an independent category. However all the Mīmāṁsakas, from Śabara to the followers of Prabhākara and Kumārila Bhaṭṭa, hold that *upamāna* is an independent *pramāṇa*. They also hold that this *pramāṇa* gives us knowledge of *sādṛśya*. The objection (1) that *sādṛśya* is not to be admitted as an independent category applies to some Mīmāṁsakas only. But the objection (2) that *upamāna* is not a *pramāṇa* which gives us knowledge of *sādṛśya* applies to all the Mīmāṁsakas.

The Buddhists, the Vaiśeṣikas and the Bhāṭṭa Mīmāṁsakas alike can raise the objection (1). In section II, however, I am to consider this objection only as it has been formulated by some Buddhist philosophers. All the schools of Indian philosophy except the Mīmāṁsakas can raise the objection (2). But we shall consider in section III the objection as it has been formulated by the Vaiśeṣikas.

While criticizing theories of *upamāna* different Buddhist philosophers have brought different arguments and objections. One may find these in texts like *Pramāṇa-Vārttika, Nyāyabindu, Tattva-Saṁgraha* and the like. In *Ratnakīrti-Nibandhāvalī* Ratnakīrti has criticized Mīmāṁsā theory of *upamāna* on the ground that there is no such thing as *sādṛśya*. How can then there be such knowledge which knows *sādṛśya*? In other words there can not be what the Mīmāṁsakas call *upamāna* (or *upamiti*).

Ratnakīrti has quoted Śabarasvāmī's statement when he criticized the Mīmāṁsā view of *upamāna*. In this matter he has taken the help of Kumārila, the internal critic of the Prābhākaras, and rejected *sādṛśya*. His argument why one may not admit *sādṛśya* is different from the Vaiśeṣika argument why *sādṛśya* is not an independent category. Again arguments of the earlier Bauddhas or the Vaiśeṣikas may be found to be different from the later Bauddhas and the Vaiśeṣikas. But we shall adopt logical approach and disregard the historical order. So the views of authors belonging to different ages may be discussed together or in a reverse order. And here disregarding the detail I am to present the general line of argument that the critics of the Mīmāṁsakas have followed or may follow.

The general position of the Mīmāṁsakas in the matter of *upamāna* may be briefly re-stated in this way. *Upamāna* is an independent *pramāṇa* required for the knowledge of *sādṛśya* (similarity). If one wants to reduce *upamāna* then one must first admit it to be a *pramāṇa*. For only a *pramāṇa* can be reduced to another *pramāṇa*. If *upamāna* is not a *pramāṇa* at all then the question of its reduction to other *pramāṇa* like *anumāna* or *śabda* does not arise. Keeping all these in mind a Bauddha critic may argue along this line. If *upamāna* is a *pramāṇa* then it must have some *viṣaya* also. The *viṣaya* of a *pramāṇa* can be either *svalakṣaṇa* or *sāmānya lakṣaṇa*. If the *viṣaya* of it is *svalakṣaṇa* then *upamāna* becomes *pratyakṣa*. If it is *sāmānya lakṣaṇa* then it will be *anumāna* or inference. On the other hand if the supposed *viṣaya* of a *pramāṇa* (say *upamāna*) is neither *svalakṣaṇa* nor *sāmānya lakṣaṇa* then that *pramāṇa* has no *viṣaya*. In that case that is not a genuine *pramāṇa*. This may be one of the possible ways in which a Bauddha philosopher can seek to prove that *upamāna* is not an independent *pramāṇa* or *upamāna* is not a *pramāṇa* at all. We shall see that Ratnakīrti has followed a slightly different line of argument to prove that *upamāna* is not a *pramāṇa* if it does not know an object as having determinate character (*niyata svabhāva*). Again some Bauddhas can argue that definition of *pramāṇa* does not apply to what is called *upamāna* (*lakṣaṇābhāvāt upamānābhāvaḥ*). These different arguments of the Bauddhas are not incompatible with each other.

We shall however argue that Ratnakīrti's way is better than the way followed by some other Bauddhas. Similarly both Udayana and Vallabhācārya argued against the Mīmāṁsakas, from the point of view of the Vaiśeṣikas. We shall, however, see that they did not offer the same criticism. It may also be noted that Vallabhācārya is a Vaiśeṣika and accepts only two *pramāṇa*s but Udayana agrees with the Vaiśeṣikas in the matter of the number of *padārthas*. According to him the number of *pramāṇas* however is four, as the Naiyāyikas say. In this chapter we will divide the following discussion into three broad divisions: (a) Bauddha objections against classical Mīmāṁsā version (Section II), (b) Vaiśeṣika objection against classical Mīmāṁsā version (Section III), and (c) Comparative assessment of Ratnakīrti's contributions (Section IV).

II

Ratnakīrti is the disciple of Jñānaśrīmitra who flourished slightly before Udayana.[1] In this section we shall discuss Ratnakīrti's critique of the Mīmāṁsā theory of *upamāna*. In other matters Ratnakīrti is directly indebted to his Guru Jñānaśrīmitra. But in his criticism of Nyāya and Mīmāṁsā theories of *upamāna*, he seems to be original. But this rejection of the Mīmāṁsā (Prabhākara?) view of *upamāna* follows to some extent Kumārila's line.

Ratnakīrti begins his critique with a short exposition of the Mīmāṁsā theory which he traces to the *Bhāṣya* of Śabarasvāmī. The statement of Śabarasvāmī he quotes has been misprinted as *upamānamapi sādṛśyam asannikṛṣṭatve buddhim utpādayati*.[2] The passage in question has been interpreted to mean this: Resemblance observed in some instance (*gavaya*) produces as

---

1. Cf. Anantalal Thakur, ed., *Ratnakīrti-Nibandhāvalī*: Introduction, p. 22. According to Karl Potter, ed., *Encyclopaedia of Indian Philosophers*, vol. I, time of Uddyotakara is CE 550-625; of Vācaspati Miśra I, CE 980; of Ratnakīrti, early eleventh century.

2. Ratnakīrti, 1957, p. 90. The editor has not noted this error. But we quote the sentence of Śabara:

   upamānamapi sādṛśyam asannikṛṣṭe 'rthe buddhimutpādayati, yathā, gavaya-darśanaṁ gosmaraṇsya. Śabarasvāmī's *Bhāṣya*, Jīvānanda edition, Calcutta, 1883, p. 12. In *Śokavārttika* ed. Dvarikadas Shastri, exactly this passage has been quoted; see p. 307 of that edition.

means (called *upamāna*), awareness about the other resembling thing cow (*go*) which is not being perceived at the moment. Suppose there are two things *X* and *Y* which resemble each other. Suppose, further, one perceives *X* and perceives in it (its) resemblance with *Y*. On the basis of this knowledge one will have another knowledge regarding the other term of resemblance, namely, the *Y* which is not being perceived at the moment. Through *upamāna* we know this other thing *Y* insofar as it resembles *X* (*sādṛśya viśiṣṭatayā*). In other words the resulting knowledge called *upamiti* has the form "that thing has resemblance with this thing."[3] Conditions that are responsible for such *upamiti* are the following: perception of one of the two resembling things and the memory of the other resembling thing which we are not perceiving at the moment. Therefore, in a situation of *upamāna pramāṇa* there are produced two separate cognitions of resemblance. One of these cognitions apprehends in one term of resemblance (the term which is being perceived at the moment) the similarity (*sādṛśya*) it has with the other term (which is *asannikṛṣṭa* or not present to senses). The second cognition which results from the first one apprehends the other term of the resemblance which is being remembered at the moment. This other term is apprehended along with its similarity with the first term present to senses. The perception of resemblance in the present object is the source or *pramāṇa*, that is, the special means of knowledge. It causes a second cognition of similarity. This second kind of cognition of similarity is believed to be a distinct kind of knowledge. It is called *upamāna* (*upamiti*). This is the Mīmāṁsā view.

Ratnakīrti expounds the Mīmāṁsā position with reference to Kumārila. He quotes what Kumārila Bhaṭṭa has said in this connection in his *Ślokavārttika*. Here again there is a misprint in *Ratnakīrti-Nibandhāvalī* so far as verse 39 of *Upamānapariccheda* of

3. *etad sādṛśya viśiṣṭa asau ityasannikṛṣṭe arthe yāṁ buddhim utpādayati tadupamānam pramāṇam iti* — Ratnakīrti, 1957, p. 91.

Ślokavārttika is concerned. This may be due to the lapse in editing or there was some other copy or edition of the text.[4] The point of the Mīmāṁsakas is this: though in the context of *upamāna* there is something which is perceived and there is something which is remembered, yet neither perception nor memory apprehends what *upamāna* apprehends.

We shall discuss the Mīmāṁsā argument for accepting *sādṛśya* as an independent category when we shall discuss the Prābhākara theory of *upamāna*. The argument which Ratnakīrti offers to show that *sādṛśya* is not an additional category appears to be decisive and radical. On this rejection of *sādṛśya* Ratnakīrti bases his conclusion: there cannot be the form of cognition called *upamāna*.[5] Here by the word *upamāna* Ratnakīrti has understood *upamiti* or a form of belief or knowledge. We need to give some argument why we think so. The word *māna* which Ratnakīrti uses is ambiguous. It may mean either belief (*jñāna*) or knowledge of some kind (*pramā*). It may also mean special means (*karaṇa*) of *pramā*. Ratnakīrti seems to have used the word *māna* in the sense of belief or knowledge. The argument he offers against *upamāna* is that there cannot be a *māna* called *upamāna*, for such *māna* cannot have any content (or *viṣaya*). Now in the direct or straightforward sense only a cognition can have object or can be *svaviṣaya*. A *pramāṇa* cannot directly be said to be *svaviṣaya* always.[6] Only when the *pramāṇa* itself is a cognition, it can be said to have a *viṣaya*. Thus Ratnakīrti's radical argument against *upamāna pramāṇa* is an argument from lack of object (*nirviṣayatva*). The question of *saviṣayatva* or *nirviṣayatva* cannot

---

4. Cf. Kumārila, 1978, p. 316, verses 38-39.

5. (*mīmāṁsakoktaṁ tāvat*) *upamānam mānam eva na bhavati*, Ratnakīrti, 1957, p. 94.

6. For example, *anumāna pramāṇa* or instrumental condition responsible for the production of inferential cognition is itself a cognition. It is *vyāpti jñāna*, i.e. the cognition having for its object the relation of *vyāpti*.

be directly relevant about a *pramāṇa* if it is not by nature a cognition. In the present case of *upamāna pramāṇa* both the instrument (*karaṇa*) and its result *pramā* are cognition. So the conclusion or the thesis of the objector can make sense whether by the word *upamāna* we understand the relevant form of cognition (*upamiti*) or its instrument. Again according to all the Mīmāṁsakas *upamāna* both in the sense of *upamiti* and *upamiti-karaṇa* is a cognition. And it is a cognition which has *sādṛśya* for its object. Ratnakīrti's argument that there is no such thing as *sādṛśya* equally affects the Mīmāṁsā theory of both *upamāna* and *upamiti*. The argument shows that there cannot be *upamāna* or means (*karaṇa*) of *upamiti;* nor can there be *upamāna* in the sense of *upamiti*.

But if both *pramā* and *pramāṇa* are knowledge then we can describe the same thing in both ways. The distinction between *pramā* and *pramāṇa* is not made (in the usual way) in the Buddhist philosophy. They define *pramāṇa* as *avisaṁvādi jñāna,* i.e. roughly speaking,[7] true belief.[8] By *pramāṇa* here one should understand both, what is known in other systems as *pramā* and what is known in some schools as *pramākaraṇa*. In a system like Nyāya the word *pramākaraṇa* (*pramāṇa*) means the condition which is instrumental in causing a *pramā*. *Pramā* or *pramāṇa phala* is the result of *pramāṇa* that is, *pramākaraṇa*. A *pramā* according to the Naiyāyikas is always a knowledge. But a *pramākaraṇa* or *pramāṇa* may be knowledge or may not be knowledge. In the Bauddha system *pramāṇa* and

7. *Avisaṁvādakatva* cannot be easily translated into English by the word true. Dharmottara in his commentary *Nyāyabindu Ṭīkā* has said many interesting things when he explained Dharmakīrti's notion of *samyak jñāna* (Dharmakīrti, 1955, p. 1). Dharmottara begins by saying *avisaṁvādakaṁ jñānaṁ samyak jñānam*. And then he explains *saṁvādakatva* as *prāpakatva*. This *prāpakatva* again is explained as *pravartakatva* (Dharmottara, 1955, p. 17f.).

8. *pramāṇam avisaṁvādi jñānam* — Dharmakīrti, 1953, p. 3.

pramā, i.e. *pramāṇa phala* are distinguished differently.[9] For the Bauddhas a *pramāṇa* and its corresponding *phala* are the same fact or entity. Two different aspects of the same state of knowledge are called *pramāṇa* and *pramāṇa phala*. We can put it differently also. The same state of knowledge can be determined differently. When it is determined in one way, it is called *pramāṇa*. When it is determined in another way the same thing is called *pramāṇa phala*. The two aspects are *vyavasthāpya* and *vyavasthāpaka* aspects of a cognition. Roughly speaking when we know a jar as a jar, the knowledge that it is a jar is the *vyavasthāpya,* and what produces the knowledge or the *vyavasthāpya* is the *vyavasthāpaka*. (A very clear exposition can be found in Durveka Mishra.[10]) Now since for a Bauddha *pramāṇa* and *pramāṇa phala* are one and the same thing, a *pramāṇa* is necessarily a cognition by nature. Jayanatabhaṭṭa has referred to the Bauddhas as those who hold that cognition alone can be *pramāṇa*.[11] This controversy relating to *pramāṇa* and *pramāṇa phala* is important so far as the nature (*svarūpa* or *svabhāva*) of *pramāṇa* is concerned.

But there is another controversy which is immediately important. This controversy is about the number of *pramāṇas*. The standard Bauddha view is that there are only two *pramāṇas*.[12] These are *pratyakṣa* and *anumāna*. One important point to note here is that some early Bauddhas admitted four *pramāṇas*.[13] It has been sometimes argued that strictly speaking nothing other

---

9. Dharmottara, 1955, p. 83.

10. Durveka Mishra, 1955, p. 17f.

11. *ye tu bodhasyaiva pramāṇatvam ācakṣyate* etc. — Jayanatabhaṭṭa, 1971, p. 14.

12. *mānaṁ dvibidham viṣaya dvaibidhyāt* — Dharmakīrti, 1968, p. 3. The names of different schools of Indian philosophy and the different *pramāṇas* which they admit have been given in many texts. See Narayana, 1975 (2nd edn.), p. 8. Also Gopinath Kaviraj, 1982, p. 116.

13. Phanibhusana Tarkavagisa, 1981, vol. 1, p. 100.

than *svalakṣaṇa* is an item of reality to be known (*jñeya*); and there is no *pramāṇa* other than *pratyakṣa*. But the standard view is that according to the Bauddhas *pratyakṣa* and *anumāna* (perception and inference) are the only *pramāṇas*. On one occasion Udayanācārya argued against the Bauddhas that the Bauddhas cannot prove momentariness either by perception or by inference.[14] So it is generally held that the Bauddhas admit only perception and inference as *pramāṇa*. But then they cannot admit *upamāna* as a *pramāṇa*. They must reduce it to one or the other *pramāṇa* they admit, i.e. to perception or to inference or they should deny altogether that *upamāna* is a *pramāṇa*.

Ratnakīrti has adopted the last alternative. Ratnakīrti argues that there is no such thing as *sādṛśya* (similarity) over and above pairs of resembling things (*sadṛśa vastudvayas*).[15] But it is this *sādṛśya* which according to the Mīmāṁsakas is the content of *upamāna*.[16] The conclusion that can be drawn from the premises is that there is no such experience as *upamāna*. For there cannot be any experience without content.[17] And if *upamāna* is devoid of content then how can we have such so-called experience of *upamiti* which is devoid of object?

Ratnakīrti himself seems to have drawn a different and a

---

14. *na vaijātyaṁ vinā tat syānna tasminnanumābhavet. vinā tena na tat siddhirnādhyakṣam niścayaṁ-vinā — Nyāya-Kusumāñjaliḥ*, 1.16.

15. Cf. Ratnakīrti, 1957, p. 95.

16. *Sādṛśya* according to the Mīmāṁsakas is the content of both *upamāna* which is a special means and *upamiti* which is the resulting knowledge.

17. No doubt this remark I state here is in a general way. The author here is not interested to raise the controversy between those who accept *sākāra-vijñānavāda* and those who do not accept it. Vijñānavādī Bauddhas are generally *sākāra vijñānavādin*. But philosophers like Naiyāyikas hold that in itself a knowledge has no *ākāra*, that is *vijñāna* is not *sākāra*. A *nirākāra* knowledge is specified or identified by the object of it. This object is something other than and outside knowledge. Cf. Udayanācārya, 1957, p. 461.

weaker conclusion. The conclusion which he draws is that *upamāna* is not a *pramāṇa* as it is devoid of object.[18] In other words Ratnakīrti concludes that *upamāna* is not a *pramāṇa* though he could have concluded that there was no such experience.[19] The object is *sādṛśya* (similarity). And if the object of a cognition does not exist then there *cannot* be any cognition. So the stronger conclusion which follows is not (ia) that where there is no *sādṛśya* there happens to be no experience. It follows that (ib) there *cannot* be experience called *upamāna* which has *sādṛśya* for its object. (ia) and (ib) will be the same for those who take *upamāna* to be knowledge of *sādṛśya*. But everyone does not take *sādṛśya* to be the object of *upamāna*. For example a Naiyāyika admits that there is a distinct kind of experience called *upamāna* but they do not think that *upamāna* cognizes *sādṛśya*. A Naiyāyika may accept the argument of Ratnakīrti which shows that there is no *sādṛśya*. He can still accept that there is *upamāna*. We have already stated that a Naiyāyika does not think that *upamāna* reveals *sādṛśya*. So it will be wrong to conclude that *upamāna* has no content and therefore there is no *upamāna* on the ground that there is no *sādṛśya* (over and above the things that are similar).[20] Considering all these Ratnakīrti perhaps thought of concluding that there is no *upamāna* which has *sādṛśya* for its object. But what he actually writes (*upamānaṁ mānameva na bhavati*) does not clearly or precisely bring out his conclusion.

---

18. *upamānaṁ mānameva na bhavati, nirviṣayatvāt asya* — Ratnakīrti, 1957, p. 94.

19. Ratnakīrti has actually said *upamānaṁ mānameva na bhavati* (cf. Ratnakīrti, 1957, p. 94). But the word *māna* may be understood to mean *jñāna* or *pramāṇa*. If *pramāṇa* means *pramā* then it is not just *jñāna* but *yathārtha jñāna*. So *mānameva na bhavati* may be taken to mean (i) *jñānameva na bhavati* or (ii) *yathārtha jñānameva na bhavati*. The (i) is stronger; the (ii) is weaker.

20. The point is, Ratnakīrti's argument can show that Mīmāṁsā *upamāna* is not there. It does not show that *upamāna* in the sense of knowledge of *śakti* is not there.

But this is only a weak defence. Again it will be wrong if Ratnakīrti means to assert in his conclusion that *upamāna*, the knowledge of *sādṛśya*, is not a *pramāṇa* or *pramā*.

In defence of Ratnakīrti one may say that the Bauddhas admit even *vikalpa vijñāna*, e.g. *saṁśaya* (doubt) and *viparyaya* (falsehood). Our cognitive experience of this type has no determinate object. The object which such experiences reveal is only indeterminate (*aniyata svabhāva*)[21] in nature. To say an experience does not have an object may mean, it has no real object; the object it has is unreal. To say that an experience has no object may again mean it does not have any object at all. The point of saying *vikalpa jñāna* to be *apramā* is this. What is real cannot be of indeterminate nature and what is not real is non-existing. Therefore strictly speaking *vikalpa vijñāna* does not have any object. Now still one can admit forms of experience which reveal objects that have no determinate character. But if so, then one can admit *upamāna* even if its object, viz. similarity, does not exist in the strict sense. But if *upamāna* is like *vikalpa vijñāna*, because it has no object (which is real or *niyata svabhāva*) then *upamāna* should not be a *pramāṇa* just as *vikalpa vijñāna* is not *pramāṇa*. And Ratnakīrti draws exactly this conclusion that . . . *upamānaṁ mānameva na bhavati*.[22]

Now it is clear that if argument for the rejection of *sādṛśya* is successful only Mīmāṁsā account of *upamāna pramāṇa* (*upamiti*) is affected. But now if the Bauddhas want to prove the more general conclusion that *upamāna* is not a *pramāṇa* then they should be able to reject the Nyāya account of *upamāna* also. But this account does not presuppose that *sādṛśya* is an additional object of the universe. Therefore it is of great importance and immediate interest how Ratnakīrti defends the Bauddha thesis that *upamāna* is not a *pramāṇa* against the Naiyāyikas. Ratnakīrti

21. See Ananta Tarkatirtha, *Vaibhāṣika Darśana* (Bengali), p. 332.

22. Ratnakīrti, 1957, p. 94.

partly owes this point to Rājakulapāda.[23]

From the above discussion it is clear that Ratnakīrti's argument against *upamāna* is that it is devoid of object. It is devoid of object in the sense that it does not have for its object either what the Mīmāṁsakas call its object or the Naiyāyikas call its object. But this is not the only way of rejecting *upamāna* (neither logically nor factually). Some Buddhist philosophers have rejected *upamāna* in a different way.

The argument that has been given by Dharmakīrti may be reconstructed thus. There are only two types of knowable items, viz. *svalakṣaṇa* and *sāmānya lakṣaṇa*. These are known respectively by perception (*pratyakṣa*) and inference (*anumāna*). Therefore there cannot be any third *pramāṇa* particularly because according to the Bauddhas *pramāṇa-vyavasthā*[24] is an undeniable truth. Therefore if *upamāna* is a *pramāṇa* then it must be another name of one of these two *pramāṇa*s or it is a myth. Now it can be said that Ratnakīrti's argument would have been identical with that of Dharmakīrti if Ratnakīrti argued that *sādṛśya* or *samākhyā sambandha* was not anything real as it was different from both *svalakṣaṇa* or *sāmānya-lakṣaṇa*. But actually Ratnakīrti offers a different argument to show that there is no such thing as *sādṛśya*. We should compare later these different ways of rejecting *sādṛśya* and *upamāna*.

Dharmakīrti explains that a *pramāṇa* is an *avisaṁvādi jñānam*.[25] But the object of it must be according to Dharmakīrti either *svalakṣaṇa* or *sāmānya lakṣaṇa*. And it is redundant to admit more

---

23. Most probably his works are not known. But according to Anantalal Thakur he is likely identical with Yuvarāja or Kumāranātha referred to by Jñānaśrī, Jñānaśrīmitra, 1959, Introduction, p. 25. See also Anantalal Thakur's Introduction to *Ratnakīrti-Nibandhāvalī*, p. 19.

24. But it is not accepted as undeniable by everyone. Cf. Vātsyāyana's *Bhāṣya* on *Nyāya-Sūtra*, 1.1.3. Vātsyāyana, 1967, pp. 182-83. See also P.K. Mukhopadhyay, 1973.

25. See note 8 above.

than one source (*pramāṇa* = *pramākaraṇa*) to account for knowledge of one type of *prameya* or object. So there can be only two distinct sources. Thus there is one to one relation between the type of *prameya* and type of knowledge on the one hand and the type of knowledge and type of source on the other. Since object or *prameya* are only of two types, there are only two fundamental types of awareness. And sources of knowledge are also two. The idea perhaps is that there is definite connection between *prameya* and *pramāṇa*; otherwise the number of *prameya* cannot determine the number of *pramāṇa* (types of veridical experience or types of source of such experience).

Now this *pramāṇa* is by definition *avisaṁvādakaṁ jñānam*. This usually means veridical cognitive experience. But there is some more meaning. According to the Bauddhas an *avisaṁvādakaṁ jñānaṁ* is a cognition which goes regularly with its object. What is meant is that if a cognition is *avisaṁvāda* then we cannot have the cognition if its object is not present at the moment. From this it follows that if one acts on a piece of *avisaṁvādi jñāna* and seeks to get the object of that *jñāna* then one gets that object. This idea has been expressed by Dharmottara in his *Nyāya-Bindu-Ṭīkā* as compatible with our common use.[26] This regular connection between veridical cognitive experience and its object is of the nature of causal relation.[27] A veridical perceptual experience is caused by the object or thing which is revealed in the experience. An object of perception is known as capable of producing perceptual cognition directly, independently, and by itself (*svena rūpeṇa*), i.e. not with the help of or through the relation with some other thing. Such objects are therefore called *svalakṣaṇa* which means determined as itself. But when an object

26. Dharmottara, 1955, p. 17. Discussion in this portion on the concept of *avisaṁvādakaṁ jñānaṁ* by Dharmottara and Durveka Mishra is very detailed and valuable. But unfortunately it is beyond the scope of this work so I am not considering the detailed discussion here.

27. Prajñākaragupta, 1953, p. 169.

causes an inferential knowledge it does so by being determined as the ground of inference or as the object to be inferred. *Sādhya* of an inference does not therefore cause knowledge just as being the thing it is. But it causes knowledge by satisfying a general description of being the object inferred. Such an object is therefore called *sāmānya lakṣaṇa*. So a *sāmānya lakṣaṇa* is an object which causes a knowledge and is revealed in it. But it is not revealed as what it is in itself. A *sāmānya lakṣaṇa* is revealed as determined by some general character. Therefore *svalakṣaṇa* means *sva* = *vyakti*, *rūpa* = *dharma*, *lakṣita* = *upa-lakṣita* = *viśiṣṭa*. Therefore the thing that is (known to be) able to know and be revealed in it as the particular thing it is, i.e. as qualified by the property it possesses as an individual is *svalakṣaṇa*. Such a *svalakṣaṇa* thing causes the knowledge directly, i.e. by the mere fact of its being there. Perception is caused in this way, so a perception is said to be caused by *svalakṣaṇa*. Or alternatively a perception has for its object *svalakṣana*. In case of inference it is otherwise. It is not enough that there should be *hetu* and *sādhya* for inference to be caused. We need *knowledge* of these things as bearer of the relevant relation. So an inference cannot be said to be caused by its object directly or as determined by the property it has as that particular thing. This is also perhaps the reason why perception has the form "*ayam* . . ." or "this . . ." as for example *ayaṁ ghaṭaḥ*. But inference does not have this form. In short, perception is caused by *svalakṣaṇa*, i.e. by things directly and not through any knowledge of it or any relevant relation. Perception depends on sense-object relation; but for such perception *knowledge* of such relation is not needed. And perception cognizes the particular jar (*ghaṭa-vyakti*) but not *ghaṭa jātīya*, or the class jar. For past and future jars are *ghaṭa jātīya* but these do not cause perception. But inference is caused on the other hand by *sāmānya-lakṣaṇa* and indirectly, i.e. by the knowledge of the relation of the thing being inferred with the ground of inference. What is known in the inference is not the fire as that particular thing but as having the general character of *sādhya* or being a term of the relation of *vyāpti*. Again mere presence of this relation of *hetu* and *sādhya* is not enough to cause inference. But inference is (indirectly) caused by the knowledge of this relation. It can be said that both perception and inference can be said to be caused by the object being known. In case of perception the object causes the knowledge directly and in case of inference the relevant object causes the knowledge indirectly.[28]

Now there are only two kinds of objects and they respectively cause knowledge directly and indirectly. The first causes perception and the second causes inference. There is no third kind of object and there is no third *pramāṇa*. But what about so-called *upamiti* and *śābdabodha*? The so-called knowledge of *śabda, upamiti,* etc. are not caused directly or indirectly by any object.[29] For in the relevant sense of the term, object here means things revealed in the knowledge. What is revealed in perception or inference has a determinate character and can therfore be said to be something real. But what is revealed in *śābdabodha* or verbal knowledge may or may not be there; it may exist or may not exist. In other words object of *śābda-jñāna* has an indeterminate character. It follows that *śābdabodha* does not reveal a thing as having a definite determinate character or *bhāvābhāvaniyata svabhāva*. But there cannot be in reality such a thing which is not

28. This roughly is the intended meaning of *Pramāṇa-Vārttika* 2.1 as explained by Prajñākara. *pratipatti bhedaśca pramāṇa bhedaḥ. sa eva ca viśayavabhedaḥ . . . yadā sākṣāt jñāna-jananaṁ prati śaktatvena pratīyate tadā asau . . . svalakṣaṇam. yadā tu pāramparyeṇa śaktatvāt tasyaiva pratīyate tadā . . . sāmānya lakṣaṇam* — Prajñākara, 1953, p. 169.

29. *keśādestu taimirika upalabdhasya śābdābhyupalabdhasya ca na arthatattvaṁ sākṣāt pāramparyeṇa vā śaktatvena apratīteḥ . . . nanu purovyavasthitaṁ gavadisadṛśarūpeṇa pratīyate; tat kim sāmānyalakṣaṇaṁ tathopamānena pratīyamānam ayaṁ sa gavaya iti; naitadasti . . . nanu yadi śabdasya viṣayah sāmānya lakṣaṇaṁ śabdopi tarhi pramāṇam sāmānya viṣayatvāt naitādasti* — Prajñākaragupta, 1953, pp. 169-70.

bhāvābhāvaniyata svabhāva.[30] Therefore *śābdabodha* does not have any object which can be said to cause it directly or indirectly.[31] The same argument, as shown below, is applicable in case of *upamāna*.

A Bauddha thinker Śāntarakṣita on the other hand offered a different type of argument. The argument is *pramāṇa lakṣaṇāyogāt.*[32] Śāntarakṣita offered this as one of the two arguments which perhaps jointly prove that there are no more than two *pramāṇas*. He argues that whatever is supposed to be a third *pramāṇa* is either not a *pramāṇa* or is reducible to one or the other of the first two. Strictly speaking here there is no argument — conclusion, or premiss — conclusion relation. For the two are the same. To say that there are only two *pramāṇas* is only another way of saying that the third is either not a *pramāṇa* or is not the third. It is not the third because it is reducible to the first or the second.

While commenting on Śāntarakṣita's argument Kamalaśīla takes the expression *pramāṇa* to mean *pramā*. By definition a *pramā* is, according to the Bauddhas, *avisaṁvādakaṁ jñānam*, i.e. factually verified cognition. Accordingly Śāntarakṣita's argument, viz. *lakṣaṇāyogāt* means *upamāna* lacks the definition of *pramā*. The definitional property of a *pramā* is *avisaṁvādakatva* or *avisaṁvādaka jñānatva*. This property is there in perception and in inference. It is not there in *śābda* or *upamiti*. One may argue that, as said above, the things which are revealed by *śabda* may or may not exist. Similarly the object of *upamāna* is at the same time both similar to and dissimilar from the same another thing. Thus *upamāna* also fails to reveal an object as having single determinate

30. *na ca bhāvābhāvābhyaṁ yukto artha jagatyasti.*

31. *keśādestu . . . apratīteḥ* — See note 29.

32. *nanu śabdopamānādipramāṇāntarasambhavāt; nirdiṣṭaṁ lakṣaṇaṁ kasmād dvayoreva-pramāṇayoḥ?* (1486) *ucyate; na dvayādnyat pramāṇamupapadyate; pramāṇalakṣaṇāyogāt yoge cāntargamādiha* (1487) — Śāntarakṣita, *Tattvasaṁgrahaḥ*, vol. I, verses 1486-87, p. 530.

character. Secondly, *upamāna* is constituted by *śabda* (*atideśa vākya*) as its necessary component. And the defect of *śabda*, or its no-*pramāṇa* character must affect *upamāna* also. In other words, *upamāna*, which involves *śabda*, cannot be a *pramāṇa*. So the Bauddhas hold that there are only two types of *pramā* or true belief, viz. perception and inference. Any true cognition is reducible either to perception or to inference. If something is not so reducible then that thing is either not cognition or it is not true. It lacks *avisaṁvādakatva* and is not a variety of *pramā*.

Now in constructing the argument against *upamāna* a Bauddha can take the word to mean *pramākaraṇa* (instrumental cause of true knowledge) or *pramiti* (resulting knowledge). Śāntarakṣita's argument *pramāṇa lakṣaṇāyogāt* has been accordingly understood to mean absence of the definition or defining property of *pramākaraṇa*. But what is the definition of *pramākaraṇa*? Why no *pramāṇa* other than perceptual and inferential means has the defining property in question? We can reconstruct the answer to this question after Gaṅgeśa's presentation in *Śabdacintāmaṇi* of the Bauddha position that *śabda* is not a *pramāṇa*. The point is this, as we have said above, that if definition of *karaṇa* does not apply to a thing then by definition that thing cannot be a *pramāṇa*. The Bauddhas argue that *karaṇa* is that after which the result necessarily occurs.[33] This argument the Bauddhas offer by way of showing that *śabda* is not a *pramāṇa*. So a Bauddha philosopher may try to prove that *upamāna* is not a *pramāṇa* in the following way. He may say that the definition of *pramāṇa* or definition of *karaṇa* does not apply to what is called *upamāna pramāṇa*. Though there is considerable disagreement about what is *upamiti*, yet the Prābhākaras and the Naiyāyikas generally agree that *upamāna pramāṇa* consists in the experience of similarity in the presented object. But how can we show that

33. *nanu śabdo na pramāṇaṁ tathāhi karaṇaviśeṣaḥ pramāṇam, karaṇañca tat yasmin sati kriyā bhavatyeva* — Gaṅgeśa, 1990 (*śabdakhaṇḍa*, vol. IV, part I), pp. 14-16.

the definition of *karaṇa* does not apply to this experience of similarity? One may argue that since neither awareness of similarity (of a particular kind) nor the knowledge of denotation immediately followed by what is supposed to be its result, this experience of similarity or *upamāna pramāṇa* fails to satisfy the definition of *karaṇa* and hence of *pramāṇa*. We can imagine a situation when we have experience of similarity (with cow not present at the moment) in a presented *gavaya*. But immediately after it there does not follow what is called by the Naiyāyikas *upamiti* (i.e. awareness that the word '*gavaya*' denotes *gavaya*). There also does not follow immediately what a Mīmāṁsaka called *upamiti*. According to Mīmāṁsakas *upamiti* is the belief that, say, the cow (not presented at the moment) is similar to *gavaya* (which is now present and is being experienced as similar).[34]

III

In this section we shall discuss very briefly some Vaiśeṣika criticisms against the classical Mīmāṁsā view. It may be noted that the classical version of Mīmāṁsā theory of *upamāna* has the following three major tenets:

(T_1) *upamāna* is knowledge of *sādṛśya*.

(T_2) *upamāna* is a *svatantra pramāṇa* (separate source of knowledge).

(T_3) *sādṛśya* is an independent category.

In Śabarasvāmī's account[35] all these three have not been clearly stated. The (T_2) is most clear and (T_1) is least clear. The (T_3) was emphasized when the Mīmāṁsā theory of *upamāna* developed in the Prābhākara school. Here, in this book I have stated the classical version of Mīmāṁsā theory. Then in this chapter mainly the discussion is done regarding the objections

34. We shall see later how such argument can be refuted by the Naiyāyikas.

35. We consider there only one sentence Śabara wrote while commenting on *sūtra* 1.1.5.

of those external critics like the Bauddhas. These Bauddha critics are mainly interested in rejecting *upamāna*. Some of their objections are (a) *upamāna* has no *viṣaya* and (b) *upamāna* does not fulfil the definition of *pramāṇa* (*pramāṇa lakṣaṇāyogāt*). (a) was supported somewhat differently following Dharmakīrti's line and following Ratnakīrti's line. In the previous section it is stated how (a) could be supported by those external critics of the Mīmāṁsakas who are Bauddhas. But the Vaiśeṣikas are not interested in rejecting *upamāna*. They want to reduce it. Here we shall consider the position of such reductionist Vaiśeṣikas.

To introduce Kaṇāda's *sūtra* 9.2.3, Śaṅkara Miśra wrote in his *Upaskāra* — *pramāṇāntarāṇi laiṅgike antarbhāvayitum prakaraṇāntaram ārabhate*. The *sūtra* is *etena śabdaṁ vyākhyātaṁ* (9.2.3). It is generally believed that in this *sūtra* Kaṇāda meant to say that *śabda* is not an independent *pramāṇa*; *śabda* is included in *anumāna*.[36] Kaṇāda's *sūtra* — *asyedamiti buddhyāpekṣitatvāt* (*Vaiśeṣika-Sūtra* 9.2.5) is believed to suggest that other *pramāṇa*s like *upamāna* should also be included in *anumāna*. Śaṅkara Miśra in his *Upaskāra* said that Kaṇāda wrote this *sūtra* to show that even *upamāna*, etc. which (philosophers of) other schools admit as *pramāṇa* and which do their job on the basis of inferential relation are included in *anumāna*.[37] Praśastapāda in his *Padārtha-Dharma-Saṁgraha* has said clearly that *pramāṇa*s like *śabda*, etc. should also be included in *anumāna*.[38] It is clear from these accounts that (1) according to the Vaiśeṣikas *upamāna* is not an independent *pramāṇa* and (2) *upamāna* is an instance of *anumāna*. So it is not said that there is no *upamāna*. In other words *upamāna*

36. Of course, in this case the text is not very clear. Some renowned Vaiśeṣika philosopher like Vyomśibācārya even has admitted *śabda* as an independent *pramāṇa*.

37. *upamānādinām api parābhimatānām avinābhāvabalapravṛttikamānāmlaiṅgika eva antarbhāva iti pratipādayitum āha*. Śaṅkara Miśra in his *Upaskāra* introduces with these words in the *Vaiśeṣika-Sūtra* — *asyedamiti buddhyāpekṣitatvāt*. 9.2.5.

38. *śabdādīnām api anumāne antarbhāvaḥ* — Praśastapāda, 1963, p. 512.

has been reduced and not rejected. So the Vaiśeṣikas cannot say that *upamāna* has no *viṣaya*. They may say that the *viṣaya* of *upamāna* also is not independent. This is however not necessary. They may hold both that object of *upamāna* is an independent category but *upamāna* is not an independent *pramāṇa*. The ground for rejection and the ground for reduction may be different.

The following questions may be distinguished:

(Q1) what is the ground of the Vaiśeṣikas for thinking that *upamāna* is reducible?

(Q2) to which *pramāṇa upamāna* may be reduced?

(Q3) which kind of *upamāna* is reduced?

The question (Q3) is important for the following reason. According to the Mīmāṁsakas *upamāna* is knowledge of *sādṛśya*. According to Nyāya, *upamāna* is knowledge of *śakti*. Kaṇāda and Praśastapāda said that *upamāna* is not an independent *pramāṇa*. Praśastapāda explicitly said it is a case of (is reduced to) *anumāna*. But they did not say whether they had the Mīmāṁsā view of *upamāna* in mind or Nyāya view of *upmāna* in mind. Thus neither Praśastapāda nor Kaṇāda gave a clear answer to (Q3).[39] And to question (Q2) Praśastapāda gives a clear answer[40] but Kaṇāda did not give a clear answer. But nobody said that Mīmāṁsā *upamāna* is not reducible. So we take the Vaiśeṣikas to be opposed to the Mīmāṁsakas also. Accordingly we include the Vaiśeṣikas among the external critics of the Mīmāṁsakas. And we take these Vaiśeṣikas also as opposed to the Nyāya theory of *upamāna*. So the Vaiśeṣika view in this matter should be separately formulated and discussed. We shall formulate the Vaiśeṣika objection in this way: (a) *upamāna* as knowledge of *sādṛśya* is reducible and (b) *upamāna* as knowledge of *śakti* is reducible. We shall now consider only (a). The ground for saying that *upamāna* is reducible cannot be the absence of *viṣaya* (whether

39. Śrīdhara, 1963, p. 531.

40. Praśastapāda, 1963, p. 530.

sādṛśya or *śakti*). For if the *viṣaya* is not there *upamāna* will also not be there. *Viṣayābhāva* (i.e. the absence of object) can be the ground for rejection but not for reduction. What can be the ground for reduction? Praśastapāda stated the ground in the words *samāna vidhitvāt*.[41] Śrīdharabhaṭṭa brings out the meaning explicitly in his *Nyāyakandalī*.[42] Accordingly *upamāna* is to be reduced to *anumāna* because when one knows by analogy one actually knows on the basis of one's knowledge of *vyāpti* (*vyāpti-graha-valena*). Śrīdhara has given an example also which suggests that knowledge by analogy is like knowledge of fire from smoke.

One may think that there is difference of opinion among the Vaiśeṣikas. Some Vaiśeṣikas appear to think that *upamāna* is reducible to *śabda*. Śaṅkara Miśra in his *Kaṇāda-Rahasya* has written, *tathāpi upamānam astu pramāṇāntaram iti cet na śabdāteva tatra . . . paricchedāt*.[43] So according to Śaṅkara Miśra in case of so-called knowledge by analogy one actually derives the knowledge from *śabda*. Similarly Praśastapāda writes: *āptena aprasiddhasya gavayasya gabā gavaya pratipādanam āptavacanam eva*.[44] From these passages one may think that the Vaiśeṣikas reduced *upamāna* into *śabda*. What is then the actual position of the Vaiśeṣikas? Do they reduce *upamāna* to *śabda* or to *anumāna*? Before we answer this question we should say that what Śaṅkara Miśra says here is not incompatible with what he said in his *Upaskāra* (*upamānādīnām api . . . laiṅgika eva antarbhāvaḥ*) or what Praśastapāda said in his *Padārtha-Dharma-Saṁgraha* (*śabdādīnām api anumāne antarbhāva*). Perhaps to remove such thought of incompatibility Śaṅkara Miśra says in his *Kaṇāda-Rahasya, śabdasya ca anumānāntara bhūtatvāt*.[45] In other words *śabda* according to the Vaiśeṣikas is included in *anumāna*.

---

41. Praśastapāda, 1963, p. 512.
42. Ibid., p. 530.
43. Śaṅkara Miśra, 1917, p. 106.
44. Praśastapāda, 1963, p. 530.
45. Śaṅkara Miśra, 1917, p. 106.

We now understand the Vaiśeṣika view in the following way: (1) what we know in case of *upamāna*, we know from words (*śabdādeva paricchedāt*).[46] And (2) *śabda* is included in or reduced to *anumāna* (*śabdasya ca anumānāntara bhūtatvāt*).[47] Thus ultimately there is no difference, from the point of view of the Vaiśeṣikas, between reducing *upamāna* to *śabda* and reducing *upamāna* to *anumāna*.

We can also view the situation in this way. The Vaiśeṣikas are criticizing the views of both (a) who hold that *upamāna* is an independent *pramāṇa* but which is of the nature of a particular sentence called *atideśa vākya* and (b) *upamāna* is a *svatantra pramāṇa* and it is not of the nature of *śabda*. Thus it follows that the Vaiśeṣikas also criticize the view according to which the knowledge we have in case of *upamāna* is derived from (certain particular) *śabda*. In other words *upamāna* in the sense of *upamiti-karaṇa* is the *atideśa vākya* itself. Praśastapāda has clearly stated, *upamānam āpta vacanam eva*.[48] The author of *Nyāyakandalī* has referred to this view as the view of Pūrva-Mīmāṁsā.[49]

Some may say that the Vaiśeṣikas cannot be taken here to criticize the classical Mīmāṁsā theory. For the Vaiśeṣikas criticize the view of *upamāna* of those who take *āptopadeśa* (or, here, the statement of analogy of authoritative person) to be *upamāna*. And this cannot be the classical Mīmāṁsā theory. For that theory was a response to the classical Nyāya theory of *upamāna*. In the classical period the Mīmāṁsakas could not accept the Nyāya view of *upamāna*. For according to this Nyāya view *upamāna* is *āptopadeśa* (*atideśa vākya*). The Mīmāṁsakas found that to hold *āptopadeśa* to be *upamāna*, was to reduce *upamāna* (*upamiti*) to *śabda* (*śābda*). The Vaiśeṣikas seem to have carried this argument

---

46. Ibid., p. 106.
47. Ibid, p. 106
48. Praśastapāda, 1963, p. 530.
49. Śrīdhara Bhaṭṭa, 1963, p. 531.

one step further. They have reduced *śabda* to *anumāna*. In any case the Vaiśeṣikas cannot be taken to criticize the classical Mīmāṁsā view.

It seems therefore the Vaiśeṣikas have the old Nyāya theory in view when they criticize *upamāna* which is *atideśa vākya*. They cannot be viewed as external critics of Mīmāṁsā. The situation may be analysed in this way. The classical Mīmāṁsakas criticized the classical Nyāya view on the ground that classical Nyāya destroys independence of *upamāna*. Now the Vaiśeṣikas show that the same objection holds against the classical Mīmāṁsā. *Upamāna* according to the classical Mīmāṁsā is reduced to *śabda*. Thus from the Vaiśeṣika texts that we have considered here it appears that the Vaiśeṣika objection is against classical Nyāya view. And at the same time we can say that the Vaiśeṣikas hold the same view about the classical Mīmāṁsā theory as well. *Upamāna* according to both these theories of Nyāya and Mīmāṁsā is actually *śabda*. So it is ultimately reducible to *anumāna*.

We shall present some textual evidences. We know according to the classical Nyāya *upamāna* is knowledge of *śakti*. If the Vaiśeṣikas say that *upamāna* in this sense is derived from *śabda* or *āptopadeśa* then they can be taken to criticize the classical Nyāya theory of *upamāna*. Now we can quote from two Vaiśeṣika texts:

(1) *āptena aprasiddhasya gavayasya gabā gavaya pratipādanāt upamānam āpta vacanam eva.*[50]

(2) *yathā gau gavayaḥ tathā — iti vākyam āptavacanam eva.*[51]

From these two quotations it is clear that in the present context the Vaiśeṣikas hold the *atideśa vākya* to be *śabda-pramāṇa*. And it is *upamāna*.

50. Praśastapāda, 1963, p. 530.

51. Śrīdharabhaṭṭa, 1963, p. 531.

(3) *āptavacanaṁ ca anumānam. tasmāt upamānam api anumāna-avyatiriktam iti abhiprāyaḥ.*[52]

From this it is clear that if *upamāna* is *śabda* or *āptopadeśa* then it is *anumāna* on final analysis. But a question remains. Is it *anumāna* of *śakti* or of *sādṛśya*?

(4) *tathāpi upamānam astu pramāṇāntaram iti cet na śabdāt eva tatra saṁjñā-saṁjñi-sambandha paricchedāt. śabdasya ca anumānāntarbhūtatvāt.*[53]

From Śaṅkara Miśra's statement it is clear that according to the Vaiśeṣikas *upamāna* in the sense of knowledge of *śakti* is reduced to *śabda* and then to *anumāna*. To be sure that the Vaiśeṣikas mean to criticize the classical Mīmāṁsakas, we need other proof. If according to the Vaiśeṣikas the Mīmāṁsakas held knowledge of *sādṛśya* to be *anumāna* then they are critics of Mīmāṁsā.

(5) *ye tāvat pūrva mīmāṁsakā banecara vacanam eva upamānam āhuḥ, teṣām idam anumānam eva.*[54]

From the statement of Śrīdhara it appears that Mīmāṁsakas particularly the Pūrva-Mīmāṁsakas held that the statement of analogy was *upamāna pramāṇa*. We have no idea who are these Pūrva-Mīmāṁsakas. Durgadhar Jha tells us in his Hindi translation of *Nyāyakandalī* that these Mīmāṁsakas are old Mīmāṁsakas (*prācīna-mīmāṁsakāḥ*).[55]

Śaṅkara Miśra in his *Upaskāra* and Vallabhācārya in his *Nyāya-Līlāvatī* have shown in some detail how knowledge of *sādṛśya* is derived from *śabda* and *anumāna* (or through *śabda* from *anumāna*). Śaṅkara Miśra says, *upamānaṁ tāvat anumānam eva śabdadvārā.*[56] Vallabhācārya in his *Nyāyalīlāvatī* has referred to

52. Ibid. p. 531.

53. Śaṅkara Miśra, 1917, p. 106

54. Śrīdhara Bhaṭṭa, 1963, p. 531

55. Durgadhar Jha, 1963, p. 531.

56. Śaṅkara Miśra, *Upaskāra* on *Vaiśeṣika-Sūtra*, 9.2.5.

Śabara by name. Referring to the theory of Mīmāṁsā in the school of Śabara he said *upamāna* is *anumāna*. His words are: *śābaraṁ tu upamānam anumānam eva*. But Vallabhācārya did not say that knowledge of *sādṛśya* comes from *atideśa vākya*. He shows directly how knowledge of *sādṛśya* can be derived from *anumāna*. He formulates the inference in the following way:

> *sa gauḥ anena sadṛśaḥ;*
> *sva sādṛśyena etat avacchedakatvāt,*
> *yadevaṁ tadevaṁ yathā bhrātā bhaginī iti.*[57]

The argument is as follows: that cow is similar to this, because (it = the cow) characterizes (*avacchedakatvāt*) this (the presented thing = *gavaya*) by its own similarity. What is so characterized has that (kind of) similarity. The example is brother and sister.

The idea is the following. According to the Mīmāṁsakas the knowledge which is *upamiti* has this form: *anena sadṛśī madīyā gauḥ*. That cow (in my village house) is similar to this (the animal which I am perceiving now). The subject of inferential knowledge, *sā gauḥ* (that cow) is *pakṣa* of the inference. The predicate of inferential knowledge is called *sādhya*. Now the ground of the inference is a little complicated. We infer the cow, which is in the village and which we do not see now (that is the *pakṣa* or P), to be similar to (or has similarity with) the animal (*gavaya*) which we are now perceiving. But how can we know that that cow is similar to this *gavaya*? Vallabha says that this *gavaya* is qualified by a similarity which has its other term 'that cow.' So from the side of that cow (*sā gauḥ*) we can say that that cow is related through its own similarity (*sva sādṛśyena*) with this animal (*etat*). In other words that cow is the *avacchedaka* (qualifier) of the similarity of its own (*sva sādṛśya*) which is there in this *gavaya*. And because that cow or the *sva* is the *avacchedaka* (qualifier). This *avacchedakatva* is the ground of the inference (*hetu*). And the *sā* is the subject of inference (*pakṣa*). And as the

57. Vallabhācārya, 1934, pp. 537-38.

pakṣa has this *hetu* so we can infer that the *pakṣa* has the *sādhya* or the predicate of the inference. In short we can infer that the cow in the village is like this animal which now I am perceiving, because that cow has the property of being the qualifier (*avacchedakatvāt*) in respect of the cow-similarity which this *gavaya* has.

Vallabha finds in brother and sister an example of the type of similarity which obtains between a cow and a bison. Sometimes we see a boy and also see in him similarity with a girl whom we know. The girl is not present at the moment. After perceiving them both we remember his sister as having similarity with this boy, there we remember her. And we see in the boy the similarity with that girl. We come to know that that girl must have resemblance with this boy. This is a new information; we never before perceived this girl to be similar to this boy. Nor do we remember that that girl is similar to this boy. We actually come to know this through inference. We go further and often infer correctly that that girl must be the sister of this boy. And the boy must be her brother. Our knowledge in case of *upamāna* is exactly like this. We infer the cow in the village to be similar to this animal (*gavaya*).

In this account of Vallabha we find Vaiśeṣika criticism of classical Mīmāṁsā view of *upamāna*. We found before that classical Mīmāṁsā view has three major tenets. Of these the first that *upamāna* is knowledge of *sādṛśya* has not been discussed. That is, Vallabha shows no interest to reject the view that *upamāna* is knowledge of *sādṛśya*. As a realist school the Vaiśeṣikas admit that we have knowledge of *sādṛśya* (they also admit that we have knowledge of *śakti*). The Vaiśeṣikas have no interest to enter into the debate whether *upamāna* is knowledge of *sādṛśya* or of something else. They find that the classical Mīmāṁsaka admit *upamāna* as knowledge of *sādṛśya*. This does not conflict with the Vaiśeṣika position if a third *pramāṇa* is not needed. The Mīmāṁsakas believed that an additional *pramāṇa* was necessary for this knowledge. And according to them this additional *pramāṇa* is *upamāna*. The Vaiśeṣikas criticize this aspect of Mīmāṁsā theory. They show that the knowledge of *sādṛśya* can be obtained through inference. This is described as Vaiśeṣika reduction of *upamiti* into *anumiti*. Now *pramāṇa* behind *upamiti* must be *anumāna* if we reduce *upamiti* to *anumiti*.

The remaining major tenets of classical Mīmāṁsā view is that *sādṛśya* is an additional category. We have not here discussed the Vaiśeṣika criticism of this tenet of the Mīmāṁsakas. For we have taken as our source of classical Mīmāṁsā theory Śabarasvāmī's statement in his commentary on *Mīmāṁsā-Sūtra* 1.1.5. In Śabara's account this tenet is not well developed. This was fully developed in the Prābhākara school by Prābhākara Miśra and his followers. We shall discuss that in the next chapter. We will discuss therefore the Vaiśeṣika rejection of the view that *sādṛśya* is a separate category after discussing Prabhākara's theory. Among the major critics of this view are Kumārila, Udayana and Gaṅgeśa. Though Udayana came after Kumārila he rejected *sādṛśya* considered as a separate *padārtha,* in a different way. But Udayana like Kumārila accepted *upamāna* as a *svatantra* (independent) *pramāṇa*. The famous Vaiśeṣika Ācārya Vallabha criticized by name this view of Udayana or the author of *Kiraṇāvalī* and rejected the view that *upamāna* was a *svatantra pramāṇa*. Later Gaṅgeśa re-established the tenet that *upamāna* is a *svatantra pramāṇa*. This tenet is accepted both in the Nyāya school (as we find in Gautama, Vātsyāyana, etc.) and in the syncretic school of Nyāya-Vaiśeṣika (as we find in Udayana).

We conclude here our discussion of the objections of the external critics of the classical Mīmāṁsā view. Before we take up the criticisms of the internal (Mīmāṁsā) critics like Kumārila we will discuss the Prabhākara view. In the next chapter we will begin our discussion of medieval and modern versions of Mīmāṁsā theory of *upamāna* with the views of Prabhākara. But before that in the next section we will give a comparative account of the views and achievement of the external critics of Mīmāṁsakas we have considered so far.

IV

It has already been stated earlier that Ratnakīrti criticized the Mīmāṁsā position in his own way. A Bauddha is to prove against the Mīmāṁsakas that there is no such thing as *upamāna*. But how can he prove it? He can prove it along the following line (of argument). There is no *upamāna* because there is no *viṣaya* of *upamāna*. But how to prove that *upamāna* has no *viṣaya*? A Bauddha may argue following Dharmakīrti (D) if there is no *sādṛśya* then according to the Mīmāṁsakas, there is no *viṣaya* of *upamāna*. And there is no similarity, for it is neither *svalakṣaṇa* nor *sāmānya lakṣaṇa*.[58] But Ratnakīrti did not follow this line.[59] He on the other hand followed a second line of argument of his own. This line of argument is stronger. Unless one is a Bauddha or accepts the Bauddha scheme that is to be either a *svalakṣaṇa* or *sāmānya lakṣaṇa* one cannot argue along the first line or Dharmakīrti line, i.e. one cannot argue in the way of (D). Ratnakīrti's line of argument may be symbolized by (R). And the line of argument is this: the supposed *viṣaya* of *upamāna*, i.e. *sādṛśya* does not exist. Now one can adopt this line of argument (R), i.e. the argument of Ratnakīrti even if one does not accept the Bauddha scheme of things. So while it is only a Bauddha who can argue along the line of (D) both a Bauddha and a non-**Bauddha** can argue along the line of (R), because this line of argument does not presuppose Bauddha scheme of things. So Ratnakīrti's argument is logically stronger. It remains valid even if Bauddha position (that things are either *svalakṣaṇa* or *sāmānya lakṣaṇa*) turns out to be wrong. To put it differently both a

58. Panchanan Shastri (1993), pp. 70, 74.

59. The line of argument which begins by accepting that there are only two types of things (*prameya dvaividdhya*), viz. *svalakṣaṇa* and *sāmānya lakṣaṇa* is narrow Buddhist way or "Dharmakīrti" way.

Bauddha and a non-Bauddha critic or Mīmāṁsā position can offer the argument (R). On the other hand it is only a Bauddha critic who can argue in the way of (D).

For a similar reason Ratnakīrti's argument is stronger than another possible line of argument. Let us symbolize it as (K). This line of argument will be valid if the Vaiśeṣika's scheme of things is accepted. A Vaiśeṣika only can say that a thing is either *bhāva* (positive) or *abhāva* (negative). And if a thing is *bhāva* it must be anyone of the six kinds of things into which *bhāva* can be logically divided. If *sādṛśya* is not *abhāva* also then *sādṛśya* is fictitious. This line of argument (which can be called Kaṇāda line of argument) showing that there is no *sādṛśya* can be adopted, only by Vaiśeṣika or his follower. But argument (R) of Ratnakīrti can be given by a non-Vaiśeṣika also. In short Ratnakīrti's argument (R) is stronger than peculiarly Bauddha (D) or peculiarly Vaiśeṣika argument (K). One can offer the argument (D) so far as he aceepts Bauddha scheme of things and he can offer the line of argument (K) if he accepts Vaiśeṣika scheme of things. On the other hand argument (R) does not need that one should presuppose the Vaiśeṣika or Bauddha view. This shows that Ratnakīrti's argument (R) is more strong than (D) or (K); for this line of argument does not presuppose any specific scheme of categories.

There is another reason why Ratnakīrti's way of criticizing Mīmāṁsā position is stronger. His argument (R) that *upamāna* has no *viṣaya* can be used to show the absence of *upamāna* both in the sense of *upamiti-karaṇa* and in the sense of *upamiti*. Some other argument may prove only the absence of *upamiti-karaṇa* or absence of *upamiti*. Ratnakīrti has noted that both *upamiti* and *upamiti-karaṇa* are knowledge. A Mīmāṁsaka holds that knowledge of one (type of) similarity is *upamiti* and knowledge of another (type of) similarity is *upamiti-karaṇa*.[60] But in any case

60. Kamalākara Bhaṭṭa, 1987, p. 74.

both *upamiti* and *upamāna* (*upamiti-karaṇa*) are, according to Mīmāṁsakas, knowledge of similarity. If now it can be shown that there is no similarity then it would follow that there is no *upamāna*. For *upamāna* is knowledge of similarity and there cannot be any knowledge without *viṣaya*. Thus Ratnakīrti's argument that there cannot be *upamāna* because it has no *viṣaya* applies both to *upamiti* and *upamiti-karaṇa*. So it is wider in scope and stronger. It remains valid if one understands by *upamāna, upamiti-karaṇa*. It also remains valid if one means by *upamāna, upamiti*.

If (R) proved absence of *upamiti* only, then it would follow indirectly that there was no *upamiti-karaṇa*. For there need not be cause or *karaṇa* if there is no *phala* or result. There cannot be *upamiti-karaṇa* for there is no *upamiti*. This will be the usual way. But Ratnakīrti's argument directly shows that there is no *upamiti-karaṇa*, for there is no *viṣaya of upamiti-karaṇa*. We can compare the usual way with Ratnakīrti way. The usual way of argument follows the following line:

Stage I

(i) There is no *sādṛśya*, the supposed *viṣaya* of *upamiti*;

(ii) Therefore there is no *upamiti*.

The principle used here is

(P_1) *sādṛśyābhāvāt upamānābhāvaḥ*.

This principle is a special case of more general principle (GP_1)

(Gp_1) *viṣayābhāvāt jñānābhāvaḥ*.

Stage II

(iii) There is no *upamiti*, the supposed effect or phala of *upamāna* (*upamiti-karaṇa*);

(iv) Therefore there is no *upamiti-karaṇa*.

The principle used here is

(P_2) *upamiti abhāvāt upamānābhāvaḥ.*

This principle is a special case of more general principle.

(GP_2) *kāryābhāvāt kāraṇābhāvaḥ.*

So we see that the general principle involved in the first stage of argument is "no knowledge without object" or *viṣayābhāvāt jñānābhāvaḥ*. The general principle in the second stage is, there is no cause without effect or *phalābhāvāt* or *kāryābhāvāt kāraṇā-bhāvah*. What is meant here is that the question of admitting a cause does not arise, where there is no effect.

Ratnakīrti's arguments may be presented in the following way.

Ratnakīrti's argument

	I		II
(i)	There is no *sādr̥śya* the supposed *viṣaya* of *upamiti*	(i)	There is no *sādr̥śya* or supposed *viṣaya* of *upamāna* (*upamiti-karaṇa*)
(ii)	There is no *upamiti.* Principle behind is (P_1) or (GP_1).	(ii)	There is no *upamāna* (*upamiti-karaṇa*). Principle behind is the same (P_1) or (GP_1)
(P_1)	*sādr̥śyābhāvāt upamānābhāva.* or (GP_1) *viṣayābhāvāt jñānābhāva.*	(P_1)	*sādr̥śyābhāvāt upamānābhāva.* or (GP_1) *viṣayābhāvāt jñānābhāva.*

Thus if one wants to prove in the usual way that there is no *upamāna* (*upamiti-karaṇa*) because there is no *sādr̥śya* then one needs four steps as we have shown earlier. In the Ratnakīrti way we need only two steps.

But here one may raise an objection. Ratnakīrti presupposes that *pramākaraṇa* must have a *viṣaya*. For then only one can say that *upamiti-karaṇa* must have a *viṣaya*. But since *upamiti-karaṇa* does not have any *viṣaya* (for there is no similarity), so there is no *upamiti-karaṇa*. This presupposition of Ratnakīrti is not accepted by all. Everyone accepts that a *karaṇa* must have a *phala* or effect. For *karaṇa* is a kind of cause and there cannot be admitted any cause if there is no effect. Ratnakīrti's presupposition will be well founded if *pramākaraṇa* is necessarily a knowledge. Philosophers like Bauddhas and Jainas hold that *pramāṇa* (*pramākaraṇa*) is necessarily a state of knowledge.[61] But a Naiyāyika[62] or a Vaiśeṣika[63] or a Mīmāṁsaka(?)[64] does not hold this. It may however be said that we can ignore all these details here. For though according to the Naiyāyikas, etc. a *pramākaraṇa* need not be a knowledge (*jñāna*) yet *upamiti-karaṇa* is admitted to be a knowledge or *jñāna* (of similarity).

The argument *viṣayābhāvāt upamānābhāva* is strong for another reason also. It is strong because it equally affects the (Mīmāṁsā) view that *upamiti* is the knowledge of similarity and the (Nyāya) view that *upamiti* is knowledge of *śakti*. For if *viṣaya* (*sādṛśya* or *śakti*) is not there then *upamiti* (*upamāna*) is not there. So the way in which Ratnakīrti tried to show that there is no *upamiti* (because there is no object of *upamiti*, that is, no *sādṛśya* is strong. And the way Ratnakīrti tried to prove absence of *sādṛśya* has also been shown to be strong.

61. *Prameya-Kamala-Mārtaṇḍa*, 1941, p. 25; See note 11 above also.
62. Cf. Jayanta, 1936, p. 14; see also Vātsyāyana *Bhāṣya* on *sūtra* 1.1.3.
63. Cf. Śrīdhara Bhaṭṭa, 1963, p. 472.
64. See Jaimini (Pūrva-Mīmāṁsā) *sūtra* 1.1.4; Bhūtanātha, 1345, p. 19.

4

Mīmāṁsā Theory of Upamāna
Medieval and Modern Versions

I

In this chapter my objective is to present the views of the medieval and modern Mīmāṁsakas. In the first chapter I have presented the classical Nyāya view of *upamāna*. In the same chapter I have also considered the views of the classical Mīmāṁsā as against the classical Nyāya view. According to classical Mīmāṁsā, the classical Nyāya view tended to reduce *upamāna* to *śabda*. So to preserve independence of *upamāna* as a *pramāṇa* Śabara offered a different definition of *upamāna*. Śabara's definition of *upamāna* suggests that there is a kind of thing called similarity and *upamāna* is the knowledge of that (similarity). But this view is not free from objections and so I have presented the objections of the Bauddhas and the Vaiśeṣikas against the classical Mīmāṁsā view. We consider the Bauddhas and the Vaiśeṣikas to be the external critics of the Mīmāṁsā theory of *upamāna*. But here one point we are to note. Śabara has not explicitly stated that similarity, what *upamāna* knows, is an independent type of existent or category. It is Prābhākara Miśra who took the responsibility of showing that similarity is an independent category. So Prābhākara went one step further. He not only accepted the view that *upamāna* is an independent *pramāṇa*, but also held that the similarity which *upamāna* knows, is an independent category. From this it appears that, Prābhākara Mīmāṁsā theory is more radical than the theory of Bhāṭṭa Mīmāṁsakas.

After Śabara the Mīmāṁsakas were divided into three schools: the Prābhākara school, the Bhāṭṭa school and the Murārimiśra school. I am to consider only the views of Prābhākara and Kumārila tradition. Discussion of these views will cover the medieval and modern periods of the development of Mīmāṁsā thought about *upamāna*. If Murārimiśra school has any distinct view about *upamāna* it is not known to me. It is in the sense that I have not been able to locate such definite or explicit reference.[1] Between the two other schools, the Prābhākaras are more radical than the (Kumārila) Bhaṭṭas. The Prābhākara school, as I have already stated, admit not only that there is an independent *pramāṇa* called *upamāna*, they also admit similarity as an independent category which *upamāna* knows. It has already been shown that the external critics like the Bauddhas and the Vaiśeṣikas challenged these tenets. Now the author is to state how the radical Mīmāṁsakas show that *upamāna* is an irreducible *pramāṇa* and the similarity it knows is an independent category. After the presentation of the Prābhākara view we are to present the view of their internal critic, the Bhāṭṭa Mīmāṁsaka. Kumārila admits *upamāna* as an independent *pramāṇa;* he also admits *upamāna* to be the means of knowledge of similarity. But he does not admit similarity as an independent category. So Kumārila differs from the Buddhists when he admits similarity. But he agrees both with the Buddhists and the Vaiśeṣikas in rejecting similarity as an independent category. Kumārila and his followers admit *upamāna* for the knowledge of similarity. Here I want to say that the Buddhists are Rejectionists, the Vaiśeṣikas are the Reductionists and the Bhāṭṭas are the Revisionists so far as the radical Prābhākara Mīmāṁsā theory of *upamāna* is concerned. The Naiyāyikas on

1. We however know that *sādṛśya* is not included in the five ontological categories which are admitted in the Murārimiśra school. See note 19 below.

the other hand are the Realists school regarding *upamāna*. But the Naiyāyikas are less radical among the realist schools. They admit *upamāna* as an irreducible *pramāṇa*. But they do not admit similarity as an additional category of thing.

It has already been noted that the familiar objection is that classical Nyāya reduced *upamāna* to *śabda*. And to avoid this Śabara offered a different definition of *upamāna*. To strengthen the view of Śabara, Prābhākara has taken the most radical way. And as a consequence he avoided the insertion of *atideśa vākya* from the description of *upamāna*. So in place of *atideśa vākya*, etc. in his *Bṛhatī Ṭīkā* Prābhākara Miśra has used the expression *anubhūta go puruṣasya* etc. This phrase means, the person who had experienced, in the past, the cow in a cow in a non-recollective way. Now he has the memory cognition of what he has experienced earlier. So Prābhākara explains the words of Śabara, *go smaraṇasya* to mean *anubhūta go puruṣasya*. According to Śabara *upamānamapi asannikṛṣṭe arthe sādṛśyabuddhimutpādayati, yathā gavayadarśanam go smaraṇasya*. It is therefore clear that when he defines *upamāna* Śabarasvāmī says that *upamāna* also generates awareness of resemblance in respect of some *asannikṛṣṭa artha*. But why does he say *gosmaraṇasya*? If we take it in its face value the text seems to be *gosmaraṇasya asannikṛṣṭe arthe buddhim utpādayati*. This statement contains answer to the question "What does *upamāna* do?" The answer is *buddhim utpādayati*. Thus Śabara says *upamāna* produces *buddhi*, i.e. belief or awareness. Awareness of what? It is awareness of *sādṛśya* or resemblance. Where does this resemblance reside? It resides in *asannikṛṣṭa artha*, i.e. in the thing which is not now in contact with the sense organ. Now the most important question is, knowledge of whom? Or to whom does this knowledge belong? Who possesses the knowledge? The statement of Śabara says *gosmaraṇasya buddhi*, i.e. knowledge of (knowledge possessed by) *gosmaraṇa*. But knowledge can be possessed by some sentient being or *cetana puruṣa*. *Gosmaraṇa* or memory of cow is a state of mind, a cognitive state. How can it be a knower? If *gosmaraṇa* cannot be a knower, it cannot have *buddhi*. How then are we to understand the expression *puruṣasya buddhi* (knowledge or belief of man) but not *gosmaraṇasya buddhi*. Prābhākara has noted this point. One awareness, memory (*gosmaraṇa*), cannot be the possessor of another awareness, the awareness of *sādr̥śya*. Prābhākara has also solved the problem. He explains *gosmaraṇasya* to mean *anubhūtagoḥ puruṣasya* (*ityarthaḥ*).[2] According to this interpretation of Śabara's view, *upamāna* is also a means or the source of knowledge. The object of this awareness is similarity. In the standard example, the man, who had earlier (non-recollectively) experienced a cow, has this awareness. But this *sādr̥śya* is known as residing in some object which is not related to sense organ at the moment. In our standard example this object is the cow; it is the same cow which the knower had non-recollectively experienced earlier, but is not perceiving now. So according to this analysis of Śabara and Prābhākara, in the context of *upamāna* the person who has recollective awareness of *go* knows the similarity in that *gau* (cow) after perceiving the similarity in the sense-presented object *gavaya* (bison). So *upamiti* is the knowledge of similarity of *gavaya* (what is presented to the senses) in the cow (what is in the recollective awareness).

Here we are to note that Prābhākara's interpretation of *gosmaraṇasya* as *anubhūta go puruṣasya* is very subtle. It would have been more natural to interpret the expression as *smaryamāṇa go puruṣasya*. It suggests that according to Prābhākara *upamiti* is not awareness of *sādr̥śya* in the object being remembered at the moment. Thus he seems to reject first two of the following three interpretations of *upamiti*. (1) Both the *go* and similarity as existing in it are remembered. (2) *go* is remembered but *sādr̥śya* is known by *upamāna*. (3) Both *go* and similarity are known by *upamāna*. The sense in which the (3) will be accepted by the

2. Prābhākara, 1934, p. 107. Accordingly Śālikanātha interprets it in his *Prakaraṇa-Pañcikā* to mean *dr̥ṣṭagauḥ puruṣasya*.

Mīmāṁsakas will become clear in the next phase of the discussion.

The next important point to note in the account of *upamāna* given by Prābhākara in his *Bṛhatī* is this. He raised and answered the question about the need for a definition of *upamāna*. The question is "What is that to exclude which this definition of *upamāna* is necessary (. . . *yannivṛtyārthamidaṁ lakṣaṇam*?)." The answer which Prābhākara gives is *sadṛśābhāṣāt*,[3] that what appears as similar. Thus according to him a definition of *upamāna* is needed so that one can distinguish what is really *upamāna* from what only seems to be (or looks like) an *upamāna*. There are things which are really similar, such as a cow and a *gavaya*. But there are also dissimilar things like cow and camel. Śālikanātha in his *Ṛjuvimalā-Pañcikā* has given the example *palālakūṭa* (pile of straw?) and an elephant. If one has the experience "this is like an elephant" about something which does not really resemble an elephant, then the experience will be about false similarity.[4]

Following Śabarasvāmī, Prābhākara then gives this account of *upamāna*. Sometimes we have genuine experience or knowledge of similarity. Sometimes one cognizes similarity in a thing which a person has experienced earlier, but which he is not experiencing at that moment. In such cases the knowledge of similarity is called *upamiti*.[5] A standard case of *upamiti* is the following. A villager who has cows in his house sometimes goes to a forest. He there perceives an unfamiliar animal. He also perceives in that animal its similarity with the cows which are familiar to him and which are there in his village house. This

3. Prābhākara, 1934, p. 108.

4. *yathā palāla-kūṭaṁ dṛṣṭvā etat sadṛśo hastī- iti jñānaṁ sadṛśābhāṣa-viṣayamiti*. Ibid., 109.

5. *upamānam api sādṛśyam*, Śabara — 1934, p. 107. *sādṛśyamiti hi sādṛśyam* — Prābhākara, 1934, p. 107. *sādṛśyam iti yatra jñānaṁ, tat sādṛśyam* — Śālikanātha, 1934, p. 107.

knowledge of similarity in the animal of the villager is a perception. It is about an unfamiliar animal which he is perceiving for the first time. He perceives in this animal similarity with familiar cows, i.e. cows which are familiar to him. The cows are familiar because he has cows in his village house, and there he had seen the cows which are familiar to him. The cows are familiar because he has cows in his village house, and there he had seen the cows so many times before. After perceiving the unfamiliar animal and familiar cow-similarity in it, the villager has, on the basis of this perception, another piece of knowledge. It is the knowledge of similarity in the cow. This last piece of knowledge is a genuine example of knowledge by analogy or *upamiti*. This *upamiti* is a knowledge about the cows. These cows are in the village, and the villager is in the forest. Therefore this knowledge of the villager is not perception of the (familiar village) cows. But these cows are not unfamiliar also. He had earlier seen the cows. Now he remembers them. But while the villager remembers the cows he also knows that these cows are similar to the unfamiliar animal he is perceiving now. To distinguish such genuine knowledge of similarity (the unfamiliar animal and the familiar cows are really similar) from false awareness of similarity (i.e. when things known are not really similar), here we need a definition of *upamāna*, or knowledge of similarity. Once we have a definition of *upamiti* we can distinguish, by applying this definition, a genuine case of *upamāna* from an awareness which simulates *upamāna*. Accoding to Prābhākara we find this definition in Śabarasvāmī's *Bhāṣya*. But the sentence of the *bhāṣya* which is taken as Śabara's definition of *upamāna* is incomplete. Prābhākara says we are to add to it the word *jñāta-sambandha*. This word has been included by Śabara in his definition of *anumāna*.[6] In the light of Śabara's definition of *anumāna*, Prābhākara suggested that Śabara's definition of *upamāna* is to be reconstructed by adding

6. *anumānaṁ jñātasambandhasya ekadeśa darśanāt ekadeśāntare asannikṛṣṭe arthe buddhiḥ* — Śabara, 1934, p. 90.

the word *jñāta-sambandha.* The complete statement of the definition has not been given by Prābhākara or Śālikanātha. But it seems the reading will be the following:

> *upamānamapi jñātasambandhasādṛśyam asannikṛṣṭe arthe buddhimutpādayati,*
> *yathā gavayadarśanaṁ gosmaraṇasya.*

The word *api* means also or as well. So there must be some other thing which causes (*utpādayati*) knowledge (*buddhiṁ*); this knowledge is the knowledge of a thing which is not in contact with sense organ (*asannikṛṣṭe arthe*). When we see a table, the thing table stands related to visual sense organ in the relation of conjunction or *saṁyoga*; it is according to the Naiyāyikas one of the six relations which generate ordinary or normal (*laukika*) perception. Śabarasvāmī has said before when he defined inference (*anumāna*), *anumānam . . . asannikṛṣṭe 'rthe buddhiḥ.* Then he said *śāstram . . . asannikṛṣṭe 'rthe vijñānaṁ.*[7] Now he says *upamānamapi . . . asannikṛṣṭe 'rthe buddhimutpādayati. . . .* If *upamāna* also, i.e. like *anumāna* and *śāstra* causes knowledge about thing which is not perceptually related then there must be some similarity between *anumāna* and *upamāna.* Following Prābhākara we now understand that this similarity is in respect of *jñāta-sambandha.* What it actually means has been stated by Śālikanātha in his *Ṛjuvimalā-Pañcikā.* Before we state that we should also mention that according to Prābhākara this *jñāta-sambandha* forms a part of the definition of *upamāna.* This *jñāta-sambandha* is the *sādṛśya sambandha* which resides in the *gavaya.* So when one perceives the *gavaya* he perceives similarity in it. One relatum of this similarity is the cow which he has perceived earlier. From the perception of this similarity in *gavaya* he now knows the similarity in the cow. This knowledge of similarity in the cow is not caused by any other *pramāṇa. Upamāna* causes this knowledge or *upamāna pramāṇa* yields knowledge of (certain) similarity.

---

7. Śabara, 1934, pp. 90, 105.

Now so far as the above discussion is concerned it is seen that the Prābhākaras have not explained *upamāna* in terms of *atideśa vākya*. In place of *atideśa vākya* or statement of analogy in the *Ṭīkā Bṛhatī* Prābhākara writes *anubhūta go smaraṇasya*. This means the person who has (non-recollectively) experienced the cow earlier. In *Prakaraṇa-Pañcikā* also we see Śālikanātha states that *sādṛśyadarśanotthaṁ jñānaṁ sādṛśyaviṣayam.*[8] The knowledge of *sādṛśya* which results from the perception of *sādṛśya* is the *upamāna*. Thus in Mīmāṁsā school or in the Prābhākara school of Mīmāṁsā *upamiti* is not said to result from *vākya*. *Śabda* or *vākya* is not the cause of *upamiti*. So it cannot be objected that the Mīmāṁsā interpretation of *upamāna* identifies *upamiti* with *śabda-jñāna*. So the objection that was brought against the definition given by Gautama cannot be brought against the Mīmāṁsā definition as formulated by Prābhākara or the Prābhākaras.

A Mīmāṁsaka can now say that the classical Nyāya theory of *upamāna* reduced *upamāna* to *śabda*. To avoid that, Śabara in classical Mīmāṁsā defined *upamāna* in a different way. Vātsyāyana's interpretation of Gautama's definition of *upamāna* in terms of *atideśa vākya* made *upamāna* identical with *śabda*. Śabara's definition is stated in such a way that it could avoid the insertion of *atideśa vākya*. As a result *upamāna* can be admitted as a distinct *pramāṇa*. One may conclude, therefore, that Śabara's definition could prevent *upamāna* from becoming identical with *śabda-pramāṇa*.

Now Śabara's definition of *upamāna* is in terms of object. He has stated *upamānamapi sādṛśyam asannikṛṣṭe arthe buddhim utpādayati*. The statement partly means, *upamāna* produces knowledge in such object which is not in contact with the senses (*asannikṛṣṭa arthe*). From this two points become clear that (1)

8. Śālikanātha, 1961, p. 267.

upamāna as a *pramāṇa* which produces knowledge (*jñānam* or *buddhiḥ*) and (2) the object of such knowledge is not a thing which is in contact with the senses. But the question is, what is that object of *upamāna* which exists as a *asannikṛṣṭa artha*? In Śabara we find only one single word *sādṛśyam*. (Remember that he said *upamānamapi sādṛśyam asannikṛṣṭe arthe buddhimutpādayati*.) But from this it is not clear that the word *sādṛśya* (similarity) stands for the object (*viṣaya*) of *upamāna*. Prābhākara Miśra in his *Bṛhatī* has explained: *sādṛśyam iti hi sādṛśyam*.[9] This may be taken to mean *sādṛśya* or similarity is what it is. But in his *Ṛjuvimalā-Pañcikā*, Śālikanātha says, *asyārthaḥ — sādṛśyam iti yatra jñānam, tat sādṛśyam*: To put it in English, where there is the knowledge of the form "there is similarity" one is to admit similarity. And this similarity as characterizing a thing which is not in contact with the senses, is the object of *upamāna*. So according to Śabara's definition, as interpreted in the Prābhākara tradition, *upamāna* is the knowledge of such similarity which characterizes an object that is not in contact with the senses.

Thus in the Prābhākara tradition of Mīmāṁsā, *upamāna* in the sense of *upamiti* is (a) knowledge of similarity;[10] (b) this knowledge has the form[11] "this is similar to . . ." or "this has similarity with"; and (c) this similarity (the object known in *upamiti*) characterizes an *asannikṛṣṭa artha*. Means of this knowledge is also called *upamāna*. And *upamāna* in this sense of means of knowledge or *pramākaraṇa* is again knowledge of *sādṛśya*.[12] *Upamiti* is non-perceptual knowledge of similarity. And it is knowledge of similarity in an object which is not in contact

9. Prābhākara, 1934, p. 107.

10. *jñānaṁ sādṛśya viṣayam upamānam* — Śālikanātha, 1961, p. 267.

11. *sādṛśyam iti yatra jñānam* [*tat upamānam*] — Śālikanātha, 1934, p. 107.

12. *sādṛśyadarśanottham jñānam* . . . upamānam — Śālikanātha, 1961, p. 267.

with sense organ (*asannikṛṣṭe arthe*). *Upamāna* in the sense of *upamiti-karaṇa* or special means of *upamiti* is perceptual knowledge of similarity; and it is knowledge of similarity in an object which is in contact with sense organ (*sannikṛṣṭe arthe*). Śālikanātha brings out all these points in one sentence: *dṛṣṭa-goḥ puruṣasya tat sadṛśam gavayaṁ paśyato yat (asannikṛṣṭa) goviṣayakaṁ gavayagata-sādṛśyajñānam, tat upamānam.*[13]

We have seen what is *upamāna* according to Śabara, Prābhākara and his followers. It is a distinct kind of knowledge about a certain kind of similarity. But what is this *sādṛśya*? Śabarasvāmī did not make any explicit statement regarding the nature of *sādṛśya*. Prābhākara has clearly stated that similarity is an independent category. He writes, *tadeva tat*. The expression literally means that is what it is. So similarity is what it is or similarity is an irreducible existent. This actually shows that according to the Prābhākaras similarity is an independent category. There are others who think that similarity is the same as universal (*sāmānya*) and so there is no need for admitting similarity over and above universal. Śālikanātha in *Ṛjuvimalā-Pañcikā* further says *sādṛśyam bhinnam*. *Sādṛśya*s which reside in different loci are different. But *sāmānya* residing in different objects is same. As for example, manness; it resides in (all) different individual men; but it is still one and the same manhood. The case is different with similarity. Thus if we take two similar things, *a* and *b*, we have two similarities. One is the similarity which exists in *a*; it is the similarity with *b*. The other similarity is the similarity which exists in *b*. It is the similarity of *b* with *a*. Again, the similarity that is there *in the cow* is different from the similarity that is *in the bison*. So similarity differs as its locus differs. Same is not the case with universals.

Another standard objection which is made against similarity

---

13. Śālikanātha, 1961, p. 267.

is this: similarity is not enumerated with the other categories like substance, etc.[14] Against this objection, two answers can be given. (1) Even if similarity is not enumerated with the other categories, it does not follow that there is no such thing (existent) as similarity. In the *Vaiśeṣika-Sūtra* Kaṇāda has not enumerated *abhāva* along with the other categories; but does this really imply that the Vaiśeṣikas do not admit *abhāva*? They in fact admit *abhāva*. In the case of similarity also, one can admit it but may not enumerate it with the other categories. (2) It may be noted that we all have (valid) experience of similarity. Corresponding to such cognition or experience there must be object of it. So one is to admit similarity. Once this similarity is admitted, it is to be admitted as an independent category; of course if it is not reducible to any other kind of thing.

Śālikanātha has shown why *sādṛśya* cannot be reduced to any of the seven Vaiśeṣika categories.[15] Gaṅgeśa Upādhyāya has also noted in his *Upamānacintāmaṇi* the argument for the supposed irreducibility of *sādṛśya*.[16] Śālikanātha says that similarity (*sādṛśya*) cannot be either substance or quality or action, because it is located in (or characterizes) quality (*guṇa*) as well as action (*karma*).[17] No *dravya, guṇa* or *karma* exists in *karma*. Again similarity cannot be regarded as universal (*sāmānya*); because it

---

14. *nedaṁ dravya-guṇa-karma-sāmānya-samavāya-viśeṣāṇāṁ anyatamam. teṣām saṁgrahe asya apāṭhāt* — Śālikanātha 1961, p. 267. *sādṛśyasya dravyādi-padārtha-saṁgrahe parigaṇanādarśanāt kathaṁ tasya tattvāntaratva* — Jaypuri Narayana Bhaṭṭa, 1961, p. 267.

15. Śālikanātha, 1961, pp. 268.

16. Gaṅgeśopādhyāya, 1983, p. 3f.

17. The fact that *sādṛśya* resides in *guṇa* alone can prove that it is different from *dravya, guṇa* or *karma*. But there are exceptional cases where *guṇa* can be said to qualify another *guṇa*. So similarity can be successfully distinguished from the things of the first three categories by the fact that *sādṛsya* resides in both *guṇa* and *karma*.

cannot produce *anugata pratīti* (uniform experience).[18] *Sādṛśya* cannot also be *samavāya* (inherence); for *samavāya* is a relation but *sādṛśya* is not a relation. According to Śālikanātha the question of reducing *sādṛśya* (similarity) to *viśeṣa* does not arise. For *viśeṣa* is no *padārtha* or category; there is no argument, according to him, to show that there is a category called *viśeṣa* over and above *pṛthaktva*. It has not been said explicitly in these texts why *sādṛśya* cannot be reduced to *abhāva*. We can imagine an argument. An *abhāva* is the content of *nāsti buddhi* that is experience to the effect "it is not" or "it does not have." We have experience of the form that a substance is not a *guṇa*. The content of this experience is *guṇābhāva*, which is an *abhāva vastu*. *Sādṛśya* is not the content of *abhāva buddhi* like *ghaṭābhāva buddhi*. It may be the *pratiyogin* (negatum) of the content of some *abhāva buddhi*; *ghaṭa* is the negatum of *ghaṭābhāva* which is the content of *nāsti buddhi* of the form "Here there is no jar." All these show, according to the Prābhākaras, that *sādṛśya* is an additional category. Let us explain. As the Naiyāyikas say both *abhāva* (absence) and *sādṛśya* (similarity) are *sapratiyogika padārtha*; they are such entities which are never known (and which can never exist) without the thing of which they are absence or with which they resemble. Thus an *abhāva* is always an *abhāva* of a jar or table or a book and the like. But we experience a jar in a knowledge of the form "this *is* a jar" or "here there *is* a jar." But the absence of jar is experienced in the knowledge which has the form "this is *not* a jar" or "here there is *no* jar." Knowledge of these last two forms are known as *abhāva buddhi* or *nāsti buddhi*. If we compare two cognitions,

18. *Anugata pratīti* may be understood as "experience having same form." We have experience of the same form "This is a cow" with respect to *different* individual cows. Though as individual animals the cows are different, they all have the same universal cowness. This explains how we can have experience of the same form "This is cow." When different particular things (like jars) or animals (like cows), etc. are uniformly experienced or experienced alike, we have *anugata pratīti*.

viz. "here there is a jar," and "here there is no jar" then we can say that an absence of jar is always known in cognition of the second form. The jar itself is known in both the cognitions. In the second cognition it is known *as the negatum* of *ghaṭābhāva* or absence of jar. But the negatum of an absence is different from the absence itself. A jar (*ghaṭa*) is never experienced as absence of jar (*ghaṭābhāva*). Now similarity is either known by itself or it is known as the negatum of its own absence. But it is not itself an absence.

We shall later see that *sādṛśya* is not admitted to be a separate kind of existent in the Kumārila school of Mīmāṁsā. In the school of Murārimiśra also *sādṛśya* is not an additional category. According to Murāri Miśra and his followers there are only five categories, viz. *dravya, guṇa, karma, sāmānya* and *śakti.*[19] The standard Nyāya view is also against the Prābhākara view; the Naiyāyikas do not admit that *sādṛśya* is an additional category. However, some of the later thinkers seem to admit *sādṛśya* to be a separate *padārtha.*[20] According to Prābhākara, in any case, we do have (*upamiti*) knowledge of similarity which is a real and irreducible category. And for such knowledge *upamāna* is to be admitted as an independent *pramāṇa* or source of knowledge.

Now I need to summarize the discussion so far stated. We wanted, to see how Mīmāṁsā theory of *upamāna* developed in the Prābhākara school. By development we understand further clarification of the three major tenets of the Mīmāṁsā theory of *upamāna* which may be found there in the Śabarasvāmī's definition of *upamāna*. These three tenets are the following:

(T_1) *upamāna* is an independent or irreducible (*svatantra*) *pramāṇa*,

(T_2) *upamāna* knows similarity (*sādṛśya*), and

---

19. Pt. Panchanan Bhattacharya Shastri, 1377 (Baṅgābda), p. 30.

20. Ibid., p. 29.

(T_3) similarity is an independent or irreducible category (*svatantra padārtha*).

But in his definition these three points have not been stated or formulated explicitly. All are not equally implicit or explicit. Some of the points are more implicit than the others. For example, the tenet (T_3) that *sādṛśya* is an irreducible (*svatantra*) kind of thing is not at all explicit in Śabara's statement of the definition of *upamāna*. One cannot be sure whether Śabara actually believed that similarity was a separate category. As a matter of fact Śabara's view of *upamāna* was developed along two different lines. Prābhākara developed it in such a way that (T_3) becomes a necessary part of the Mīmāṁsā theory of *upamāna*. But Kumārila developed Mīmāṁsā theory of *upamāna* in a different way. He did not find in Śabara's statement any indication that he believed (T_3). We have seen that in his *Bṛhatī*, Prābhākara commented upon Śālikanātha in his *Ṛjuvimalā-Pañcikā*. The important things that have been said are the following. (T_1) *upamāna* is an independent *pramāṇa*; . . . *iti pramānāntaram*.[21] (T_2) *upamāna* knows similarity. (T_3) *sādṛśya* is an independent category or irreducible kind of thing; it is not reducible to things like *sāmānya* or universal. Prābhākara writes, *atra sāmānyam eva kaiścit sādṛśyam uktaṁ. na tat sādṛśyam. kiṁ tarhi? tadeva tat.*[22] Another tenet related to (T_2) is (2a) unlike *sāmānya sādṛśya* differs if the loci differ. One can have this suggestion from Prābhākara's remark *gotvāderekatvāt.*[23] Śālikanātha in his commentary has stated the point more clearly and broadly and also gave an argument. His words are: *atra vadanti-sādṛśyam nāma*

21. Prābhākara, 1934, p. 108.

    Śālikanātha brings out Prābhākara's point more explicitly in his *Ṛjuvimalā-Pañcikā*. He writes . . . *idaṁ pramāṇāntaram upamānam* — Śālikanātha, 1934.

22. Ibid., p. 109. By things like *sāmānya* we mean all the other six types of things which the Vaiśeṣikas admit.

23. Prābhākara, 1934, p. 109.

na kiñcit asti dravya-guṇa-karma-sāmānya-samavāya-viśeṣātiriktaṁ tadantarbhūtaṁ vā, teṣām saṁgrahe apathitatvāt-iti padārthavidāḥ.[24] From the expression *atra vadanti* it is clear that Mīmāṁsā view is just the opposite. That is to say, Prābhākara Mīmāṁsā holds that (T_3) *sādṛśya* is an additional entity. Śālikanātha concludes his elucidation of Prābhākara's commentary on Śabara's statement of *upamāna* with a question. He quotes the passage to show *upamāna svarūpam*. The relevant part of the quoted passage is . . . *sādṛśya-viṣayakaṁ jñānam upamānam taducyate.*[25] Śālikanātha is one of the greatest scholars in the school of Prābhākara. And from what we have just stated in the summary it is clear that all the three major tenets of the Prābhākara theory of *upamāna* have been separately and clearly stated by Prābhākara and Śālikanātha in connection with the interpretation and development of Śabarasvāmī's thought which is contained in the statement of the definition of *upamāna*.

It is now time we make transition to how Kumārila interpreted and developed the thought of Śabara. The Mīmāṁsā theory of *upamāna* as developed by Kumārila and his followers differs from the theory of *upamāna* as developed by Prābhākara. Kumārila and his followers do not accept *sādṛśya* or similarity to be an additional category. But before we pass on to Kumārila's views, we should note another work of Prābhākara Mīmāṁsā literature. Rāmānujācārya, the author of *Tantra-Rahasya* who flourished as late as in eighteenth century is a follower of Śālikanātha, He had little to add to the account of *upamāna* left by his predecessors of the Prābhākara school. But he has clearly shown the form of *upamiti* according to the Mīmāṁsakas. Taking the example of *go* and *gavaya* he says that the form of *upamiti* is *anena sadṛśī madīyā gauḥ*. In the second place he has shown why *upamāna* as a *pramāṇa* cannot be reduced to such other *pramāṇa*

24. Śālikanātha, 1934, p. 107.

25. Ibid., p. 109.

as *pratyakṣa* or *anumāna*.[26] We shall however show later that a Naiyāyika can argue that it can be reduced to another *pramāṇa* which the Mīmāṁsakas admit, viz. *arthāpatti*.

II

In this section my objective is to discuss Bhāṭṭa version of the Mīmāṁsā theory of *upamāna*. Our source in this respect is the section on *upamāna* of Kumārila Bhaṭṭa's *Śloka-vārttika*. But we have also consulted Parthasarathi's *Nyāyaratnākara* and *Śāstradīpikā*, Gāgābhaṭṭa's *Bhāṭṭacintāmaṇi* and Ramakrishna Mishra's *Yuktisnehaprapūraṇī*. Besides these, I have consulted Umbeka's *Tātparyaṭīkā* and Sucharita Mishra's *Kāśikā*; both these works are on *Ślokavārttika*. *Mānameyodaya*, the well-known elementary text by Nārāyaṇa Bhaṭṭa (etc.), and *Mīmāṁsā-Kutuhalam* by Kamalākara Bhaṭṭa have also been consulted.

In our discussion we shall emphasize Kumārila's role as an internal critic. As an internal critic Kumārila accepts in all essence the Mīmāṁsā theory of *upamāna*. But he does not accept the radical formulation of the theory. He would rather *revise* the radical version. Prābhākara on the other hand is inclined to accept or advance a radical formulation. According to this radical version there is not only a separate, independent and irreducible *pramāṇa* like *upamāna* but what it knows, i.e. similarity is also an independent irreducible category. We have discussed this radical formulation in connection with our exposition of Prābhākara's views. The difference between the accounts of the radicals and the revisionists is that while the radicals accept similarity as an additional category though they admit the independence of *upamāna*, the Bhāṭṭa revisionists[27] hold that knowledge by analogy is knowledge of similarity. But while *upamāna* is an

26. Rāmānujācārya, 1956, p. 12.

27. It should be remembered that it has been said earlier that the author is not making historical statement.

independent means, which gives us knowledge of similarity, similarity itself is not an independent category. More progressive among the Bhāṭṭa revisionists are even ready to admit that *upamāna* may sometimes be knowledge of something other than similarity.[28] Kumārila Bhaṭṭa himself however accepts the standard Mīmāṁsā view that *upamāna* is the knowledge of *sādṛśya*.

Though Śabarasvāmī himself accepts that *upamāna* is the knowledge of similarity, yet Kumārila finds some difficulty with his view. As an internal critic of the Mīmāṁsā school, Kumārila therefore criticizes Śabara. He also criticizes the view, known as the view of Prābhākara school. Kumārila's objection against Śabarasvāmī is that he has failed to show that *upamāna* is a *pramāṇa*. Earlier Kumārila and following him Parthasarathi in his *Nyāyaratnākara* had shown why Śabara defined *upamāna* in a different way.[29] The reason is this that the alternative definition given by the Naiyāyikas turn *upamāna* or knowledge by analogy into *śabda,* i.e. knowledge by verbal testimony. For *upamāna* consists in *āptopadeśa* or statement of analogy which is uttered by some person. This statement produces as means the knowledge called *upamiti*. Because it is produced by statement or *śabda, upamiti* is a case of *śābda-buddhi*. And the *atideśa vākya* which produces it is a *śabda-pramāṇa*. So far Śabara is justified in not accepting this account of the Naiyāyikas. For to accept this account is to admit that *upamāna* is not an irreducible means of knowledge (*svatanatra pramāṇa*). But all the Mīmāṁsakas accept *upamāna* to be a *svatantra pramāṇa,* i.e. a means which cannot be reduced to any other means of knowledge.

But Kumārila finds Śabara's own definition to be equally defective. Parthasarathi says, *bhāṣyakāraṁ api lakṣaṇam ākṣipati*.[30]

---

28. Gāgābhaṭṭa, 1933, pp. 45-46.
29. Kumārila 1978, pp. 307-08 and Parthasarathi 1978, pp. 307-08.
30. Parthasarathi, 1978, p. 308.

What is *bhāṣyakāra's lakṣaṇam* (Śabarasvāmī's definition)? What according to this *lakṣana* is the nature of *upamāna*? Parthasarathi finds some indication about the reply in the last part of Śabara's statement of definition, i.e. *gavaya-darśanaṁ go-smaraṇasya iti*. This portion in Sanskrit may be taken to mean, perception of *gavaya* [qualified by (cow) similarity] causes memory of cow (*gabi smaraṇam utpādayati*); the memory so produced has been said to be *upamāna* (*tadutpāditam ca smaraṇam upamānam ityuktaṁ*).[31] Kumārila has also taken this to be the answer of Śabara to the question stated above.[32]

The above quotation from Parthasarathi's elucidation of verse 4 of Kumārila's *Ślokavārttika, Upamāna Pariccheda* is important. Umbeka takes this verse to be Kumārila's explanation of Śabara's passage *yathā gavaya-darśanaṁ gosmaraṇaśya*. It is clear that Śabara gives here an example of *upamāna*. He defines *upamāna* in the first part of the sentence *upamānam api*, etc.; *gavaya-darśanaṁ*, etc. is the second part of this sentence. Umbeka has said *upamānamudāhṛtam*. Following Kumārila, Umbeka, Sucharita and Parthasarathi all have taken this example to show that memory about cow (*gabi smaraṇam*) is produced by the perception of *gavaya* (*gavaya-darśanam*) which is similar to cow (*go sadṛśa*). If this memory of cow is the example of *upamiti* then one can raise the objection against Śabara that he has turned *upamāna* into memory. And no memory cognition is a *pramāṇa*. So *upamāna* cannot be *pramāṇa*. Kumārila therefore asks how *upamāna* can be a *pramāṇa*? For it is cognition (*mati*) of the second of the two similar things (*sadṛśāntare*), and it is produced by the perception of the first of the two similar things. This view is different from the standard Mīmāṁsā view of *upamāna*. According to the standard Mīmāṁsā view *upamāna* is knowledge of similarity (of *gavaya*) in unperceived or remembered cow; but it is not a

31. Parthasarathi, 1978, p. 308.

32. *sadṛśāt upajāyate yā matiḥ sadṛśāntare* — Chapter on *upamāna*, 1st half of verse 4, *Ślokavārttika*, 1978, p. 308.

memory cognition. This will become clearer below. [It may be noted that Gāgābhaṭṭa (Viśveśvara Sudhi) gave some other examples of *upamāna*. Some of these he gave following modern Mīmāṁsakas.] Kumārila's objection against this account of *upamāna* has been formulated in the form of a question *dhyānādiḥ smṛti-tulyatvāt sa pramāṇam kathaṁ bhavet*? The idea is this: Śabara's account turns *upamāna* into memory and so it cannot be a *pramāṇa* at all. For memory is not a case of *pramāṇa*. Here *pramāṇa* means *pramā* which is non-recollective knowledge or knowledge of thing not known before (*ajñātārtha-viṣaya-jñānam*). In case of meditation also no novelty is there. Some known thing is known again and again. It is a repetition or practice of the same thing. And such meditation is not regarded as a *pramāṇa*. But it is a case of memory. Similarly *upamāna* which is a case of memory cannot be regarded as *pramāṇa*.

Against this objection brought by himself Kumārila considered some replies also. He found many of these answers unacceptable. But this does not mean that Kumārila does not follow the line of Śabara and followed the Naiyāyikas whom Śabara criticized. After discussing many points Kumārila states his final position in the middle of the chapter on *upamāna*. He writes:

> *tasmāt yat smaryate tat syāt sādṛśyena viśeṣitam*
> *prameyam upamānasya sādṛśyam vā tadanvitam.*

This is the verse no. 37 of the chapter on *upamāna* of *Ślokavārttika*. While introducing this verse Parthasarathi wrote: *evaṁ naiyāyikamataṁ dūṣayitvā bhāṣyoktaṁ eva lakṣaṇam pūrvākṣiptaṁ samarthayate.* Umbeka Bhaṭṭa has also said in his *Tātparyaṭīkā* that in the verse in question Kumārila has defended the definition quoted before (*bhāṣyakārodāhṛtameva samarthayitumāha vārttikakāraḥ-tasmāt iti.*[33] This therefore seems to be the point of

---

33. Umbeka, 1940, p. 382.

Kumārila. The acceptable view of *upamāna* (according to Mīmāṁsaka) is that *upamāna* is the knowledge of a thing which is remembered as qualified by similarity (*sādṛśyena viśeṣitam yat smaryate tat prameyam upamānasya*), or the object of *upamāna* is similarity which is related to that (*tat*) — *sādṛśyaṁ vā tadanvitaṁ prameyam upamānasya*. In simple words *upamāna* is (1) the knowledge of the cow, which is being remembered and which has similarity (with *gavaya*); or it is (2) the knowledge of similarity in the cow (which is now remembered) of *gavaya*. In other words *sādṛśya-viśiṣṭa-smaryamāno gauḥ* or *smaryamāṇa-go-gata-gavayānvita-sādṛśyam* is the object of *upamāna*.[34]

We now understand that it will be acceptable to Kumārila if one defines *upamāna* as knowledge of remembered thing (cow) qualified by similarity. It will not be acceptable if *upamāna* is defined as memory of a thing (cow). Knowledge of a thing being remembered at the moment as *having similarity* (*sādṛśya-viśiṣta-smaryamāṇa-vastuviṣayaka-jñānaṁ*) cannot be memory. It may even be an additional *pramāṇa*.

One thing is not clear. If Kumārila accepts the view that *upamāna* is the knowledge of *sādṛśya viśiṣṭa smaryamāṇa vastu* (remembered thing as qualified by similarity), then why Kumārila raised objection against Śabara? From his objection it appears that according to Śabara memory of a thing like cow is *upamāna*. But Śabara did not say this. And he talked about *sādṛśya* also. Here the following solution can be offered. Kumārila's purpose was to bring out clearly the acceptable account of *upamāna* from Śabara's statement. Śabara's statement itself is not very clear. Some may get from it the idea that *upamāna* is the memory of *gau* produced by the perception of *gavaya* having similarity. One gets this impression from the example (*dṛṣṭānta*)

34. See the elucidation of Parthasarathi and Umbeka Bhaṭṭa on verse no. 37 of *Ślokavārttika, Upamāna Paricchedaḥ*.

which Śabara has given in the passage *gavaya-darśanaṁ gosmaraṇasya iti*. This we have discussed above. Against such a view one may also bring some objection. Kumārila showed what objection could be brought against Śabara's account so understood. Finally he formulated the intended view of *upamāna* in the unobjectionable but in the Mīmāṁsā way. In this way Kumārila actually developed Śabara's view of *upamāna* as a faithful follower. Earlier reference is given to show that according to Umbeka Bhaṭṭa and Parthasarathi, Kumārila finally meant to defend Śabara. Umbeka has further shown that in verse 38 of *Upamāna Pariccheda*, the author of *Ślokavārttika* has answered the charge[35] which was brought against Śabara's definition in the verse 4.

To conclude this topic for the present it is important to note the following. Kumārila does not deny that in case of *upamāna* similarity is perceived. And one of the two similar things (*go*) or cow is remembered. How can then *upamāna*, as Kumārila formulates it, be a *pramāṇa*? How can it be an additional *pramāṇa*? Kumārila himself has given answer to this question. The central point is this. Cow as characterized by similarity is the object of *upamāna*. The cow, so characterized is not remembered. For the cow so characterized was not perceived before. If the knowledge of the cow qualified by similarity with *gavaya* is not memory then it may be *pramāṇa*. And if this knowledge is not perception (we shall see that it is not also inference and the like), it can be regarded as an additional *pramāṇa*. And if this knowledge is not perception (we shall see that it is not also inference and the like), it can be regarded as an additional *pramāṇa*. Kumārila has

35. The charge was ". . . *dhyānādi-smṛti-tulyatvāt sā pramāṇaṁ kathaṁ bhavet*" verse 4. In answer it has been stated in verse 38, ". . . *upamānapramāṇatā*." Umbeka introduced this verse 38 with the remark *yat punaridam uktam-pratyakṣeṇeti*. Umbeka 1940, p. 382, *pratyakṣeṇāvabuddhe 'pi* . . . Kumārila, *Upamāna Pariccheda* of *Ślokavārttika*, verse 38.

given an example to show that the knowledge of a qualified thing is different from both the knowledge of the thing and the knowledge of the qualification. We present below in Kumārila's own words, the answer he has given and the example he has cited.

> *pratyakṣenāvabuddhe 'pi sādṛśye gabi ca smṛte*
> *viśiṣṭasyā 'nyato 'siddherūpamānapramāṇatā.*
>
> — verse 38

To translate:

> Even if similarity is perceived and the cow is remembered, yet since the cow as qualified by the property is not known. That is known by *upamāna*.

The idea is this. We can know separately by two different means a thing (such as a cow) and its qualification (such as *sādṛśya* or similarity). But the knowledge of the qualified thing may need a third separate means. In other words even when one knows similarity in *gavaya* through perceptual means and known cow in his town through memory, the knowledge of this cow characterized by similarity is obtained through the separate means of *upamāna*. It should not be thought to be an ad hoc explanation discovered by the Mīmāṁsakas to justify their view that *upamāna* is a separate (*svatantra*) means of knowledge (*pramāṇa*). For what is said here about *upamāna* is nothing new. The same is true about *anumāna* or inference. So Kumārila illustrates his point with the example of *anumāna*. He writes —

> *pratyakṣe 'pi yathādeśe smaryamāṇe ca pābake*
> *viśiṣṭa-viṣayatvena nānumānapramāṇatā.*[36]

To translate:

> Even though the place (*deśa*, here the hill) is perceived and fire

36. Kumārila 1978, p. 316. But there is some difference in the reading of this verse, see Kumārila, 1940, p. 383.

> is remembered, knowledge of the qualified thing (that is, the hill having fire), is not known otherwise; so *anumāna* is a *pramāṇa*.

The idea is this. When one infers that a hill has fire, one can know separately the hill, by perception, and fire, in memory. For he has contact of visual sense organ with the hill. The fire also was known by him earlier when *vyāpti* was known. So the fire can now be remembered. But the hill as qualified by fire was not (non-recollectively) known before. So it cannot be remembered now. It cannot be known by perception also. Because the part of it the fire is not in contact with any sense organ. So the knowledge of hill as qualified by fire is derived from some other *pramāṇa*. This is *anumāna* (inference); it is different from perception, memory or any other *pramāṇa*.

For the knowledge of the qualified hill (i.e. the hill as qualified) we need a separate means which is inference. Similarly for the knowledge of the cow in the town or village having similarity with *gavaya*, we need a separate *pramāṇa* which is *upamāna*. Kumārila has extensively discussed why *upamāna* cannot be reduced to *anumāna* in verses 43-45. Without going into detail we will simply note one argument of Kumārila. He says when one knows that the cow in the town is similar to *gavaya*, conditions like *pakṣadharmatā* do not obtain. So this knowledge cannot be said to be inference. Following Umbeka, however, we give the formulation of the argument below:

> *gavaya sadṛśa gauḥ iti vijñānam, anumānādbhinnaṁ pakṣadharmādi anaṅgatvāt, pratyakṣavat.*[37]

One major point of the Mīmāṁsā theory of *upamāna* as formulated by Kumārila is the following. *Sādṛśya* is not a new kind of entity or existent. It is to be carefully noted that Kumārila does not say like the Buddhists that there is no such thing as

37. Cf. Umbeka Bhaṭṭa, 1940, p. 384.

sādṛśya. Buddhist Ratnakīrti has shown the consequence of the view that there is no *sādṛśya*. The consequence is that since the *prameya* or the object to be known is not there (*prameyābhāvāt*) there cannot be *upamāna*, that is, the knowledge of it (this *prameya*). And if the knowledge is not there, there cannot be (or need not be) admitted a means of knowledge like *upamāna* for it.[38] Kumārila's point is that

> *sādṛśyasyāpi*[39] *vastutvam na śakyam apabādhitum.*
> (verse 18)

According to Kumārila then there is a thing like *sādṛśya*. So we cannot argue that there is no *upamāna* because there is no object to be known (or *prameya vastvabhāvāt ca nābhipretā pramāṇatā*). From our discussion it follows that according to Kumārila, *upamāna* is an independent and irreducible means of knowledge. The resulting knowledge or *upamiti* is also a distinct kind of knowledge. This *upamiti* knows as its object similarity. This similarity of course, according to Kumārila, is not a new category of being.

IIA

But then the question is, what is this *sādṛśya* accoding to Kumārila? Parthasarathi has given the answer. He writes, (*sādṛśyam*) *na tvavastu, nāpi tattvāntaraṁ.*[40] The Bauddhas could argue that *sādṛśya* is not real (*vastu* or *vastu sat*) because it is known in *svavikalpaka pratyakṣa*. But this type of *pratyakṣa* is not, in the strict sense, a case of knowledge. But object of knowledge (*abādhita pratīti*) alone can be said to be real.[41] Kumārila says in reply that the reality of *sādṛśya* cannot be denied. *Sādṛśasya api vastutvam na śakyam apabādhitum* (verse 18). While explaining this verse

38. See above Chapter 3, Note 18.
39. In the Umbeka edition there is *ca* in place of *api*.
40. Parthasarathi, 1978, p. 311.
41. Umbeka, 1940, p. 378

Parthasarathi brings reference to *jāti*. He says, *sarvadā tu abādhita pratyakṣa-buddhiḥ jātivat sarva-vikalpa-nirākaraṇena sādṛśyam upasthāpayati iti*. Our knowledge of universal (*jāti*) which exists in many individuals (e.g. our knowledge of the form "this is a cow" or "this has cowness") is not falsified or contradicted by any other knowledge. So as the object of non-contradicted experience we admit universal to be real. In the same way our experience of similarity such as the following are uncontradicted (*abādhita*). Yajñadatta is like Devadatta; a cow is like *gavaya;* the fragrance of this flower is similar to the fragrance of rose; the twins are similar to each other, and so on. *Sādṛśya* as an object of such uncontradicted experience must be admitted to be real.[42] Umbeka has gone further and shown that *sādṛśya* is real (*sat*) even in the Bauddha sense of the term. According to the Bauddhas a thing is real if it is *arthakriyākārī,* i.e. if it produces some effect. And Umbeka says that *sādṛśya* or similarity produces at least two effects or does at least two things. As object it produces its own knowledge, i.e. knowledge of *sādṛśya*. Again it makes possible the meaningfulness of such scriptural injunction as *gavaya sadṛśeṇa yajeta*[43] or *gavayena idṛśena yajata.*[44] Sucharita Mishra has noted some other arguments in favour of the Bauddha thesis that *sādṛśya* is unreal.[45] We shall not go into those. The reasons why *sādṛśya* cannot be unreal have been noted.

One argument why it cannot be an additional *padārtha* or category (*padārthāntara* or *tattvāntara*) is the following. If it were an independent entity it could be known independently. We could then have the knowledge that *gavaya* is similar (*gavayaṁ sadṛśam iti*) without reference to cow.[46] There is another reason

42. Umbeka, 1940, p. 378.

43. Ibid.

44. Ibid., fn. 7, p. 378.

45. Sucharita Mishra, 1943, pp. 12-43.

46. Sucharita Mishra, 1943, p. 143.

why the Prābhākara Mīmāṁsā view that *sādr̥śya* is an independent category cannot be accepted. If *sādr̥śya* were an independent category then a thing would be *sadr̥śa* (similar) or not *sadr̥śa* (not similar). But it could not be more similar or less similar. Let us take the case of universal or *jāti* like cowness. *Jāti* is an independent category (*padārthāntara* or *tattvāntara*). Either a thing has cowness or it does not have it. Accordingly, either a thing is a cow or is not a cow. It cannot be less (of a) cow or more (of a) cow. Parthasarathi in his *Śāstradīpikā* has noted this argument. He has said in addition that there is no argument whatsoever to show that *sādr̥śya* (similarity) is an additional category. *ye tu . . . anyat eva tattvaṁ sādr̥śyaṁ manyante, teṣāṁ prakarṣāprakarṣabhedaḥ kiṁ nimitta iti cintanīyam. na ca tattvāntaratve pramāṇam api kiñcit asti iti āstāṁ tāvat.*[47]

Kumārila believes that *sādr̥śya* is real but it is not an additional category. What is it then? Kumārila answers, *bhūyo- 'vayava-sāmānya-yoga-jātyantarasya tat* (verse 18). *Jātyantara yogibhiḥ avayava sāmānyairyo jātyantarasya yogaḥ tat sādr̥śyam.*[48] Similarity (*sādr̥śya*) is that (*tat*) relation (*yoga*) which things of a certain kind (*jātyantarasya*) have to the common parts (*avayava sāmānya*) of things of another class (*jātyantara yogibhiḥ*). Umbeka Bhaṭṭa has written, *bhūyasām avayava sāmānyānāṁ . . . jātyantara upalakṣite avayavini yo yogaḥ tat sādr̥śyam.*[49] The commentators including Sucharita Mishra agree that the reference to *jāti* and *avayava* in Kumārila's account of *sādr̥śya* should not be taken literally. Similarity need not be always in respect of parts. For things which have no parts can be similar to each other. Fragrance or *gandha* which is a quality (*guṇa*) has no parts. But fragrance of one thing can be similar to the fragrance of another thing. Therefore though Kumārila explicitly speaks of similarity in

47. Parthasarathi, 1913, p. 212.

48. Parthasarathi, 1978, p. 311.

49. Umbeka, 1940, p. 378.

respect of parts or *avayava, avayava* is here representative of *guṇa* (quality), *kriyā* (action), *jāti* (universal), etc. Therefore, two things can have similarity in respect of parts or quality, or action or universal. Again just as substances having parts can be similar to each other so also qualities (*guṇa*) or actions (*kriyā*) can be similar to each other. Between two sacrificial rites or *yāga* (which are actions) there can be similarity in respect of *dravya, guṇa* and so on.[50] Kumārila himself has said all these in verse 20. We are also to note that reference to *jāti* in verse 18 is not to be taken literally. Similarity may obtain between things which do not belong to different classes as cow and *gavaya*. Similarity can obtain between two individuals of the same class. We experience similarity and speak of similarity between two brothers, who obviously belong to the same class.

It is to be noted, however, that if similarity is understood in this way then we can easily explain our experience and usages regarding quantitative differences of similarity or different qualities of similarity. We can say about two things that they are more or closely similar if they have greater number of common parts or qualities or actions, etc. If two things have less number of common parts, etc. then we say that they are less similar.

IIB

The last two points which we want to note about Kumārila's account of *upamāna* in his *Ślokavārttika* are closely related. Kumārila suggests that *atideśa vākya* or statement of analogy does not play any essential role in *upamāna*. One can have *upamāna* or knowledge of similarity even where no *atideśa vākya* has been uttered:

śrutātideśavākyatvaṁ na cātībopayujyate.
— verse 10

50. Parthasarathi, 1978, p. 312.

ye 'pi hyaśrutatadvākyāsteṣāmapi bhavatyayam
pratyakṣadṛṣṭagotvānāṁ bane gavayadarśinām.

— verse 11

If thus *atideśa vākya* is not necessary for *upamāna* according to the Mīmāṁsakas, then nobody can even say that *upamāna* according to the Mīmāṁsakas is a case of *śabda*. A Naiyāyika may object that if *atideśa vākya* is not uttered or heard then one can never know the thing in question (*gavaya*) to be the meaning or reference or denotation of the word *gavaya*. So Kumārila says in the second place that *upamāna* is not the knowledge of the relation of word to its meaning (*saṁjñā-saṁjñi sambandha*, or, in short, *śakti*) as the Naiyāyikas say. *Upamāna* is rather the knowledge of similarity. A question will arise here. We certainly have knowledge of *śakti*. If we do not get it from *upamāna*, do we get it from still another *pramāṇa*? In that case there will be one more *pramāṇa*. In answer Kumārila says:

na ca śabdārthasambandhaḥ prameyo 'tra tadeṣyate
sādṛśyavādhṛte vākye vākyādvagato hyasau.

— verse 13

Śakti is not admitted to be the object of the knowledge called *upamāna*. But the statement of analogy which is about *sādṛśya* gives the knowledge of *śakti*. Therefore, according to Kumārila, the hearer of the *atideśa vākya* comes to know *saṁjñā-saṁjñi sambandha* from words (*śabda*). According to Kamalākara Bhaṭṭa the knowledge of *śakti* comes from perception as associated with *śabda* (*śabdānubiddha pratyakṣa*).[51] It may be noted here that according to Gāgābhaṭṭa some later Mīmāṁsakas believe that perception of the animal having cow similarity (*gosādṛśya-viśiṣṭa piṇḍa-darśanaṁ*) is the special means or *karaṇa*; memory of the content of the statement of analogy is the *vyāpāra* and the knowledge of meaning is the resulting knowledge. This view is very close to the Nyāya view.

51. Kamalākara Bhaṭṭa, 1978, p. 74.

One question still remains. What use *upamāna* has in Mīmāṁsā or for the Mīmāṁsakas? Following some Prābhākara thinkers, we have shown that sometimes one may need the knowledge of similarity of some animal with *gavaya*. This happens to be the case when the sacrificial rite (*yāga*) to be performed involves the use of something like *gavaya*. Writers of the Kumārila *Prasthāna* here make reference to the discussion by Jaimini and Śabara in chapter 7, *pāda* 4 of *Mīmāṁsā Darśanam*. The *sūtra* 7.4.1 of Jaimini is *itikarttavyatā 'vidheryajateḥ pūrvavattvam*. Śabarasvāmī in his commentary on this *sūtra* writes, *anārambha-kiñcit śruyate, śauryyaṁ caruṁ nirvapet brahma-varcasakām iti.*[52] Referring to this discussion the greatest Mīmāṁsaka of our time, Pattabhirama Shastri, has written in his *Mīmāṁsānyāyamañjarī* the following.[53] The result obtained here from *upamāna pramāṇa* is not the knowledge of that name and what is named (*vācya-vācaka-bhāva*); the result obtained is rather the knowledge of type-instance relation based on similarity (*sādṛśyāt prakṛti-vikṛti-bhāva-niścaya*). The point is this. In the injunction quoted by Śabara the rite to be performed (*śaurya*) and the result to be obtained (*brhmavarcasa*) have been stated. But how the rite is to be performed, i.e. the *itikarttavyatā* has not been stated. But the knowledge of that is necessary. And the knowledge is obtained in this way. In consideration of similarity of the things used in the rites it is ascertained that *śaurya-yāga* comes under the type called *āgneya-yāga. Āgneya-yāga* is therefore the *prakṛti* (type) *yāga* and *śaurya-yāga* is the *vikṛti* (instance or special case of a type) *yāga*. Once this is known, one comes to know from *alaukika* means called *vidhi* or *dharma* how *śaurya-yāga* is to be performed. It is to be performed in the way *āgneya-yāga* is (or is to be) performed.

---

52. Śabarasvāmī, *Mīmāṁsādarśanam*, Jīvānanda Vidyāsāgar, Kolkata, 1883, vol. II, p. 57.

53. Pattabhiram Shastri, 1984, *Pariśiṣṭam*, p. 5.

III

In this concluding section of this chapter I want to make some critical observations about the Mīmāṁsā theory of *upamāna pramāṇa*. For this purpose I need to state briefly the development of the discussion so far. The discussion started with the initial statement of the classical version of Nyāya theory of *upamāna*. This view was opposed by the Mīmāṁsakas. The representative version of the classical Mīmāṁsā theory and Mīmāṁsā objection against Nyāya theory of *upamāna* were found in Śabara's commentary. Mīmāṁsā theory of *upamāna* was further developed by Prābhākara and his followers on the one hand and by Kumārila and his followers on the other. Prābhākara gave more positive and radical formulation to the Mīmāṁsā theory of *upamāna*. Kumārila's approach was that of a revisionist. So far as the definition of *upamāna pramāṇa* is concerned Kumārila defended, then criticized, and finally supported Śabara's account of *upamāna* as an independent means of knowledge of *sādṛśya*. *Sādṛśya*, however, is not a distinctive category according to Kumārila. But so far as Śabara's criticism of (classical) Nyāya view of *upamāna* is concerned, Kumārila seems to have little to add. He, however, endorsed the criticism. In the next chapter I want to discuss the Bauddha and the Vaiśeṣika criticism of Nyāya theory of *upamāna*. Here I have pointed out that the Mīmāṁsā criticism or the criticism of Kumārila against Nyāya which the author has discussed so far cannot be supported. For the view which, according to Parthasarathi, Śabara and Kumārila criticized as Nyāya view is not Nyāya view at all. The view or the theory of *upamāna* which has been criticized as the Nyāya theory of *upamāna* has two tenets: (a) *Atideśa vākya* or statement of analogy is the *upamāna pramāṇa* in the sense of means of *upamiti*; and (b) the object of the resulting knowledge of *upamiti* (knowledge by analogy) is similarity. On account of (a) the alleged Nyāya theory is held to reduce *upamāna* (*upamiti*) to *śabda* (*śābda*). When the Mīmāṁsakas bring this charge against the Naiyāyikas, they mean to say that the Naiyāyikas turn the knowledge of similarity (by analogy) into *śābda*. Against this we would like to say the following. One may find something in the writing of Vātsyāyana in his *Bhāṣya* which may suggest that the statement of analogy (or the *atideśa vākya*) is the *upamāna pramāṇa*. One who receives this suggestion is likely to object that the Naiyāyikas turn *upamiti* into *śābda*. For *upamiti* is the result of *upamāna*. And if *upamāna* is *śabda* (*atideśa vākya*) then the resulting knowledge is *śābda*, i.e. verbal or linguistic. So far Mīmāṁsā objection against Nyāya may be valid. But there is hardly anything in the writing of Vātsyāyana or any other Naiyāyikas which can suggest that according to the Naiyāyikas *upamāna* is the knowledge of similarity. But it seems that some Mīmāṁsakas and perhaps Kumārila also thought that the Naiyāyikas held that view.[54] At least in their criticism of Nyāya view these Mīmāṁsakas did not discuss the view that *upamāna* (*upamiti*) is the knowledge of the relation of words to their meaning (*śakti*). We shall show, however, that the Bauddha and the Vaiśeṣika critics of Nyāya criticized the view that *upamāna* is the knowledge of *śakti*. It may be noted in passing that the author of *Nyāyakandalī* demonstrated that the Mīmāṁsaka account of *upamāna*, turned *upamāna* into *śabda*. Then he showed that *Mīmāṁsā-upamāna* is reducible to *anumāna*.[55]

We, however, find that one Mīmāṁsā writer has drawn very carefully the sharper and finer distinction. Umbeka Bhaṭṭa in his elucidation of *Ślokavārttika* did not confuse Nyāya view with the view that *upamāna* is the knowledge of *sādṛśya*. He has distinguished three views. The first view which turns *upamāna* into *śabda* or knowledge by testimony is the view, according to Umbeka not of the Naiyāyikas but of the *laukika*.[56] The second

54. See Parthasarathi's explanation of verse 6 of *Upamāna-Pariccheda* of *Ślokavārttika*. We shall see below that this interpretation has some support in the writings of Vātsyāyana.

55. Cf. Gaurinatha Shastri, Introduction in *Pragalbhācārya*, 1983, p. *ca*.

56. *tasmāt laukikasya āgamatvam* — Umbeka, 1940, p. 382.

view is the view of the Naiyāyikas. The objection against it is not that it turns *upamāna* into *śabda*, but that it turns *upamāna* into *pratyakṣa*.[57] The third view reduces *upamāna* into memory.[58]

But there is some doubt whether the third view was Śabara's own view. Umbeka carefully refers to this view as the view quoted by the *bhāṣyakāra*. Ramakrishna, we noted earlier, explicitly says that this view is the view of Upavarṣa. Most probably Pandit Ramakrishna got his clue from Umbeka. Taking this to be the view of Śabarasvāmī an objection was initially brought against the view that it turns *upamāna* into memory cognition.[59] Thus Umbeka distinguishes three views and he did not attribute to the Naiyāyikas the view which turns *upamāna* into *śabda*. Umbeka's interpretation here differs from the interpretation of Parthasarathi. But it is not clear whether according to Umbeka, Śabara stated his own opinion about *upamāna* or quoted the view of others when he (Śabara) wrote, *upamānamapi sādṛśyam asannikṛṣṭe arthe buddhiṁ utpādayati, yathā gavayadarśanaṁ gosmaraṇasya iti*. For Umbeka writes, *bhāṣyakāra udāhṛtasya*[60] and also he writes, *upamānamapi . . . utpādayati 'iti bhāṣyam*.[61]

It may, however, be noted that Vātsyāyana himself discussed in his *Bhāṣya* the objection against the Nyāya theory of *upamāna*, that this *upamāna* is actually a case of perception (*pratyakṣa*). But when Vātsyāyana considered this objection, he

---

57. *naiyāyikoktasya ca pratyakṣatvam iti nopamānaṁ pramāṇāntaram* — Umbeka, 1940, p. 382.
58. Ibid., p. 382.
59. *bhāṣyakāriyam api lakṣaṇam ākṣipati . . . tat ca smaraṇatvāt pramāṇam eva na bhavati* — Parthasarathi, 1978, p. 308.
60. Umbeka, 1940, p. 382.
61. Ibid., p. 374.

considered it as an objection against the view that the knowledge that the *gavaya* is similar to cow, is *upamāna*.[62] From this it appears that prior to or during the time of Vātsyāyana, some thinkers brought against the Naiyāyikas the charge that the knowledge that *gavaya* is similar to cow could be known by perception; that *upamāna* has nothing to do here. Therefore it cannot be said that it was wholly unfounded to say that the Naiyāyikas of the classical period held knowledge of similarity to be *upamāna*. These Naiyāyikas also held *atideśa vākya* to be *upamāna pramāṇa*. So it was objected against them that they turn *upamiti* or the knowledge of similarity into *śābda*. Again it can also be said that this knowledge is derived from the perception of *gavaya* when the man goes to forest. Both these objections have in fact been brought against the classical version of Nyāya theory of *upamāna* by the Mīmāṁsakas.

Our final criticisms of Kumārila relate to the following two points: (1) Kumārila's objection following Śabara that the Naiyāyikas failed to preserve the independence of *upamāna pramāṇa* and (2) Kumārila's positive view that *upamāna* is an independent *pramāṇa* which gives us knowledge of similarity. His third important thesis that *sādṛśya* is not an additional category, however, is quite acceptable to us.

Against Kumārila's point (1) above we would like to say that this point is based on (i) taking *atideśa vākya* to be *upamāna pramāṇa* according to the Naiyāyikas and (ii) taking knowledge of similarity to be *upamiti* according to the Naiyāyikas. But a careful study of Vātsyāyana's commentary shows that he did not hold these views; he had anticipated these as objections and rejected them also. He has quite explicitly stated that according to Nyāya position *upamiti* is the knowledge of *śakti*. This *śakti* is

62. *kiṁ punaḥ atra upamānena kriyate? yadā khalu ayaṁ gavā samānadharmaṁ pratipadyate tadā pratyakṣataḥ tamarthaṁ pratipadyata iti* — Vātsyāyana, 1985, p. 169.

the relation between the words and their meanings. This knowledge has not been shown to be either a case of *śābda* or a case of perception. It is not easy to prove that.

So far as the point (2) is concerned, we would like to say that for the knowledge of similarity in question we do not need a separate *pramāṇa* like *upamāna*. We do not deny that one may have the knowledge that the cow in the town is similar to the *gavaya* being perceived now in the forest. But a Mīmāṁsaka can explain this knowledge in terms of *arthāpatti*. For they admit *arthāpatti* as a separate *pramāṇa*. And in this case they admit that one has through perception the knowledge that the *gavaya* in front (in the forest) is like the cow (in town). Now it is a matter of simple reason (*yukti*) that if the cow there (town) were not like this *gavaya*, then this *gavaya* could not be like that cow. So this knowledge that the cow in the town is like the *gavaya* in the forest is of the same type as the knowledge that Devadatta must be eating during night. Because if he did not eat in the night, then he could not have been fat (for he does not eat during the day time). Perhaps such a criticism was in the mind of Udayana when in *Nyāyakusumāñjaliḥ* he wrote on behalf of the Vaiśeṣikas, *arthāpattiḥ asau vyaktam iti cet prakṛtaṁ na kim.*[63]

63. See Udayana's *Nyāyakusumāñjaliḥ*, 1962 chapter 3, verse 9.

Part Three

Critical Development of the Nyāya Theory of Upamāna

5

Bauddha and Vaiśeṣika Objections against the Nyāya Theory of Upamāna

I

In parts One and Two the following things are considered: (a) the classical version of Nyāya theory of *upamāna*, (b) criticisms of the Nyāya theory by the Mīmāṁsakas of the classical period, (c) statement of the classical Mīmāṁsā version of *upamāna*, (d) criticisms of the Mīmāṁsā theory by the rejectionists Bauddha, the reductionists Vaiśeṣikas, and by the revisionists Bhāṭṭa Mīmāṁsakas (or the internal critics of the Mīmāṁsā position). The development of the classical Mīmāṁsakas and (e) the Bhāṭṭa Mīmāṁsakas has also been discussed, and (f) some critical observations also are given.

It is clear that the third of the three major positive tenets of the Mīmāṁsā theory of *upamāna* cannot be accepted. Among the three tenets the third is that similarity is an additional category. This (T_3) has been criticized by the Buddhists, by the Vaiśeṣikas and also by the Mīmāṁsakas themselves. Among the Mīmāṁsakas only the Prābhākaras accept *sādṛśya* as an additional category. As we have stated it is not so accepted in the school of Murāri Miśra. The Bhāṭṭas explicitly criticized (T_3). The Naiyāyikas also do not accept *sādṛśya* as an additional category. (T_2) is the other major positive tenet of the classical Mīmāṁsā theory of *upamāna*. (T_2) states that *upamāna* is the knowledge of *sādṛśya* or it is the means of knowledge of *sādṛśya*. In other words according to the Mīmāṁsakas when we admit *upamāna* in the sense of *upamiti,* we admit it for the knowledge of similarity. To account for such knowledge we need to admit *upamāna* as an additional source of knowledge or *pramāṇa.* We have shown in our critical observation that this argument cannot be accepted. For we can have some knowledge of similarity through perception. Mīmāṁsakas themselves admit this. Again sometimes we can know similarities through *arthāpatti.* We may also have knowledge of *sādṛśya* through inference.[1] It is said that still *upamāna* is needed. *Iti kartavyatā* (procedure of performance) in respect of *yāga* like *śaurya,* may also be non-secular (non-*laukika*) way. But the Mīmāṁsakas hold that the need for *upamāna* may be found in case of rites like *śaurya.* We would like to quote from Ramaswami Shastri's Introduction to his edition of Sucharita Mishra's *Kāśikā.*[2] In the introduction some of the uses of *upamāna* of the Mīmāṁsakas are shown. "The importance of *upamāna* as a separate *pramāṇa* in the interpretations of the Vedic texts is emphasized by the *vārttikakāra* at the end of the *upamāna* section. The *atideśa* by which the accessories of a *prakṛti* sacrifice are transferred to a *vikṛti* on the basis of similarity is nothing but *upamāna pramāṇa.*" But one may say to the Mīmāṁsakas that all these may be valid ground for *upamāna.* But these will not show that *upamāna* is an independent source of knowledge. *Upamāna* may rather be viewed as another Mīmāṁsā nyāya in addition to the familiar ones like *upakarma, upasaṁhāra,* etc. It should not be counted among *pramāṇa*s (or means of knowledge) like perception, inference, etc. which fall within the scope of epistemology. From all these it follows that *upamāna* is not needed for the knowledge of *sādṛśya* whether or not *sādṛśya* is an additional kind of entity or *atirikta padārtha.* For other uses of *upamāna* including knowledge of *sādṛśya* one may be referred to Ramaswami Shastri's Introduction noted above.

---

1. Kamalākara Bhaṭṭa, 1987, p. 74.
2. Ramaswami Shastri, 1943.

Should we now draw the conclusion that there is no such *pramāṇa* like *upamāna*? This conclusion does not follow. What follows from the previous discussion is that *upamāna* in the sense of means of knowledge of *sādṛśya* is not there. If *upamāna* means only knowledge of similarity or source of knowledge of similarity then we could conclude that there is no *upamāna*. Therefore everything now depends on whether there is any other sense in which *upamāna* has been admitted or can be admitted. As a matter of fact the Naiyāyikas, the only realist school of Indian philosophy other than Mīmāṁsā, admit *upamāna* in a different sense. According to them, as it has been stated earlier, *upamāna* (i.e. *upamiti*) is not a knowledge of *sādṛśya* (similarity). They hold that *upamāna* is the knowledge of the relation of the words to their meanings. Meanings are the things which correspond to the words. We now turn to the examination of this Nyāya theory of *upamāna*.

It may be remembered that Kumārila criticized Nyāya theory of *upamāna* according to which *upamāna* is the knowledge of (or the means of knowledge of) *śakti*. According to him we get knowledge of *śakti* from *śabda*. And Kamalākara Bhaṭṭa said that the meaning relation can be known from the *śabda* aided by perception. These criticisms will be discussed. But we shall not always refer to the Bhāṭṭa Mīmāṁsakas. We shall discuss the points in a general way. Many other criticisms of Nyāya view will also be discussed. We hope to show finally that Nyāya theory of *upamāna* may be defended against all honest criticisms. Some of these criticisms are brought by the Bauddha rejectionists, and some others by the Vaiśeṣika reductionists. Some criticisms are brought by the philosophers of the sister realist school of Mīmāṁsā. Finally some criticisms have been brought by a section of thinkers who belong to the Nyāya school itself.

The major positive tenets of the Nyāya theory of *upamāna* are (T_i) *upamāna* is an independent *pramāṇa;* (T_{ii}) *upamāna* is needed to account for our knowledge of the meaning relation or *śakti*.

(T_{iii}) *śakti* is not an additional category. It is rather a kind of quality. By "meaning" we are to understand here word-meaning. Bauddha critics say against (T_{ii}) that there is no such thing as *śakti*. Therefore (T_i) must also be wrong; for there is no *upamiti* in the sense of knowledge of *śakti*. From this it follows that there is no *upamāna* in the sense of special means or *karaṇa* of knowledge of *śakti*. The Vaiśeṣikas on the other hand are ready to admit that we have knowledge of word-meaning or relation between a name and the object named. But this knowledge can be obtained from inference. The Mīmāṁsā opponents would say that this knowledge is obtained from the means or *pramāṇa* called *śabda*. A Vaiśeṣika cannot really say here what the Mīmāṁsakas say. For they do not admit *pramāṇa* other than perception and inference. Therefore even if sometimes a Vaiśeṣika is found to say that the knowledge of *śakti* is obtained from *śabda-pramāṇa* they will ultimately reduce this *śabda-pramāṇa* to inference (*anumāna pramāṇa*). Some section of the Naiyāyikas become internal critics of the standard Nyāya theory of *upamāna*. For example Bhāsarvajña and his followers would say that we do not need to admit a separate *pramāṇa* called *upamāna*. All that is said to be obtained from *upamāna* are obtained from other *pramāṇas*. But we find that there is another objection which seems to be most difficult to answer. Our point is this, it may be admitted that we have knowledge of *śakti*. And there may not be any objection in principle against admitting a separate *pramāṇa* like *upamāna* for the knowledge of this *śakti*. But according to the standard Nyāya view one can have the knowledge of *śakti* from different sources. There are as many as eight different sources for the purpose. Some of these sources are actually inference. So the Naiyāyikas themselves appear to hold that the *śakti* can be known by *upamāna, anumāna* and also from *śabda*. This shows *upamāna* is not necessary for the knowledge of *śakti*. The Nyāya theory of *pramāṇa* (knowledge) would be more economical if they could drop *upamāna* as a *pramāṇa*. We have found still another objection. By admitting *upamāna* in their scheme of *pramāṇas* the Naiyāyikas have turned their scheme of *pramāṇas* anomalous. Again if Nyāya is not regarded simply as a logical or epistemological theory but as *mokṣaśāstra* then one may wonder what utility can *upamāna* has in *mokṣaśāstra*. Answers to some of these charges have been found in the writings of Vātsyāyana and his followers. Answers to some other charges have been found in the writings of thinkers like Jayanta, Udayanācārya and Gaṅgeśa Upādhyāya. I have tried to offer our own answers to some objections. I have also discussed some relation between the views about *sādṛśya* on the one hand and universal on the other. I have also tried to show some relevance of the discussion of *upamāna* in the present-day context.

II

In this section I am to discuss Ratnakīrti's criticism of the Nyāya theory of *upamāna*. The chapter in which Ratnakīrti criticizes the Nyāya and also Mīmāṁsā view of *upamāna* has the title — *Pramāṇāntarabhāvaprakaraṇa*. This suggests that the Bauddhas mean to reduce *upamāna* to some other *pramāṇa* just as the Vaiśeṣikas. But in that case they deny only the distinctive character (*atiriktatva*) of what is called *upamāna pramāṇa*. If this is so the Bauddhas are not denying either that there is what is called *upamāna* or that it is a *pramāṇa*. They only deny distinctness of *upamāna*. But in the same chapter Ratnakīrti advances certain argument which suggests that according to him there is no experience called *upamāna*. Ratnakīrti's real intention may not be to say that there is no cognitive experience here; he may have simply meant that the experience in question is not true. In any case the Bauddhas, unlike the Prābhākaras, admit certain cognitions which are false. They admit *vikalpa vijñāna*. *Saṁśaya* (doubt) is such a form of experience. But *saṁśaya* lacks the character of *pramāṇa*.[3]

3. Ananta Tarkatirtha, Kolkata, p. 332.

The Bauddhas may argue in the following way. If an experience shows that an object has incompatible properties then that experience cannot be veridical. This will be admitted by Dharmakīrti who, according to Ananta Tarkatirtha, has not given a definition of *pramāṇa* as such.[4] Before we explain the Bauddha argument let us try to understand Ananta Tarkatirtha's remark. He has said that Dharmakīrti has not given any general definition of *pramāṇa* either in his book *Pramāṇa-Vārttika* or in his book *Nyāyabindu*. One may be puzzled by this remark. For we find in two standard editions of *Pramāṇa-Vārttika* explicit statement of definitions of *pramāṇa* as such. In one edition the definition is *pramāṇam avisaṁvādi jñānam.*[5] In the other edition it has been stated *avisaṁvādī jñānaṁ pramāṇam.*[6] While introducing this definition Manoratha Nandin has stated, *prathamaṁ pramāṇa sāmānya lakṣaṇam āha.*[7] Prajñākaragupta introduced the definition with the comment *sāmānyena pramāṇalakṣaṇam nirdiśati.*[8] In view of all these there seems to be two solutions of the puzzle. (1) The editions of *Pramāṇa-Vārttika* in question were not available to Ananta Tarkatirtha. Or the editions he used did not contain any definition of *pramāṇa* as such. (2) Ananta Tarkatirtha in his book *Vaibhāṣika-Darśana* meant to say that there is no known general definition of *pramāṇa* given by the Vaibhāṣika Bauddhas. The definition of *pramāṇa* in general which one finds in the works of Dharmakīrti is (either from Yogācāra point of view or) from the Sautrāntika point of view.

The remark of Ananta Tarkatirtha, is important. Ananta Tarkatirtha holds that according to the Bauddhas *pramāṇa* is the knowledge which does not reveal the object (which it knows)

4. Ananta Tarkatirtha, Kolkata, p. 329.
5. Dharmakīrti, 1953, p. 3.
6. Ibid.
7. Manoratha Nandin, 1968, p. 3.
8. Prajñākaragupta, 1953, p. 3.

as having incompatible properties. For according to the Bauddhas a thing which is real cannot fail to have a determinate and consistent character (in this respect they differ from the Jainas). Nothing that is real can have incompatible nature. A thing cannot be by nature both a positive and a negative entity. It cannot have *aniyata svabhāva*. Things that are (or are experienced to be) *aniyata svabhāva* must be unreal. Therefore if some cognitive experience reveals certain things as having *aniyata svabhāva* that experience does not reveal the reality or the truth. Such experience must be false or must lack truth (*prāmāṇya*). *Saṁśaya* or doubt is a case in point. Such experience is regarded by the Bauddhas as *vikalpa vijñāna*.[9]

Besides, strictly speaking veridical cognition takes for its object *svalakṣaṇa* and from this point of view even inference has *prāmāṇya* only in some indirect or derivative sense. For *anumāna* cognizes *sāmānya lakṣaṇa*. So far as *upamiti* and *śābda* are concerned the Bauddhas will reject their *prāmāṇya* as they do not take *svalakṣaṇa* as their object.

Vikalpa vijñāna or *adhyavasāya* are experiences which lack *prāmāṇya*. It may be said that in order to be considered as false experience, something must be an experience first. And to be an experience it must have a content.[10] But no false experience can have *svalakṣaṇa* as its *viṣaya*. And every experience which reveals *svalakṣaṇa* directly must be a *pramā*. But the important point is that even a false experience must have a content. If now it can be shown that (what is alleged to be) *upamāna* is an experience which does not have any content whatsoever then it will be proved that there is no such thing as *upamāna* (*pramāṇa*).[11] Let us explain. Remaining within their own system a Buddhist may

9. Ananta Tarkatirtha, Kolkata, p. 332.

10. This we can say even if we admit the Yogācāra point that the content of a cognitive experience need not be outside the experience itself.

11. *yasya na viṣayavattvaṁ na tasya prāmāṇyam.* — Ratnakīrti, 1957, p. 94.

say that there is no such *pramāṇa* as *upamāna*. For there can be at the most two *pamāṇas* for there are only two (kinds of) objects, viz. *svalakṣaṇa* and *sāmānya lakṣaṇa*. And the two *pramāṇas* which know them are respectively *pratyakṣa* and *anumāna*. So *upamāna* must either be a form of *pratyakṣa* or *anumāna* or it cannot be a *pramāṇa* at all. If a Bauddha wants to argue against *upamāna* without presupposing their own scheme of *pramāṇa* or *prameya* then he will argue in the following way. He will say to a Vaiśeṣika or the Mīmāṁsaka "what you call the object of *upamāna*, viz. *śakti* or *sādṛśya*, does not exist. And if its object is not there, there cannot be *upamāna*."

Ratnakīrti offers against the Naiyāyikas the same sort of argument which he offered against the Mīmāṁsakas. His argument against the Mīmāṁsakas was that *upamāna* is not a *pramāṇa* because it is devoid of object.[12] According to the Mīmāṁsakas the object of *upamāna* is *sādṛśya* (similarity) and Ratnakīrti has shown that this *sādṛśya* is non-existent. And as this *sādṛśya* is non-existent so there is no reason for admitting the specific *pramāṇa* called *upamāna* to account for the knowledge of non-existent *sādṛśya*. Ratnakīrti's argument against the Naiyāyikas is of the same nature. Here also he shows that the so-called *upamāna* admitted by the Naiyāyikas is devoid of object (*nir-viṣaya*). The object of *upamāna* according to the Naiyāyikas is not *sādṛśya* or similarity but the relation (*sambandha*) between a term (*pada*) and its meaning (*padārtha*). Ratnakīrti says that this relation between a term and its meaning does not exist; there is no such thing as relation between a term and its meaning,[13] because, this relation, according to Ratnakīrti, can neither be identical with nor different from the relata. If the

---

12. *naiyāyika parikalpita upamāna nirākaraṇārtham api ayam eva prayoga draṣṭavyaḥ, tasya api nirviṣayatvāt.* — Ratnakīrti, 1957, p. 95.

13. *pratyākhyāto vācya-vācaka-lakṣaṇaḥ sambandhaḥ.* — Ratnakīrti, 1957, p. 93. Also *sa (samākhyā sambandha) ca paramārthato nāsti* — Ibid., p. 95.

relation were different from the relata we could not say that it is the relation of or between these relata?[14] The point is this. If the relata *a* and *b* as well as the relation *R* are all independent then *R* is not necessarily related to either *a* or *b*. But when we say relation of or between *a* or *b* we signify that *R* is related to *a* and *b*. So either *R* is not separate or independent or the usage "relation of *a* to *b* or relation between *a* and *b*" must be false. If it is said that the usage in question can be accounted for by postulating a second relation which connects the first relation with its relata then by the same logic a third relation and a fourth will have to be admitted. The process will continue endlessly. In other words if the relation between a word and its meaning is different from its relata then there would be an infinite regress. It seems that the only way to avoid this infinite regress is to hold that the nature of the first relation is such that it can get related with its terms without (needing) a second relation for the purpose. There are examples to show that it is possible. A lamp which reveals an object does not need a second lamp to reveal itself. Similarly one may argue in support of the Naiyāyikas that the relation that connects a word with the corresponding thing does not require a second relation to connect the first relation with its relata. Ratnakīrti rejects this defence. His argument is interesting but very difficult to explain in English. It can be stated in the following way. We may postulate that a thing has certain peculiar nature by virtue of which it can do something. But we can postulate a character if the thing is already accepted as real. In other words, if the thing is not itself postulated (but real) then we can postulate a character of it, when necessary. The idea is this. Suppose a thing has evidence (*pramāṇasiddha*) in support of it; and it is therefore accepted by both the contesting parties (*pūrvapakṣa* and *siddhānta pakṣa*). In respect of such a thing one of the contesting parties can, for the

14. *yadi bhinnastadā tayoriti kutaḥ?* — Ibid., p. 95.

purpose of explanation, postulate that the thing has a certain character which was so long unknown or unacknowledged. In the context of *upamāna* also we cannot postulate that the relation of meaning has the special characteristic of relating itself to its relata without another relation. First there should be the relation (of *śakti*) itself. Thus a Naiyāyika cannot appeal to the nature (*svabhāva*) of *samākhyā sambandha*, so long as this *sambandha* is not proved independently. So infinite regress cannot be avoided. First there should be the relation of *samākhyā*. But Ratnakīrti argues we cannot admit such a relation. This relation is not *pramāṇasiddha*. We do not have any real awareness of this particular relation, when we do not have any valid awareness of such relation, how can we say that there is such a relation? And if the reality or existence of the relation itself is disputed we have no scope to postulate in respect of this relation a peculiar nature or *svabhāva*. So if this relation is different from its relata we shall have to admit a second and a third relation; and so on. As a result we cannot avoid infinite regress. In other words analogy with lamp drawn by a Naiyāyika is a bad analogy. For while a lamp is undisputedly an existing thing, relation between word and object is a disputed entity. So far the charge of infinite regress cannot be answered on the basis of the said analogy.[15]

The Naiyāyikas may say in reply that it is unjustified to think or to say that there is no evidence for the existence of *samākhyā sambandha*. For, what can be an evidence for the existence of a relation? Experience or awareness of relatedness (*sambandha jñāna* or *viśiṣṭa buddhi*) is the ground for our admitting relation. And nobody will dispute that we have such awareness. It is phenomenologically given and certain. Ratnakīrti himself has noted that we have experience of relatedness in either of these two forms: "This is the relation between the two" (*ayam anayoḥ*

---

15. *na ca yathā pradīpaḥ . . . yad vānāsti eva ayam iti* — Ratnakīrti, 1957, p. 95.

sambandhaḥ) or "These two are related" (*sambandhau etau*). So far as the particular relation, viz. *samākhyā sambandha* or word-meaning relation is concerned we have experience of appropriate kind of relatedness. The great poet Kālidāsa compared this relation with the relation between God Śiva and Goddess Pārvatī.[16] A Naiyāyika may argue that the existence of *samākhyā sambandha* is as evident (*siddha vastu*) as a lamp. Our awareness of the relation between a word and its object is the evidence for admitting the relation called *samākhyā*. Since this relation is evident or *pramāṇa pratīta* we can postulate it to have such a special nature or character that it can be related with the terms it relate.

Ratnakīrti says in reply that the evidence cited above by the Naiyāyikas is not conclusive. We can have experience of relatedness even where there is no relation over and above the two terms which are believed to be related. We can give an example also. We speak of warmth of fire; we have the usage like "The city of Kolkata." In cases like these there is no relation as an extra entity corresponding to the word "of" and obtaining between the two terms where there are two terms. Perhaps with such examples in mind Ratnakīrti says that the awareness of relatedness may be produced even by just the terms related. If this is correct then the Naiyāyikas cannot say that the awareness of relatedness implies that there is a relation which causes this awareness and which is over and above the relata. So it may be admitted that we have experience that words and objects are related, but we can yet deny that there is any relation called *samākhyā* as a third term between a word and its meaning. In other words we can still say that there is no evidence for the existence of *samākhyā sambandha*. And for such non-existing *samākhyā sambandha* we cannot postulate any special character of

---

16. *vāgarthāviva samp̥rktau vāgarthapratipattaye jagataḥ pitarau vande pārvatī-parameśvarau.* — *Raghuvaṁśam, śloka* 1.

it. Accordingly we cannot postulate it to have the nature or character of being self-relating just as a lamp is self-revealing. Therefore the charge of infinite regress remains unanswered. We cannot accept a relation as different from the terms related. We should now turn to the other alternative.

Can it be said that the relation of *śakti* (which according to the Naiyāyikas is the content of *upamāna,* i.e. *upamiti* or knowledge by analogy) is identical with the relata it relates? If one says yes, then there cannot be any relation called *samākhyā*. For every genuine relation is distinct from the terms it relates. If there is no relation as *śakti* or there is (according to the Naiyāyikas) no object of *upamāna*, the charge that *upamāna* is *nirviṣaya* would be valid. It will also be proved that *upamāna* is not a *pramāṇa* or that there is no *upamāna*. The Bauddha objection remains equally sound if one says that *sambandha* (such as *samākhyā*) does not mean (a) what is different from the relata but (b) it relates the relata. It rather means the property of causing the awareness of relatedness. For either this property is identical with the relation (*samākhyā sambandha*) or different from the *samākhyā sambandha*.[17] Ratnakīrti has shown that none of these alternatives can be accepted. And he finally concludes, *naiyāyikasyāpi nirviṣayam upamānam . . . nirākṛtam.*[18]

Kamalaśīla in his *Pañjikā* has also noted this objection against the Nyāya theory of *upamāna*: *sambandhi vyatiriktaḥ sambandho 'paro nāsti.*[19] This he writes while explaining verses 1577-78 of *Tattvasaṁgrahaḥ* by Śāntarakṣita. Some other objections have also been discussed in these texts. I shall note only one of them. It has been said that the real or *svalakṣaṇa* is not the meaning of any word.[20] What can have name therefore is actually

17. Ratnakīrti, 1957, p. 96.
18. Ibid.
19. Kamalaśīla, 1968, p. 555.
20. Ibid., p. 554.

the unreal "thing." Therefore the awareness of the relation between word and its meaning cannot be knowledge or *pramāṇa*. On the basis of such awareness we cannot accept *saṁjñā-saṁjñin sambandha* as an existent thing or reality. Therefore we cannot admit a separate *pramāṇa* like *upamāna* for the knowledge of such a relation. Instead of going into further details about these objections we may pass over to the objections brought by the Vaiśeṣikas. There is one difference between the Bauddhas and the Vaiśeṣikas. The Bauddhas are the rejectionists. They deny *upamāna* altogether. They say that there is no such thing as *upamāna*. But the Vaiśeṣikas do not reject *upamāna* altogether. They are reductionists. They reduce *upamāna* to other *pramāṇa*.

III

The Nyāya and the Vaiśeṣika systems are very close to each other. Regarding most of the things they hold the same view; so they are known as sister systems of Indian philosophy. But as these two schools have their own separate identity so they have some points of difference as well. The issue regarding the number of *pramāṇa*s is a point where these two schools of philosophy differ. The Vaiśeṣikas admit only two *pramāṇa*s: perception and inference, while the Naiyāyikas admit four: perception, inference, analogy and testimony. However, as we have already stated, unlike the Cārvākas and the Bauddhas the Vaiśeṣikas are reductionists in respect of the last two of the four *pramāṇa*s of the Naiyāyikas. So they do not reject *upamāna* altogether but they reduce *upamāna* to another *pramāṇa* (*anumāna*). Regarding *śabda-pramāṇa* they hold the same view, that is to say, they think that *śabda* is also reducible (to *anumāna*).

But the question is, what does this reductionism mean in this context? Is the resulting knowledge believed to be reducible or the instrumental cause of such knowledge? This question arises because we speak of *antarbhāva* (reduction of *upamāna* to *anumāna* or of *upamāna pramāṇa* to *anumāna pramāṇa*. But each of the two words *upamāna* and *anumāna* are used in two different senses. Either they stand for the resulting knowledge (*pramā*) or they stand for the instrumental cause of such knowledge (*pramāṇa*). A Vaiśeṣika philosopher shows both that (*upamiti*) is reducible to *anumiti* and *upamāna* is reducible to *anumāna*. This means knowledge by analogy (*upamiti*) is not an independent kind of knowledge, rather it is reducible to some other variety of knowledge; and secondly, *upamāna pramāṇa* is not an independent accredited source of knowledge but is reducible to some other source. As a result the purpose that may be served by *upamāna* will be served by this other *pramāṇa* in which *upamāna* is reduced.

A reductionist philosopher can state his position with regard to *upamāna* in the above way. But there is one difficulty; the difficulty is this. *Upamāna* and *upamiti* are not admitted in the same sense in such schools like Nyāya and Mīmāṁsā where *upamāna* has actually been admitted. In Indian tradition we all know that it is only the Naiyāyikas and the Mīmāṁsakas who admit *upamāna* as an independent *pramāṇa*[21] both in the sense of *upamiti pramiti* and in the sense of *upamāna pramāṇa* (knowledge and accredited source of knowledge). But they have difference. It has already been stated that the Naiyāyikas admit *upamiti* as the knowledge of the denotative relation of word to its corresponding object (*samākhyā sambandha*). The Mīmāṁsakas admit *upamiti* as the knowledge of similarity (*sādṛśya*) of the perceptible object in the imperceptible object. With regard to the corresponding *pramāṇa* (*upamāna*) or accredited source of knowledge they have some subtle difference, but both of them think that the *pramāṇa* (*upamāna*) is also of the nature of knowledge.[22] So the knowledge called *upamiti* results from

21. Of course there are exceptions both among the Naiyāyikas and among the Mīmāṁsakas.

22. Cf. Subrahmanya Shastri, 1961, pp. 34-35.

another piece of knowledge.[23] Let us explain the point. Both the Naiyāyikas and the Mīmāṁsakas admit that, like inference, *upamiti* also results from a process which involves other knowledge. This process consists of three different knowledges: (1) perceptual knowledge of certain sentence uttered by some reliable person (*atideśa vākya śravaṇa*). This sentence in case of *upamiti* is the statement of analogy or *atideśa vākya*; (2) the perception of similarity (*sādṛśya pratyakṣa*); and the (3) memory of the meaning of the sentence of the reliable person (*atideśa vākyārtha smaraṇa*). None of these knowledges is able to produce the resulting knowledge of *upamiti* independently. But they jointly produce *upamiti*. Among these three knowledges one is regarded as the instrumental cause or *upamāna pramāṇa*. But the philosophers differ as to which one is the instrumental condition. Among the Naiyāyikas themselves there is no unanimity here. But in any case the word *upamāna* is taken to mean both *upamāna pramāṇa* and *upamiti pramiti*. So when a Vaiśeṣika philosopher tends to reduce *upamāna* he is to keep all the above-mentioned differences in his mind. And so far as he is a reductionist he is to reduce *upamāna* and *upamiti* taking each of them in Nyāya as well as Mīmāṁsā sense of the term. If he is unable to do that he cannot claim to have proved his position of reductionism.

But if we consult the texts like *Praśastapāda Bhāṣya* or *Nyāyakandalī* or *Nyāyalīlāvatī* we find that the respective authors have always stated in detail their position or explained why *upamāna* is not an independent *pramāṇa* or why *upamiti* is not an independent *pramiti*. For example, in the text *Padārthadharma-saṁgrahaḥ* of Praśastapāda it is stated that *upamāna* is nothing but *āptavacana*, i.e. statement of a reliable person.[24] In such context

---

23. Inference, knowledge by analogy and testimony are all *jñānakaraṇakaṁ jñānam* while perception is *jñānākaraṇakaṁ-jñānam*. Cf. Viśvanātha Nyāya Pañcānan, 1377 (Baṅgābda), p. 261.

24. *āptena aprasiddhasya gavayasya gavā gavayapratipādanād-upamānam āptavacanameva* — *Praśastapāda Bhāṣya*, 1963, p. 530.

upamāna is taken in the sense of *karaṇa*, and, negatively speaking, not in the sense of resulting knowledge. But in other texts like *Līlāvatī*, etc.[25] *upamāna* is identified with the resulting knowledge, i.e. *upamiti*. From this one may get the impression that either the Vaiśeṣika philosophers were not always very conscious about such differences or they were conscious but they did not bother to distinguish the points. The first alternative is unacceptable. For the difference in question is very common and is generally accepted by the philosophers of Indian tradition. If the second alternative is true then the Vaiśeṣika philosophers' position remains somewhat vague. It could not be known whether they have reduced both *upamiti* and *upamiti-karaṇa*.

In two ways it can be justified. First in some Vaiśeṣika texts the word *upamāna* is taken both in the sense of *upamiti-karaṇa* and in the sense of *upamiti*. Secondly, it can be said that if a philosopher is able to show that *upamiti* is nothing but *anumiti* or *śābda* then from that it will not be difficult to show that their respective *karaṇa*s are identical with *anumāna* or *śabda*. The distinctive nature of a piece of knowledge can be determined by certain criterion.[26] And once the nature of the knowledge is determined then one can easily show which is the distinct *pramāṇa* or special cause of such knowledge. According to the causal principle a particular effect is also produced from a specific cause. So if there is difference in the nature of the knowledge, which is the effect, we can think that their respective causes are also different. On the other hand if the nature of the knowledge which is produced is the same then from that we can assume that their causes are also same. So if once one is able to show

25. *upamānaṁ ca na mānāntaram anumānādeva tadartha-siddhyeḥ* — Vallabhācārya, 1934, p. 531. *gavayatvena pravṛtti-nimittena gavaya-pada-vācya ayam iti parābhimato upamāna phalam anumānāt eva bhavati iti na upamānaṁ pramāṇāntaram iti āha upamānam iti.* — Śaṅkara Miśra, 1934, p. 531.

26. P.K. Mukhopadhyay, 1984, chap. II, pp. 21-26.

that *upamiti* is nothing but *anumiti* then one can say that what is cause of *anumiti* is also the cause of *upamiti*. Again since *anumāna-pramāṇa* is the cause of both *anumiti* and *upamiti* these two types of knowledge are really the same. So from *anumāna* is the *karaṇa* of *upamiti*, it follows that *upamāna* is nothing but *anumāna*. In *Nyāyalīlāvatī* Vallabhācārya or in *Nyāyakusumāñjaliḥ* Udayanācārya used *upamāna* mainly in the sense of *upamiti*. So they have considered whether *upamiti* is *anumiti* or *upamiti* is *śābda*.

Many philosophers are there who do not admit verbal testimony (*śabda*) as a *pramāṇa* but admit inference in this sense. If they want to reduce it they would reduce *upamāna* to inference. Exactly this has been done by the Vaiśeṣikas. But those who, like the Mīmāṁsakas, admit *śabda* as an independent *pramāṇa*, can reduce some version of *upamāna* to *śabda*. Śabara and, following him, Kumārila have done that. Again the Sāṁkhya philosophers admit *śabda-pramāṇa* but do not admit *upamāna pramāṇa*. But instead of reducing it to *śabda* Vācaspati Miśra in his *Sāṁkhya-Tattva-Kaumudī* has shown how *upamāna* is reduced to *anumāna-pramāṇa*.[27] In *Nyāyalīlāvatī* Vallabhācārya has referred to this text of Vācaspati Miśra. Thus not only the philosophers like the Vaiśeṣikas, who do not admit *śabda-pramāṇa*, reduce *upamāna* to *anumāna*; even those who, like Sāṁkhya philosophers, admit *śabda* sometimes reduce *upamāna* to *anumāna*. In any case the Vaiśeṣikas think that if *anumāna* is admitted then that itself can serve the purpose of *upamāna*. Whatever is accountable by *upamāna* is accountable by *anumāna*. So there is no need to admit *upamāna* in addition to the other *pramāṇas*.

It may be interesting to discuss why the Vaiśeṣikas reduce *upamāna* to inference. One may think that for a Vaiśeṣika there is no other option. For, they find independence (*svātantrya*) of *upamāna* is unacceptable. For, they find knowledge of *śakti* to be

27. Vācaspati, 1982.

a genuine kind of knowledge. So they must reduce it. But a *pramāṇa* can be reduced to another *pramāṇa*. The Vaiśeṣikas admit only two *pramāṇas*: perception and inference. So they must reduce *upamāna* either to perception or to inference. But it cannot be reduced to perception. Therefore they reduce it to inference. From this one may think that Vaiśeṣikas reduce *upamāna* to inference as they admit *anumāna* as the only *pramāṇa* in addition to perception. But it would be wrong if one thinks like this. For, Praśastapāda who is a Vaiśeṣika thinker reduced *upamāna* into *śabda* in the first place.[28] Some Sāṁkhya philosophers on the other hand have reduced *upamāna* to *anumāna* even though they accept *śabda-pramāṇa* in addition to *pratyakṣa* and *anumāna-pramāṇa*. The only general rule which we can therefore admit is this. A reductionist reduces a *pramāṇa* in one or the other of the *pramāṇa* he admits. A Vaiśeṣika who does not admit *śabda-pramāṇa* reduces *śabda-pramāṇa* into *anumāna*. He also does not accept *upamāna-pramāṇa*. He can reduce *upamāna* directly to *anumāna* or he can reduce *upamāna* to *śabda* and then *śabda* to *anumāna*. If therefore some other reductionists reduce *upamāna* to a *pramāṇa* which they admit and which is other than *anumāna* then the Vaiśeṣikas will reduce that other *pramāṇa* into *anumāna*.

It has already been stated that *upamāna* cannot be reduced to *pratyakṣa*. The Jainas have reduced it to *pratyabhijñā*.[29] This *pratyabhijñā* is, according to the Jainas, one type of *parokṣa-jñāna*.[30] But this *pratyabhijñā* is a type of perception according to the Naiyāyikas. Secondly why according to the Naiyāyikas *upamāna*

---

28. Ultimately, however, Praśastapāda reduces *śabda* itself into *anumāna*, see Praśastapāda, 1963, p. 512.

29. *upamānasya hi pratyabhijñāne antarbhāvo vakṣyate.* — Prabhācandra, 1941, p. 193.

30. *etacca parokṣabhede pratyabhijñāyām antarbhāvyam* — Guṇaratna 1986, p. 206. According to the Jainas *pratyabhijñāna* is one of the five types of *parokṣa-jñāna*. Ibid., p. 209. See also Hemcandrācārya, 1939, p. 33.

cannot be reduced to perception (including *pratyabhijñā*) will be discussed when we shall discuss Udayana's view.[31]

Granted that *upamiti* is reducible to *anumiti*. But now it becomes an imperative on the part of the Vaiśeṣika philosophers to show the nature and form of such *anumiti*. To understand the Vaiśeṣika position we also need to understand the process of *upamāna*. Let us briefly state the process of *upamāna*.

First one hears a statement of analogy from a reliable person. This is known as *atideśa vākya śravaṇa*. Then one perceives some object which has similarity with some known object. After such perception one remembers the meaning of the sentence which one heard earlier from a reliable person. The second and third are respectively known as *sādṛśya pratyakṣa* and *atideśa vākyārtha smaraṇa*. All these conditions constitute according to (both the Mīmāṁsakas and) the Naiyāyikas the process of *upamāna*. The philosophers differ so far as the nature and form of the resulting knowledge is concerned. According to the Mīmāṁsakas the resulting knowledge is the knowledge of certain similarity, while a Naiyāyika will say that the knowledge which results from the above mentioned conditions will be knowledge of denotation. Differences so far relate to the nature of the object of the knowledge which finally results from the stated conditions. But the philosophers who do not admit *upamāna* but reduce it to *anumāna*, e.g. the Vaiśeṣikas, will say that the nature of the knowledge (which results from the above-mentioned conditions) is inference; and the object of that knowledge is denotative relation (as is admitted by the Naiyāyikas also). To put differently the point of the Vaiśeṣikas is that the so-called conditions of *upamāna* are, when properly viewed, are steps of an inference.

We shall try to understand how the Vaiśeṣika philosophers reduce Nyāya *upamiti* to inference. We all know that the

31. See chap. 8, note 17.

Naiyāyikas do not admit *upamāna* for the knowledge of any and every kind of denotative relation but they admit *upamāna* when such knowledge depends on the three conditions mentioned earlier.

Now the Vaiśeṣika philosophers will say all the three conditions enumerated may be accepted. But these conditions produce the knowledge called *upamiti* through the knowledge of *vyāpti* (concomitant relation). It is for this reason the resulting knowledge should be called inference.

Now those who hold such view, as for example, the Vaiśeṣika must be able to answer the following questions: (i) what is the form of the inference which is involved when one comes to know (or have the knowledge) that this (animal) is called *gavaya* (*ayaṁ gavaya-padavācya*)?; (ii) what use the three conditions of *atideśa vākyaśravaṇa*, etc. have in generating the inference that yields the knowledge of meaning relation?; and (iii) is there any difference between learning the meaning of a word from what is called *vṛddha vyavahāra* and what is called *upamāna*?

Now in answer to the question (i) Vaiśeṣikas have shown that the inference in question will have the following form.

yo yatra asati vṛttyantare prayujyate sa tasya vācakaḥ,
yathā "go" śabda gojātīyasya.[32]

Long before Vallabhācārya the same inference was alternatively formulated by Vācaspati Miśra in his *Sāṁkhyatattvakaumudī* in the following way:

yo hi śabda yatra vṛddhaiḥ prayujyate,
so 'sati vṛttyantare tasya vācakaḥ yathā go śabda gotvasya.[33]

The idea of the inference may first be generally stated.

---

32. Vallabhācārya, 1934, p. 531.

33. Vācaspati, 1982, pp. 63-64.

That (thing) is the referent (*vācya*) of an expression (*tasya*) to which (*yatra*) the expression applies (*prayujyate*) independent of such other (*antara*) word-meaning relation (*vṛtti*, as *lakṣaṇā*); an example is the word "cow" which applies to the thing (animal) which has the property of being a cow. That is:

jat padaṁ tadarthasya vācakam
asati vṛttyantare tatra prayujyatvāt yannaivaṁ tannaivaṁ
yathā anya-padam arthāntarasya.[34]

The same inference will take the following form in the particular case under reference:

gavaya-padaṁ gavayatva viśiṣṭa arthasya vācakam,
asati vṛttyantare tatra prayujyatvāt,
yathā go-padam (gotva-viśiṣṭasya vācakam).

Now when one has all the three conditions like *atideśa vākya śravaṇa*, *sādṛśya-pratyakṣa* and *vākyārtha-smaraṇa* one understands that all reliable usages have corresponding denotation. Then as he heard the word *gavaya* so he understands that the word must have denotation. If it does not have any direct relation it must have some indirect relation to that denotation. As for example, the word "cow" has some normal use; it has direct relation to its object. The word *gavaya* if it is used by some reliable person and if we do not perceive any object corresponding to it even then we are to understand that there must be some animal corresponding to the word *gavaya*. Fully formulated this is a case of inference and the result is the knowledge of denotation. So the Vaiśeṣika philosophers are of the opinion that one has the knowledge of denotation from inference. This is the reduction of *upamāna* to inference. That means the resulting knowledge of *upamiti* is explainable by inferential knowledge.

But now if it is true then a Vaiśeṣika philosopher is to face the second question, what use the three conditions of *atideśa*

---

34. The example we are offering here is negative.

vākya śravaṇa, etc. have in generating the inference that yields the knowledge of meaning relation? In answer a Vaiśeṣika philosopher is to say either of these two things: (i) the conditions like *atideśa vākya*, etc. cause the knowledge of *vyāpti* which in its turn produce the inferential knowledge of *śakti* or (ii) these conditions themselves produce the said inferential knowledge. If anyone of these answers is correct then it will follow that the process of *upamāna* is nothing but *anumāna*. To explain, if the Vaiśeṣika philosopher accepts the first alterntive he is to say that in the situation first the hearer has the knowledge from *atideśa vākya* and perception of similarity, then the person has the knowledge of *vyāpti* and then he has the inferential knowledge of the denotation. This view of the opponent may be found to violate the law of parsimony. For, on this view the *atideśa vākya* and perception of similarity are not sufficient for the knowledge of *śakti*; we require in addition knowledge of *vyāpti*. But on the theory of one who believes in *upamāna* the conditions of *atideśa vākya* and knowledge of similarity are sufficient condition; on this theory therefore knowledge of *śakti* results from less number of conditions. This theory is therefore logically more economical. If now a Vaiśeṣika philosopher admits the other alternative and says that the process of *upamāna* is the process of inference then he is to explain how the knowledge of similarity first from *atideśa vākya* and next from perception amounts to knowledge of *hetu* and knowledge of *vyāpti* which together finally yields the inferential knowledge of *śakti*. The Vaiśeṣika philosopher may say that the perception of similarity is the perception of *hetu*. And though not the *śravaṇa* of *atideśa vākya* yet the memory of *atideśa vākya* is equivalent with memory of *vyāpti*. So there is no difficulty if now one claims that he has inferential knowledge, in understanding that the process involved in *upamāna*, the conditions that are operative here are equivalent to the conditions of *anumāna*. Now one can easily say that the knowledge which results from this process is *anumiti*.

And if the resulting knowledge is inferential then no need is there to admit another independent *pramāṇa* called *upamāna*.

One point remains to be explained. It has been shown above what could be perception of *hetu* and what could be memory of *vyāpti*. But before memory of *vyāpti* there should be *anubhava* of *vyāpti*. Where is *anubhava* or non-recollective awareness of *vyāpti*? Now it may be said that when a hearer hears from a reliable person that "*gavaya* is like *gauḥ*" he has the *anubhava* of *vyāpti*. He understands that wherever there is similarity with *gauḥ* there is *gavaya-pada-vācyatva*. Now after having this knowledge (*anubhava*) of *vyāpti* when the person perceives cow-similarity in an animal he remembers the *vyāpti* which he knew earlier from the reliable person. So the process of *upamāna* actually shows that first a person has thc non-recollective knowledge of *vyāpti* then if later he happens to perceive the *hetu*, he remembers the *vyāpti* and derives knowledge of *śakti*. This resulting knowledge cannot be knowledge by analogy; it is inferential knowledge. Now the Vaiśeṣika philosophers can accept inference in this sense. The author later will discuss Nyāya answer to the Vaiśeṣika objection that *upamāna* is *anumāna* in the sense explained here.

Now the discussion is regarding the third question noted above. The question arises for this reason. The Naiyāyikas think that the relation of a word to its meaning is known by different means. Two of these means are *upamāna* and what is called *vr̥ddha vyavahāra*. Now *upamāna* is claimed to be an independent means of knowledge. Whatever is known must be known through certain *pramāṇa* or means of knowledge. If *vr̥ddha-vyavahāra* knows the meaning relation then it must be a *pramāṇa*. But there is no such *pramāṇa* as *vr̥ddha vyavahāra*; it is not one among the four *pramāṇa*s admitted in the Nyāya school. The Naiyāyikas hold that *vr̥ddha vyavahāra* is really a case of inference. If so then a Naiyāyika also admits that the meaning relation can be known by means of inference. And the Vaiśeṣikas also claim that it is through inference that meaning relation is known. So two questions arise: (1) How Naiyāyikas can admit independence of *upamāna*? In other words how can they then say that *upamāna* is an independent source of knowledge of meaning relation? and (2) If the Vaiśeṣikas admit that the meaning relation is known through inference as explained above and if *vṛddha vyavahāra* is an inference how these two are related?

The Vaiśeṣikas would say either that *vṛddha vyavahāra* and *upamāna* are same or that these two are different. The question is important. Because both *vṛddha vyavahāra* and *upamāna* are admitted for the knowledge of denotation. Now if the two are same then as *vṛddha vyavahāra* is reducible to inference so also *upamāna* the Vaiśeṣikas will say, will be reducible to inference. But this will not really negate the Naiyāyika view of *upamāna*. Because the Naiyāyikas do not say that the cases of knowledge by *vṛddha vyavahāra* are the cases of knowledge by *upamāna*. They say that only in some cases our knowledge of denotation comes from *upamāna*; in some other cases we do have knowledge of denotation through *vṛddha vyavahāra*.

Now to conclude this point a Vaiśeṣika will say that when one knows the meaning relation from *vṛddha vyavahāra* (or so called *upamāna*) one knows the meaning relation through inference. The form of inference may be different in case of *upamāna* and in case of *vṛddha vyavahāra*. But the Vaiśeṣika position stands. The relation of words to the things which they mean is known through *anumāna*. There is no need to admit a separate *pramāṇa* like *upamāna*. If what is called *upamāna* knows the meaning relation then that *upamāna* is really inference.

Before closing this section which includes the Vaiśeṣika criticisms of the Nyāya view of *upamāna* it is important to note a point. The form of the inference to which a Vaiśeṣika reduces *upamāna* is already shown. The Naiyāyika criticism of the Vaiśeṣika objection will be discussed later. But one criticism which Vallabha has anticipated and tried to answer may be briefly discussed. This criticism was stated by Udayanācārya in his *Nyāyakusumāñjaliḥ*.

In *Nyāyalīlāvatī* Vallabhācārya has anticipated or raised a provisional objection against inference. The objection is this: As the knowledge is on the basis of *gosādṛśya* so one has no other alternative than to accept *go-sādṛśya* as the qualifying property of *sādṛśya*. But Vallabhācārya has raised this objection that between two such properties, viz. *gavayatva* and *gosadṛśatva* if one takes *gosadṛśatva* as the qualifier one will violate the law of parsimony. So one is to take *gavayatva* as the qualifying property; the qualifier.[35]

In answer to such objection Vallabhācārya has defended the Vaiśeṣika position and states: in case of such sentence as "*gaṅgāyām ghoṣaḥ*" we understand the inhabitants of a certain village on the bank of the river Ganges. Here we take the word *Gaṅgā* in its indirect meaning. So also in this case we can understand *gavayatva* in place of *go-sādṛśya* as the qualifying property. And if once we can take *gavayatva* as the qualifying property of the referent then the object as having this property can be the denotation of the word *gavaya*. And accordingly by inference one will be able to understand the animal which has *gavayatva* to be the denotation of the word *gavaya*. So the inference can give us knowledge of the meaning relation between the word *gavaya* and the thing (animal) *gavaya*. And *gavayatva* though not directly yet indirectly will be the qualifier of the property of being denotation, i.e. *śakyatāvacchedaka*.

But this view is objectionable from the Nyāya standpoint. If there is no hindrance or difficulty in understanding a sentence by taking words in it in their literal and direct sense then we cannot take any of these words in its indirect sense or *lakṣaṇā*.

---

35. Annaṁbhatta, 1390 (Baṅgābda).

How then can one understand the word (*gosadṛśa*) in the sentence *gosadṛśa gavaya* in indirect sense of *gavayatva*? How can *gavayatva* be the qualifier or the property determination of the property of being denotation? So one cannot get by inference the knowledge that thing having *gavayatva* is the meaning of *gavaya*.

The Vaiśeṣikas may answer in this way: A property cannot be the determining property if it is more complex than another. So far its being more complex acts as the hindrance in cases of *gosādṛśya*. If one takes *gavayatva* in place of *gosadṛśatva* one can avoid that.[36] And accordingly from the above inference and from this consideration of logical economy one can come to know that the meaning of *gavaya* is the animal which has *gavayatva*. There is no need for *upamāna-pramāṇa*.

It may be said in the last place that the criticism or rejection of Vaiśeṣika reductionism will not prove the Nyāya position that *upamāna* is an independent *pramāṇa*. To say that the Vaiśeṣikas are wrong is not to say that the Naiyāyikas are correct. Naiyāyikas need to show that the rejectionists and the reductionists are wrong. They are to show in addition that there are positive arguments which prove that *upamāna* is an independent *pramāṇa* which knows *śakti*. They must also show that there is such a thing as *śakti*. And in this connection they are to state clearly whether *śakti* is an additional category.

---

36. Of course, Raghunātha Śiromaṇi in his *Avacchedakatva nirukti* has shown that in some cases a complex property (*gurudharma*) can as well be the determining (*avacchedaka*). *Gauravapratisandhāna-daśāyāmapi kambugrībādimānnāstīti pratītivalāt gūrurapi dharma avacchedakaḥ pratiyogitāyāḥ* — Raghunātha, 1968, p. 125.

6

Development of the Nyāya Theory of Upamāna

SOME objections against the Nyāya theory of *upamāna* are considered. Over centuries critics brought these objections. The author is not going to offer all the answers to these objections one by one. The objective here rather is to show how the Nyāya theory developed in course of time. The Nyāya theory developed in response to various objections which were brought against it. The development in this sense started from the time of Vātsyāyana or even before. It continued up to the time of Gaṅgeśa and afterwards. The history of development is divided into two periods: development till the time of Udayana and development from the time of Udayana. The three major objections against Nyāya theory of *upamāna* which we have already noted are the following. (i) The Naiyāyikas have failed to preserve the independence of *upamāna* as a *pramāṇa*. For they say that *upamiti* results from *atideśa vākya*. This makes *upamiti* a case of *śābda*. (It may be agreed that only when we come to Navya-Nyāya, the role of perception of similarity is clearly stated to be the *karaṇa* of *upamiti*.) (ii) There is no such thing as *upamāna-pramāṇa*. Because *upamāna* is admitted for knowledge of *śakti*. But there is no such entity like *śakti*. (iii) The Naiyāyikas wrongly believed that *upamāna* is an independent *pramāṇa*. Actually speaking, it is inference or according to some it is perception. According to some other it is nothing but memory.

Buddhists and perhaps also the Cārvākas are rejectionists in respect of *upamāna*. They have shown that *upamāna* is not to be considered as a *pramāṇa*. For some of them, there is no such object for the knowledge of which *upamāna* may be necessary. Reductionist philosophers like the Vaiśeṣikas or the Jainas on the other hand have denied independence of *upamāna* as a *pramāṇa*; they have reduced it to the other *pramāṇa* like inference or *pratyabhijñā*.[1] However these philosophers did not always discuss the definition of *upamāna* which has been offered by Gautama in the *Nyāya-Sūtra* 1.1.6.[2]

Gautama himself (in the second chapter of *Nyāya-Darśana*, i.e. in the *Parīkṣā Prakaraṇa*) examined definitions of *pramāṇa*s given by himself earlier. In this connection he has considered some objections against his own definition of *upamāna*. The purpose is to defend the way in which he has defined *upamāna*. For it is a common belief with the Indian philosophers that *ekākinī pratijñā hi pratijñātuṁ na sādhayet*, i.e. mere statement of it (doctrine or position) does not prove one's doctrine or position. So after offering the definition of *upamāna* in the *sūtra* 1.1.6 Gautama himself has considered the probable objections against the definition in *sūtra*s 2.1.45 to 2.1.48.

Gautama's definition of *upamāna* consists of two parts: (1) *prasiddha sādharmyāt* and (2) *sādhya sādhaṇam*. In the first place these two expressions are to be understood or interpreted. By way of interpreting these expressions and answering the objections of the opponents Gautama defended his own (or Nyāya) theory of *upamāna*. This theory has the following two major tenets:

(1) *upamāna* is a *pramāṇa*; and

(2) *upamāna* is an independent *pramāṇa*.

In his *sūtra* 2.1.44 Gautama has anticipated the objection that *upamāna* is not a *pramāṇa*. And in *sūtra* 2.1.46 he has hinted at the

1. See note 29 of chapter 5.

2. *prasiddhasādharmyātsādhyasādhaṇam upamānam* — *sūtra* 1.1.6.

objection that even if *upamāna* is accepted as *pramāṇa* it cannot be said to be an independent *pramāṇa*; it is nothing but *anumāna*.[3] It may be said that the expression *prasiddha sādharmyāt* shows that *upamāna* is a *pramāṇa* and the expression *sādhya sādhanam* shows that *upamāna* is an independent *pramāṇa*. Accordingly now our task is to show how Gautama and his commentators have anticipated or formulated the objections. And we also want to show if and how such objections can be answered from the Nyāya point of view. The intended definition of *upamāna* is this: *upamāna* is the knowledge of denotation resulting from the knowledge of similarity. So according to Gautama when one derives the knowledge that x is the denotation of a term w, from the knowledge of similarity one has the knowledge by analogy. An example of such knowledge is the knowledge of the relation of denotation of the word *gavaya* to the animal *gavaya* (i.e. Bosgāvaeus)[4] on the basis of the knowledge of similarity of *gavaya* with cow.

The objector says that one cannot have the knowledge of denotation from the (knowledge of) similarity. For the similarity on the basis of which one may have the knowledge of denotation can be of three types. But none of these three kinds of similarity can yield knowledge of denotation. Similarity can be (i) total (*ātyantika*) or (ii) close (*prāyika*) or (iii) only partial (*ekadeśa*). On the basis of these similarities one cannot have the knowledge of denotation. If total similarity were the basis of knowledge of denotation then one could know a second cow (*gavāntara*) to be the meaning of the word *gavaya*; because the second cow has total similarity with the first cow. But from the knowledge of total similarity (in a second cow) we do not have the knowledge of meaning of a word *gavaya*. We do not come to have the

3. *astu tarhi upamānamanumānam* (Vātsyāyana, 1985, p. 529). *pratyakṣ-eṇāpratyakṣasiddheḥ* — Gautama, *Nyāya-Sūtra*, 2.1.46.

4. Cf. Satish Chandra, 1978, p. 94.

knowledge that (the second) cow is the meaning (referent) of the term *gavaya* or "Bosgāvaeus." In other words we do not say "*go* is *gavaya* or bosgāvaeus," i.e. *go* or cow is the referent of the word *gavaya*. On the basis of close similarity also we cannot have knowledge of what is the denotation of a word. Uddyotakara has interpreted *prāyika* to mean *bhūyaḥ*.[5] The word *bhūyaḥ* literally means many. We translated it as close. Such similarity is present between a buffalo and an ox. But Vātsyāyana says that such similarity cannot make *upamāna* possible. Uddyotakara says one does not say a cow is a buffalo. But they have close resemblance. Again partial similarity is present between a mountain and a mustard seed. But on the basis of it one does not acquire the knowledge (by analogy) that mountain is (the denotation of) *sarṣapa* or "mustard seed." But *upamāna* according to the Naiyāyikas is knowledge from similarity. It now follows that on the basis of none of the three types of similarity one can have the knowledge of denotation. So one cannot say *upamāna* is the source of knowledge of denotation on the basis of knowledge of similarity.

Vācaspati Miśra in his *Tātparya-Ṭīkā* has shown the deeper implication of the above objection. According to him the importance of the objection is not only to show that from such three different kinds of similarity we cannot have knowledge by *upamāna*. Because in some cases one does have knowledge by *upamāna* after one hears *atideśa vākya* or the statement of similarity. This has been shown by Uddyotakara. In his *Vārttika* Uddyotakara has shown that there are actual examples where *atideśa vākya* or statement of analogy signifies respectively total similarity (*atyanta sādharmya*), large-scale or close similarity (*bhūyaḥ sādharmya*) and merely, partial similarity (*ekadeśa sādharmya*). As example of the first Uddyotakara quoted a portion of a verse from *Kabi Ratna*. The verse states that the battle which

5. Uddyotakara, 1985, p. 527.

was fought between Rāma and Rāvaṇa could be compared with that fight only.[6] Uddyotakara says *bhūyaḥ sādharmyeṇāpi bhavati* and *ekadeśādharmyādapi.*[7] According to Uddyotakara if time and context are suitable then each of the three types of similarity can be the basis of *upamāna.*[8] Vācaspati Miśra has brought out the real point of the objector. The objector says that no one of this type of similarity can be made the basis of our knowledge of denotation. If in the context of the statement "*gavaya* is like cow" similarity is understood to mean total similarity then to be the denotation of *gavaya* a thing must be totally similar to cow. But then the second cow which has total or complete similarity with the first cow, experienced before, would become the meaning or the denotation of *gavaya.* In other words *gavaya* will become a description of a cow or a cow will be called *gavaya.* Similarly, the objector will argue that even though large-scale or close similarity obtains between an ox and a buffalo yet one does not know "ox" to be the name of a buffalo. This shows the similarity asserted by *atideśa vākya* cannot be understood as very close or large-scale similarity. In other words, one cannot take the *atideśa vākya* to tell us that the reference of a word is what has close similarity with the (some) other familiar thing. Lastly nobody knows "mountain" to be the name of a mustard seed, though between the two there is partial similarity and there may be such *atideśa vākya* as *yathā merustathā sarṣapa.* Both the mountain and the mustard seed are substances and they both exist; there are many such points of similarity between the two.

---

6. *sarvathābhāvāccātyantasādharmyādupamānam-siddhyati, tatkriyayiva tatkriyopamīyate. yathā rāma rāvaṇayoryuddhaṁ rāma rāvaṇayoriva iti* — Uddyotakara, 1985, pp. 528-29.

7. Ibid., p. 529.

8. Vācaspati Miśra has shown this in detail. He says, *prakaraṇādyapekṣaṁ hi vākyam svārthaṁ pratipādayati na kevalam. tadvaśāt ca kvacit atyanta sādharmyaṁ pratīyate kvacidbhūyaḥsādharmyaṁ kvacidekadeśasādharmyaṁ.* — Vācaspati Miśra, 1985, p. 528.

Everything may have some similarity with every other thing. If *ekadeśa sādharmya* could be the basis of *upamāna* then *sarveṇasarvamupamiyata iti.*[9] This shows similarity asserted or stated in the *atideśa vākya* cannot simply be partial similarity.

When interpreted in the above way the objection is very strong no doubt. But the above objection cannot disprove the Nyāya theory of *upamāna*. According to the Naiyāyikas *upamāna* is not the knowledge of denotation from the knowledge of any one of the above three kinds of similarity. And the *atideśa vākya*, partly from which word-meaning relation is known, does not assert anyone of these three kinds of similarity necessarily.

To a Naiyāyika *upamāna* is the knowledge of denotation from the *known* similarity. It is not knowledge from *total, close* or partial (*occasional*) similarity. In other words *upamiti* is not knowledge from total (*ātyantika*), large-scale (*prāyika*) or partial (*ekadeśa*) similarity but it is knowledge from known (*prasiddha*) similarity. Now what will count as known similarity depends on what similarity one comes to know from the statement of similarity; and this will depend on the context of utterance. So Vācaspati says depending on the relevant context *atideśa vākya* can mean *atyanta* or *bhūyaḥ* or *ekadeśa sādharmya*. A reliable person tells a man that "a *gavaya* is like a cow." Suppose this man already knows an ox; he will understand the statement of analogy to mean that a *gavaya* is an animal which is both different from an ox and similar to cow. When this man later perceives some animal which is other than ox but like cow he remembers what he was told. Then if he understands that this animal is called *gavaya*, he has this knowledge by *upamāna* or analogy (or known similarity). So the objection is that *upamāna* is not possible, because none of the three kinds of similarity can be the basis of knowledge of meaning relation. But this objection cannot do any harm to the Nyāya position. In *sūtra* 2.1.44 Gautama has

9. Vātsyāyana, 1985, p. 528.

hinted at the above objection and in *sūtra* 2.1.45 he himself has hinted at the answer to that.[10]

Uddyotakara in addition has pointed out a logical defect in the argument of the opponent. The opponent wants to prove that there is no *upamāna* or that *upamāna* is not possible.[11] But Uddyotakara says, what the opponent has actually shown is that *upamāna* is not possible from total, almost total (*prāyika*) or partial similarity. But to say that *upamāna* which depends on these similarities is not possible is not to say that *upamāna* as such (*upamānamātra*) is not possible.[12] Secondly Uddyotakara comments that the implication of what the objector really says is that (*upamāna* from these types of similarity is not possible but) *upamāna* is possible in some other form or in some other sense. The objector should show what is that other form or how that can be possible. Thus to imply *upamāna* is possible in a different sense, is not to show that *upamāna* is not possible.[13]

If the objector really wants to eliminate *upamāna* as such he will have to offer some other argument. Uddyotakara has shown the type of argument which will be necessary. He says that the opponent must say that *upamāna* is not *pramāṇa* because it does not give us knowledge of anything.[14] In fact, this kind of argument we actually find in the Buddhist literature. As we have stated earlier, according to the Buddhists real objects are only of two kinds. It is either *svalakṣaṇa* or it is *sāmānya lakṣaṇa*. *Upamāna* reveals neither *svalakṣaṇa* nor the *sāmānya lakṣaṇa*, so it cannot be said to reveal any thing (any real object) at all. This

10. *prasiddhasādharmyādupamānasiddher-yathoktadoṣānupapattiḥ* — 2.1.45, Gautama, 1985, p. 528.

11. . . . *upamānāsiddhiḥ* . . . — *Nyāya-Sūtra* 2.1.44, Gautama 1985.

12. *atyantādi* . . . *na punarūpamāna-mātrasya pratiṣedhaḥ* — Uddyotakara, 1985, p. 527.

13. *evaṁ sati anyathā upamānaṁ, tatsvarūpam vaktavyam* — Ibid., p. 527.

14. *upamānam apramāṇam, arthāpratipādakatvāt* — Ibid., p. 528.

argument is the same as the Bauddha argument from the absence of object which we find in Ratnakīrti. *Upamāna* is devoid of real object and therefore is not *pramāṇa*. We shall discuss this objection. But this objection against *upamāna*, that it has no object to know, has not been considered by Gautama. He has considered, as we have already mentioned, the objection that *upamāna* is not possible from anyone of the three varieties of similarity. And he has also answered the objection.

From all the above discussions it follows that *upamāna* is possible. Gautama therefore finally shows in the *Parīkṣā-Prakaraṇa* that *upamāna* is possible. Discussion so far may be summarized here. In his *sūtra* 1.1.3 Gautama first mentioned *upamāna* by name. Then in the *sūtra* 1.1.6 he offered the definition of *upamāna*. Long after in *sūtra*s 2.1.44-48 he examined *upamāna*. Because there intervened a big gap and many different subjects are discussed in between, Gautama must find some excuse for taking up *upamāna* for examination now. Gautama has not himself shown what excuse he finds there. The author of *Vṛtti* explicitly stated that Gautama found *avasara* to take up *upamāna* for *parīkṣā* after *anumāna*.[15] In the *Parīkṣā-Prakaraṇa* Gautama first noted an argument against *upamāna* which an opponent may offer. It is that, *upamāna* from any of the three varieties of similarity is not possible.

Vācaspati Miśra in his *Tātparya-Ṭīkā* has very nicely shown the possible intention of Gautama. Gautama's intention was not to suggest that similarity is only of three different kinds. Gautama wanted to show that even if *upamāna* from such three different kinds of similarity is not possible, it may still be possible. *Upamāna* does not necessarily need one of these three different kinds of similarity. What is important is that the similarity should be *known* similarity if it is to be the basis of

---

15. *athāvasareṇa kramaprāptamupamānaṁ parīkṣitum . . .* — Viśvanātha, 1985, p. 528.

knowledge by analogy. One may ask the question how one can know similarity? Vācaspati Miśra has given the answer. He said it will be known from *atideśa vākya*, the meaning of which is determined by the context. So a man who knows from a reliable person that *gavaya* is like *go* may later go to the forest and perceive an animal which is a buffalo. If he knew buffalo to be like cow before *atideśa vākya* was told to him he will not have the knowledge by *upamāna* that buffalo is the meaning or denotation or *vācya* of the word *gavaya*.

We distinguished on page 134 two points. Of these we have so far discussed the first point. We shall now discuss the second point. Granted that *upamāna* is a *pramāṇa*, is it irreducible to other *pramāṇa*? Is it a *svatantra pramāṇa*?

Now to show that *upamāna* is an independent *pramāṇa* one is to show that it is not reducible to any other *pramāṇa* which one already admits. Accordingly as a Naiyāyika admits perception, inference and testimony (other than *upamāna*), it is to be shown that *upamāna* is not reducible to any of these three *pramāṇas*, which a Naiyāyika admits. And if a Naiyāyika is able to do that then he can claim the independence of *upamāna*. The Naiyāyikas of ancient and classical age have done exactly this. In the *Parikṣā-Prakaraṇa* of his *Nyāya-Darśana* Gautama has shown how irreducibility can be demonstrated. His successors including Udayana have followed him in this respect. But when Udayana discussed irreducibility in his *Nyāyakusumāñjaliḥ* he treats the matter in a slightly different way. We shall discuss this at the appropriate place. In addition to *upamāna* the Naiyāyikas admit perception, inference and testimony. In his *Vārttika* on the *Parīkṣā-Prakaraṇa* of *upamāna* Uddyotakara explicitly stated that *upamāna* cannot be reduced to either perception or inference or testimony.[16] To show that this knowledge is not accountable by

16. *evaṁ ca nopamānamāgamo na pratyakṣam, . . . na caivamanumānam* — Uddyotakara, 1985, p. 531.

either perception or testimony Uddyotakara writes that, in case of *upamāna* one does not have knowledge of the form "this is *gavaya*" either from perception or from *śabda*.[17] In case of *upamāna* one has the knowledge of the form *ayaṁ gavayaḥ* or *gavaya gavaya-padavāccya*.

One may accept this as an answer to the attempt to reduce *upamāna* into perception or testimony. Yet one may say that the knowledge under consideration may not be perception or verbal but may be inferential. This objection has been anticipated also. Gautama and his followers have shown that *upamāna* is not reducible to even inference. It is a separate *pramāṇa*. If one wants to reduce *upamāna* to *anumāna* then one must say the following. In case of inference one knows fire from perception of smoke. Similarly in case of so-called *upamāna* (i.e. in case of *go-gavaya*) one knows the *gavaya* from the perceptual knowledge of cow. So there is no need to admit *upamāna* as a separate source of knowledge. Rather the knowledge one has is nothing but inference. So *upamāna* is not at all necessary as an independent and additional source. *Upamāna* is reduced to *anumāna*. Uddyotakara states this position of the opponent in the words *astu tarhi upamānam anumānam*. The words mean, let then *upamāna* be *anumāna*. In other words even if *upamāna* is a *pramāṇa* but is not reducible to perception or testimony it can be inference. To put it otherwise *upamāna* is a *pramāṇa* but not a separate *pramāṇa*. It is reducible to *anumāna*. This view is known as *anumānāntarabhāva* of *upamāna*.

But Uddyotakara states that the above-mentioned two cases are not similar. Knowledge of fire from smoke and knowledge of (*viśiṣṭa*) *gavaya* from cow (*go*) are different. In case of inferential knowledge the *sādhya*, i.e. fire is not perceived while in case of *upamāna* one perceives the *gavaya*. But from this one

17. *Na hi ayam āgamāt pratyakṣādvā 'yaṁ gavaya iti pratipadyate.* — Uddyotakara, 1985, p. 531.

may have the impression that according to the Naiyāyikas what we know through *upamāna* is a percept. To say this is to say that *upamāna* is nothing but perception. We therefore gain very little. In our attempt to resist the reduction of *upamāna* to *anumāna*, we have actually reduced *upamāna* to *pratyakṣa*.

Uddyotakara himself has given the answer to this problem. He says that *gavaya* is perceptible no doubt. But the object of *upamāna* is not the perceptible *gavaya*. The actual object in this case is the relation between the name *gavaya* and its corresponding thing (animal) *gavaya*. So it is true that in case of *upamāna* one knows (the perceived) *gavaya* as the referent of *gavaya*. Object of *upamāna* is actually the *meaning relation* between name and the object. So Uddyotakara states, *yā asau saṁjñā-saṁjñi-sambandha pratipattiḥ sa upamānārthaḥ*.[18] The result (*phala* or utility), i.e. *artha* of *upamāna* is the knowledge (*pratipatti*) of the relation (*sambandha*) of name (*saṁjñā*) to its referent (*saṁjñin*). So though apparently it may seem that *upamāna* is nothing but a kind of inference yet actually, as we have shown, *upamāna* is different from *anumāna*. Accordingly such objection that *upamāna* is nothing but *anumāna* does not stand.

Vātsyāyana has noted another argument why *upamāna* cannot be reduced to *anumāna*. He has stated very explicitly in his commentary the view of those who think that there is a basic difference between an inference and an *upamāna*. *Upamāna* is made always for others while *anumāna* is made for his own self also. And in other words *anumāna* is of two kinds — *svārthānumāna* and *parārthānumāna* — while *upamāna* is always for others. When one utters (*atideśa vākya*) the statement of analogy he does so for others, i.e. from this utterance the hearer will understand the meaning relation (of course, there are other conditions). But sometimes one derives from inference one's own knowledge. In such cases *anumāna* is of course *svārtha* and

18. Uddyotakara, 1985, p. 531.

not *parārtha*. Some thinkers therefore are of the opinion that on this ground we can resist the attempt to reduce *upamāna* to *anumāna*. *Anumāna* is either *svārtha* or *parārtha* but *upamāna* is always *parārtha*.

Against this Vātsyāyana says, though not very explicitly, that this distinction does not really obtain between *anumāna* and *upamāna*. For, those thinkers who thought that *upamāna* is different from *anumāna* thought that *upamāna* is made for others. But this cannot be the point of difference of *upamāna* from *anumāna*. An inference is also made for others. So this cannot be the point of theirs. They actually mean to say that *upamāna* is only for others, i.e. it is not for one's own self. But *anumāna* is there both for others and also for one's own self. Vātsyāyana says that from *upamāna* or *atideśa vākya* the hearer as well as the utterer himself get the same (similar) knowledge. As for example, when one utters the statement of analogy that "*gavaya* is like *go*" one has, Vātsyāyana says, the same knowledge which the other (*para*) or the hearer has.[19] Thus like *anumāna, upamāna* is both *svārtha* and *parārtha*.

One may ask Vātsyāyana "Is there no difference between *anumāna* and *upamāna* according to a Naiyāyika?" Anticipating such a question Vātsyāyana has said that we do not deny that the hearer has knowledge (*nādhyavasāyaḥ pratisidhyate*) from statement of analogy one utters, but this knowledge is not what we call the result of *upamāna* (*upamānaṁ tu tanna bhavati*).[20] When one utters the statement for others it is true that the person himself has also knowledge. But the person can have knowledge of similarity. But according to a Naiyāyika this knowledge of similarity is not what is called *upamiti* or the result of *upamāna*.

---

19. *bhavati ca bhoḥ svayam adhyavasāyaḥ yathā gourebaṁ gavaya iti.* — Vātsyāyana, 1985, p. 531.

20. Ibid.

But the result of *upamāna* is the knowledge of the meaning relation which is not revealed by the statement of analogy.

In answer it may be said that the knowledge cannot be perceptual, because here the knowledge is not of the nature of the thing. It is not the knowledge "this is *gavaya*." Nor even this is *āgama*. If it were so then one should have the knowledge that *gavaya* is like cow. For, the utterance of the reliable person was to that effect. But as we all know *upamiti* according to the Naiyāyikas is not the knowledge of similarity. It is the knowledge of the denotation of the word *gavaya*. It is the knowledge that the yonder animal is the thing called *gavaya*. Thus the knowledge of the meaning relation does not result just from sense object contact; nor just from *āgama*. It results from the combination of *āgama*, perception and also memory cognition. So when one perceives a *gavaya* and perceives similarity in it, one actually does not have a mere perception. One has certain particular perception. It is a perception of similarity (*sādṛśya pratyakṣa*) caused by the memory (*smṛti*) which in its turn is caused by corresponding disposition (*saṁskāra*). This disposition is left behind by the non-recollective knowledge produced by the utterance (of similarity) of some reliable person (*āgamāhita*).[21]

Anyway, from such special perception (of similarity) there results what is called knowledge by analogy. And that knowledge has for its object meaning relation. In the case of *upamāna* in question the resulting knowledge is not the mere perception of similarity with cow in the bison; it is the knowledge of denotation of the word *gavaya*.[22]

---

21. *āgamāhita saṁskāra smṛti sāpekṣaṁ svārūpya pratyakṣam* — Uddyotakara, 1985, p. 532.

22. *tasmāt pratyakṣa eva gavaye gavayatvasya pratyakṣatvāt saṁjñā-saṁjñi sambandha paricchedaḥ pramāṇārthaḥ*. — Vācaspati, 1985, p. 530.

So we must admit a fourth (kind of) source of knowledge. Even if all the three, perception, etc. are somehow involved in this fourth *pramāṇa*, still this fourth *pramāṇa* cannot be said to be either perception or inference or testimony. This shows that the fourth *pramāṇa* will be an irreducible *pramāṇa*. *Upamiti* or the knowledge we have here (*go-gavaya* case) is accountable by *āgamāhitasaṁskāra smr̥ti sāpekṣa pratyakṣa jñānam*. And this is called *upamiti-karaṇa* or *upamānam*.

Part Four

Some More Objections from Internal and External Critics

7

Nyāyaikadeśī View on Upamāna (Bhāsarvajña)

I

THERE are both external and internal critics of the Nyāya theory of *upamāna*. Bauddhas are among the external critics while the Vaiśeṣikas or Mīmāṁsakas are the internal critics.[1] This shows that *upamāna* is really a dubitable *pramāṇa* in the Indian tradition. But once a view is admitted by the founder of a system, it is generally accepted by the followers of that system. So when in his *Nyāya-Sūtra* Gautama accepted *upamāna*, the other Naiyāyikas are expected to accept it. Same is the case so far as the Mīmāṁsakas are concerned. But Bhāsarvajña is an exception. He is a Naiyāyika who lived long before Udayana and probably after Vācaspati (CE 875 to 925). So even being a Naiyāyika Bhāsarvajña has become a critic (but it seems that Bhāsarvajña himself thinks that he has not violated the intention of the *sūtrakāra*; he is rather a more close follower of Gautama), an internal critic of Nyāya theory of *upamāna*. In his *Nyāyasāraḥ* he has explicitly mentioned that there are three *pramāṇas*.[2] He is not only the internal critic but is also a reductionist so far as his

---

1. Of course, of the Vaiśeṣikas and the Mīmāṁsakas are internal critics in two different senses.

2. *evametāni trīṇyeva pramāṇāni* — Bhāsarvajña, 1961 (2nd part, 3rd chapter), p. 33. *trividhaṁ pramāṇam pratyakṣamanumānamāgama iti* — Ibid. part I, p. 105. See also Bhāsarvajña, 1968, p. 80. *tathācopamānādināmatraivāntarbhāvam pratipādayaiṣyāmaḥ*.

criticism is concerned. He has also spoken about reductionism (*antarbhāva*) of the other *pramāṇas* into these three.[3]

But the question is, to which *pramāṇa upamāna* may be reduced? Bhāsarvajña has stated clearly that *upamāna* is to be reduced to *śabda*. And he has stated *upamānaṁ śabde antarbhūtam*. Bhāsarvajña has not only stated this, he has also stated that *tatra yathā gau-evaṁ gavaya ityupamānaṁ śabde antarbhūtam*. Bhāsarvajña has not given any further analysis on the point. In his commentary Aparārkadeva has written, *yeṣām etādṛśam atideśa vākyam eva upamānaṁ teṣāṁ tacchabda evāntarbhūtaṁ vākya-rūpatvāt, agnim ānaya ityādi vākyavat*.[4] Now we know that the word *upamāna* is taken both in the sense of resulting knowledge and also in the sense of instrumental cause of such knowledge. The point of Aparārkadeva is that, for those who think that *upamāna*, in the sense of instrumental cause, is a sentence like "as is cow so is *gavaya*" *upamāna* is nothing but *śabda*. "As is cow so is *gavaya*" is nothing but a sentence like such other sentence as "bring the fire." And if the resulting knowledge (wrongly) called *upamiti* is produced by such sentence then the knowledge is nothing but *śābda* or knowledge by verbal testimony. So *upamāna* (resulting knowledge) is nothing but *śābda* as it is produced by sentence. Aparārkadeva has only said that *upamāna*, according to those who think *upamāna* to be the sentence called *atideśa vākya*, is reducible to *śabda*. But Aparārkadeva has not clearly stated who are those philosophers[5] who think *atideśa vākya* itself is the *upamāna-pramāṇa*. We have found before that according to some thinkers this view was held by the *jaḍannaiyāyikas*. We

3. *eṣuevopamānārthāpattisambhavābhāvaitihyādīnām antarbhāvaḥ tasmāt triṇyeva pramāṇāni* — Bhāsarvajña, 1968, p. 417.

4. Aparārkadeva, 1961, part II, p. 33.

5. The way Bhāsarvajña and Aparārkadeva reduced *upamāna-pramāṇa*, shows that they had the Naiyāyikas in mind. But none of these authors explicitly said that according to the Naiyāyikas *vākya* is the *upamāna-pramāṇa*.

have also seen that there is some doubt about who exactly is (are) the *jaḍannaiyāyika*(s). Some think Bhāsarvajña and others think that Jayanta is a *jaḍannaiyāyika*. Some again think some predecessors of Jayanta are *jaḍannaiyāyikas*.[6]

In any case Bhāsarvajña is the earliest and the most famous among the Naiyāyikas who admitted a threefold division of *pramāṇa*. In *Sarvasiddhānta-Saṁgrahaḥ*, as noted by Gopinath Kaviraj, it is written that *catvāryatra pramāṇāni nopamānaṁ tu kasyacit*. Gopinath Kaviraj thinks that the term *kasyacit* in the above sentence of *Sarvasiddhānta-Saṁgrahaḥ* refers to Bhāsarvajña. Gopinath Kaviraj is also of the opinion that the word *nyāyaikadeśinaḥ* occurring in the following *Kārikā* of Sureśvarācārya's *Mānasollāsaḥ* refers to Bhāsarvajña: *pratyakṣamekam cārvaka . . . nyāyaikadeśino 'pyevaṁ*.[7]

Sometimes it has been said that the author of *Bhūṣaṇa* is the Naiyāyika who held that the number of *pramāṇa*s was three. But Bhūṣaṇakāra and Bhāsarvajña are one and the same person. For *Bhūṣaṇa* is a work by Bhāsarvajña.[8] So it comes to this that according to this Nyayāikadeśin, the *pramāṇa*s are three in number and *upamāna* is to be reduced to *śabda*. Gopinath Kaviraj believes that in restricting the number of *pramāṇa*s to three Bhāsarvajña was not so much influenced by Sāṁkhya philosophers who also admit three *pramāṇa*s. He was influenced by the Yoga philosophy.[9]

So far we see that Bhāsarvajña has reduced *upamāna* as it is understood by the Naiyāyikas. He reduced it to *śabda*. And accordingly, the number of *pramāṇa*s to be admitted by him becomes three. But he did not reduce *upamāna* as understood by the Mīmāṁsaka to *śabda*. Bhāsarvajña has made a definite

6. Gopinath Kaviraj 1982, p. 116, note 2.
7. Gopinath kaviraj, 1982, p. 116.
8. Ibid. p. 116.
9. Ibid., p. 4.

statement to the effect that *upamāna* as it is viewed by the Mīmāṁsakas is a case of memory or *smṛti*. He did not refer to the Mīmāṁsakas by name. But he has given an example of *upamāna* (*upamiti*) which clearly shows that he had Mīmāṁsā view in mind. For he writes, *anena sadṛśī madīyā gouriti upamānamiti cet, na, tasya smṛtitvāt.*[10]

But *smṛti* is not a *pramāṇa;* it is not admitted as a *pramāṇa* by the philosophers of the Sāṁkhya, Yoga, or Nyāya school in general or by Bhāsarvajña. So from this we can say that in relation to the Nyāya theory of *upamāna* Bhāsarvajña is a reductionist as he reduces such Nyāya *upamāna* to *śabda*. But so far as the Mīmāṁsā view is concerned Bhāsarvajña becomes a rejectionist. He does not consider Mīmāṁsā *upamāna* to be a *pramāṇa* at all. It is rather a case of *smṛti* (memory cognition). And according to these philosophers *smṛti* (or memory cognition) is not a *pramāṇa*.

Bhāsarvajña's argument that the Mīmāṁsā *upamāna* is really a case of *smṛti* has freshness and novelty about it. The ordinary argument is the following. The Mīmāṁsakas hold that the cow which one knows in case of an *upamāna,* to have *gavaya-sādṛśya,* is a remembered cow. It is a cow which is being remembered at the moment. It is the very same cow which was perceived before. The standard reply from the Mīmāṁsā standpoint against this line of argument is that though the cow was previously perceived, yet the cow as having *gavaya sādṛśya* (i.e. *gavaya-sādṛśya-viśiṣṭa-go*) was never perceived before. But this reply cannot meet the argument of Bhāsarvajña. Bhāsarvajña says (that not only *go* but) even *gavaya-sādṛśya-viśiṣṭa-go* was perceived previously. The reason for his saying so is that there is no reasons to think that it (*sādṛśya viśiṣṭa go*) was not perceived. In this case he says more. He says, we have both positive and negative reasons to think that it was perceived. The positive reason as

10. Bhāsarvajña, 1961, part II, p. 33.

stated by Bhāsarvajña for his thesis, that *sādṛśya-viśiṣṭa-go* was perceived previously,[11] is *upalabdhiyogyatvāt*. We can make this positive reason explicit in this way:

> *sādṛśya-viśiṣṭa-gopiṇḍaḥ pūrva-upalabdaḥ upalabdhiyogyatvāt.*

The point of Bhāsarvajña is the following. If a thing is perceptible and if the conditions for perceiving it are present then that thing will be perceived. Since the man perceived *go* previously it cannot be denied that the conditions of perception obtained at that time. For otherwise he could not have perceived even the cow. The Mīmāṁsakas could say that though the *go* was perceived yet the *sādṛśya-viśiṣṭa go* was not perceived if only they could say that *sādṛśya* was not perceptible. But this they cannot say. And here Bhāsarvajña gives his negative argument. He says, *ayogyatve ca na kadācit upalabhyeta adṛṣṭavāt*. Aparārkadeva in his *Nyāya-Muktāvalī* has brought out the force of this argument. He says if *sādṛśya* was imperceptible then *gavayaṁ dṛṣṭvā gāṁ paśyato 'pi tena sadṛśī ayam ityanubhavo na bhavet gavayagataṁ ca sādṛśyaṁ na cakṣuṣā nirīkṣetetyarthaḥ.*[12] The argument in short is this: If *śādṛśya* was not perceptible then the man could not perceive *go-sādṛśya viśiṣṭa-gavaya* even when he perceived *gavaya*. But Mīmāṁsakas agree with the Naiyāyikas on the point that when the city dweller goes to the forest and perceives *gavaya* he does perceive *gavaya* as possessing cow-resemblance. Let us conclude Bhāsarvajña's argument. According to Bhāsarvajña similarity must be admitted as perceptible or knowable (*upalabdhiyogya*). Accordingly the city dweller peceived *sādṛśya-viśiṣṭa go* before he comes to have the belief *anena sadṛśī madīyā gauḥ iti*. What therefore is known in *upamiti* according to the Mīmāṁsakas is not a new thing. It was known before. It is only remembered

---

11. *pūrvam eva hi sādṛśya viśiṣṭa upalabdho go-piṇḍaḥ* — Bhāsarvajña, 1961 (part II), p. 33.

12. Ibid., pp. 33-34.

now. In this way *upamāna* as it is conceived by the Mīmāṁsakas is reduced to *smṛti*.

One point remains unclear. If something is reduced to *smṛti* then it is not a *pramāṇa;* nor can it be reduced to any *pramāṇa*. How can then Bhāsarvajña say that *upamāna* like *arthāpatti,* etc. are reducible to one or the other of the three *pramāṇas*? Perhaps according to Bhāsarvajña *upamāna* is reduced to *śabda-pramāṇa* when it is conceived of as *atideśa vākya*. In other words *upamāna* as conceived by the *jaḍannaiyāyika,* and not as conceived by the Mīmāṁsakas, was reduced to *śabda-pramāṇa*. This interpretation tallies with the following known fact. The Mīmāṁsakas brought against the (old) Naiyāyikas the objection that they turned *upamāna* into *śabda*.

There is a second point also which remains unclear. If Bhāsarvajña is right then the city dweller must have perceived *sādṛśya* or similarity when he perceived the cow. And he perceived the cow long before he came to have *upamiti* of the form *anena sadṛśī madīyā gauḥ*. But this is not corroborated by the actual knowledge which the city dweller has. He has knowledge of the form *gauḥ* and not the knowledge of the form *sadṛśī-viśiṣṭa-gauḥ*.[13] But this point has not been left wholly undiscussed. We cannot go into the details. But the main point may be stated in this way: Bhāsarvajña admits that the town man had earlier perceived *sādṛśya* or *sādṛśya-viśiṣṭa-go*. He also accepts the agreed fact that the form of the knowledge of that man was not *gavaya-sadṛśa-go* (cow resembling *gavaya*) or *sādṛśya-viśiṣṭa go* (cow having similarity). But how both can be true? Bhāsarvajña says that the man's perception of similarity was indeterminate or *nirvikalpaka jñāna*. This is the reason why his *nirvikalpaka jñāna* is not represented in the form of knowledge or language *sādṛśya-viśiṣṭa-gauḥ*. It is more accurate to say that the man had known *gauriti*.

---

13. This difference is very important from the theoretical point of view.

But the Mīmāṁsakas can say now if *sādṛśya* was known only in *nirvikalpaka* (indeterminate perception) then it cannot be remembered now. But the city dweller then has the belief, *anena-sadṛśī-madīyā-gauḥ* or he has the belief that the cow (in the town) has similarity with *gavaya*. This knowledge is then *upamiti*; it cannot be a case of memory. To say this is to say *antarbhāva* or reduction of what a Mīmāṁsaka calls *upamiti* into memory cannot be possible. Bhāsarvajña had anticipated this objection and he said in reply, *nirvikalpakopalambhe 'pi sahakārisāmarthyāt abhāvādiṣu savikalpaka smṛtirdṛṣṭā.*[14] We shall not explain this in detail. Bhāsarvajña's point is, if suitable (auxiliary) conditions obtain then even things that were known in *nirvikalpaka* perception may be remembered.

We have seen how Bhāsarvajña argues in favour of reducibility of *upamāna* into *śabda* or *smṛti*. The *upamāna* which according to him is reduced to memory is the *upamāna* as it is viewed by the Mīmāṁsakas. Bhāsarvajña is a Naiyāyika and it is natural for a Naiyāyika to argue that *upamāna* as admitted by the Mīmāṁsakas is not an independent *pramāṇa*. But Bhāsarvajña goes further and shows that *upamāna* as conceived even by the Naiyāyikas is not a separate *pramāṇa*. To hold such a view is to go against the explicit evidence of the *sūtra* text of Gautama. In fact the charge of *sūtra virodha* has been brought against Bhāsarvajña. We shall soon return to this.

According to the Naiyāyikas knowledge by analogy is the knowledge of the relation of meaning (*śakti sambandha*) which the words bear to the corresponding things. According to Bhāsarvajña this knowledge of the meaning relation or (the relation the names bear to the things named (*saṁjñā-saṁjñi sambandha*) is a result of the statement of analogy made by some

14. Bhāsarvajña, 1961, part II, p. 34. Aparārkadeva in his *Nyāyamuktāvalī* explained, *tatra abhāve tāvannirvikalpakānubhūte savikalpakaṁ smṛtimupapādayisyāmaḥ.*

authoritative person.[15]

The supporting argument Bhāsarvajña offers for his thesis is: *tathā praśnottarābhidhānāt*. Aparārkadeva explains this argument. Suppose a man has learned the meaning of the word *gavaya* from the conditions like the utterance of statement of analogy and perception of cow-similarity in *gavaya*. Suppose we ask the man "How did you come to learn the meaning of the word *gavaya*?" In reply he will (normally) say that he had learnt the meaning relation from what he was told by the forester; this forester was in a position to know what thing or animal is called *gavaya*. But the man will not (normally) say that he learnt the meaning of it from *upamāna-pramāṇa*. This is one of the arguments of Bhāsarvajña.

Bhāsarvajña offered another argument. Men are found to take the name of three *pramāṇa*s (and Bhāsarvajña admits these three *pramāṇa*s). The names of these three *pramāṇa*s are *pratyakṣa* (perception), *anumāna* (inference) and *śabda* (word). Thus we hear people say "I perceive a jar," "I infer fire," "I came to know about gods and heaven from the words of the scriptures." But we never hear people say "I have known such and such from *upamāna*." We therefore cannot admit *upamāna pramāṇa* though we can admit *pratyakṣa, anumāna* and *śabda*.

In reply it may be said that it will be wrong to say that from *śabda* we derive such knowledge as "the word *gavaya* is the name of this (animal)."[16] The idea perhaps is this, the *atideśa vākya* or the statement of analogy asserts a sort of general relation between the word *gavaya* and what has similarity with cow. For the form of the sentence is "as is cow so is *gavaya*."[17] A sentence

15. *saṁjñā-saṁjñi-saṁbandha-pratipattiḥ api āptavacana-kāryā* — Bhāsarvajña, 1961, p. 36.

16. *asyą gavayaśabdaḥ saṁjñā iti pratipattau upamāna-siddhiḥ, tathā śabdāśravaṇāt.* — Bhāsarvajña, 1961, part II, p. 37.

17. *yathā gourevaṁ gavaya* or *yādṛśo gauḥ tādṛśo gavayaḥ.* — Aparārkadeva, vol. II, 1961, p. 36.

of this form cannot give us knowledge to the effect "this animal is called *gavaya.*" On the other hand the form of *atideśa vākya* is not admitted to be *asya gavaya-saṁjñā* (that is to say), this has the name *gavaya*.

Bhāsarvajña argues that the point of the opponent seems to be this. The knowledge that the particular thing over there is the referent of the word *gavaya* was not or could not be had from utterance (of statement of analogy). So *upamāna* as a *pramāṇa* is to be admitted as necessary.[18]

Bhāsarvajña's reply is that if for the knowledge of a particular thing (a particular *gavaya*) we need a separate *pramāṇa* (*upamāna*) then we would need another *pramāṇa* for the knowledge of another particular thing (or animal, viz. a particular cow or another particular *gavaya*), as the referent of the name "cow."' This however cannot be said.

But how would Bhāsarvajña account for our knowledge of the form *asya gavaya-śabda-saṁjña iti* or the word *gavaya* is the name of this (particular thing)? Bhāsarvajña says that this can be known on the basis of the intention of the speaker. In the context of conversation a hearer as a matter of fact understands that the speaker refers to a particular thing when he uses a particular name.

Bhāsarvajña also noted the point that the relation of naming (*saṁjña-saṁjñi-sambandha*) need not have to be known in case of perceptible things only. For we know the relation of naming which the word *śakra* bears to the Being called *śakra*. This being however is imperceptible.

II

We now return to the objection *sūtra virodha*. If Bhāsarvajña holds that *upamāna* is not a *pramāṇa* or that it is not a separate *pramāṇa*

---

18. *asya gavaya-śabdaḥ . . . pramāṇam uccyata iti* — Aparārkadeva, vol. II, 1961, p. 37.

then he will go directly against the evidence of *Nyāya-Sūtra* 1.1.3. In this *sūtra upamāna* has been admitted as a *pramāṇa;* it has also been admitted as a separate *pramāṇa*. Bhāsarvajña says to this objection that in the *sūtra* 1.1.3 Gautama has separately enumerated *upamāna*. But this does not prove that *upamāna* is not included in any of the other three *pramāṇa*s which have also been enumerated in the same *sūtra*. Gautama has enumerated sixteen *sat* (real) *padārtha*s in *sūtra* 1.1.1. Vātsyāyana has shown that though the last fourteen (i.e. *saṁśaya* through *nigrahasthāna*) have been separately enumerated yet they are included in the first two namely *pramāṇa* and *prameya* as the case may be). He has also shown why the last fourteen *sat padārtha*s had to be enumerated separately. Referring to this discussion Bhāsarvajña says that *upamāna* (as it was conceived by the old Naiyāyikas) is reducible to or is included in *śabda*. Yet Gautama felt it necessary to enumerate it separately. *Śabda prāmāṇya samarthanaṁ* is the need why Gautama enumerated *upamāna* separately.[19] This point has been explained by Aparārkadeva. The point is this. In some cases at least *upamāna* enables or helps *śabda* to function as *pramāṇa*. Let us explain.

Some critics may hold that *śabda* cannot be a *pramāṇa*. For it is supposed to give us knowledge of the relation between *padārthas*.[20] But if *padārtha*s (meaning of the words of the sentence) are not known then *śabda* cannot give us the knowledge of the relation. In case the *padārtha*s in question are ordinary perceptible things then perception can yield knowledge of *padārtha*s and *śabda* can give us the knowledge of their relation. But where the *padārtha*s are imperceptible things like *śakra, devatā, svarga,* etc. then *śabda* cannot yield knowledge of their relation. Bhāsarvajña says, *upamāna* is separately enumerated to answer such objection.

---

19. Bhāsarvajña, 1961, part II, p. 41.

20. This is the standard view. But Bhāsarvajña represents the opponents as holding *vākyārthastu prasiddhārthānāṁ padānām anvayamātram.* — Bhāsarvajña, 1961, part II, p. 42.

Thus *upamāna* makes it possible for *śabda* to yield knowledge of the relation between *padārtha*s even when these *padārtha*s are imperceptible things. To show that even in these cases *śabda* is a *pramāṇa* Gautama has enumerated *upamāna* separately. This is the point of Bhāsarvajña when he says, *śabda prāmāṇya samarthanam* (*upamānasya prayojanam*).

So far we have critically described and defended the view of Bhāsarvajña about *upamāna*. The position of Bhāsarvajña in the Nyāya tradition reminds us of the position of Vyomaśivācārya in the Vaiśeṣika tradition. The Vaiśeṣika philosophers in general do not admit *śabda* as a separate *pramāṇa*. But Vyomaśivācārya has admitted *śabda* as a separate and irreducible source of knowledge. Similarly the Naiyāyikas in general admit *upamāna* in addition to *pratyakṣa, anumāna* and *śabda;* but Bhāsarvajña reduced *upamāna* to *śabda*. Here we shall not criticize in detail Bhāsarvajña's views about *upamāna* from the standard Nyāya position. We have discussed in the chapters on Jayanta and Udayana why *upamāna* cannot be reduced to *śabda*. In the chapter on Gaṅgeśa we shall again show that *upamāna* is an irreducible *pramāṇa*. We shall only discuss against Bhāsarvajña's position the objection of *sūtra virodha*. We shall state the objection and defence from the side of Bhāsarvajña. Then we shall show why this defence is unacceptable.

Against Bhāsarvajña, objection of *sūtra virodha* is raised. It is said that Bhāsarvajña's acceptance of three *pramāṇa*s goes against the *sūtra* 1.1.3 of Gautama. In the *sūtra* 1.1.3 Gautama mentioned as we have already said names of four *pramāṇa*s. Now if Bhāsarvajña accepts that *pramāṇa*s are three in number then he goes against the evidence of this *sūtra*. But Bhāsarvajña belongs to the Nyāya tradition. So he is to think on the line of Gautama. It will be a major fault on the part of Bhāsarvajña if he goes against the *sūtra* of Gautama. And as a result Bhāsarvajña's analysis will not be acceptable.

In answer to this it has been said that if we understand the *Nyāya-Sūtra* 1.1.3 in the proper perspective, we shall see that Bhāsarvajña's analysis does not go against the *sūtra*. We can understand the *sūtra* in two different ways:

(1) It is true that Gautama has mentioned the names of four *pramāṇas*. But that does not mean that *pramāṇas* are really four. In the *indriya vibhāga sūtra* 1.1.12 of Nyāya, Gautama has mentioned the names of five sense organs and he has mentioned the name of *manas* in the other *sūtra* 1.1.16. From this the other Naiyāyikas do not think that sense organs are five in number or *manas* is not a sense organ. They all, on the other hand, think that according to Gautama sense organs are six in number. In the case of the *sūtra* 1.1.12, the names of the sense organs do not determine the number of the sense organs. In *sūtra* 1.1.3 also the names of the four *pramāṇas* do not imply that *pramāṇas* are really four in number. But we are to understand the *sūtra* to mean that *pramāṇas* are actually three in number. So far it follows that in *vibhāga sūtra* the names of the *vibhāgas* (divisions) are mentioned. But these names in the *vibhāga sūtra* do not tell us the exact number of the divisions. We cannot make an *avadhāraṇa* of the *saṁkhyā* (number) of the thing divided. But there remains a question. What does the *vibhāga sūtra* then? Bhuṣaṇakāra and following him Aparārkadeva think that *vibhāga sūtra* removes the doubt about the more or less (*nyūnādhikya śaṁkā*).

(2) Aparārkadeva in his *Nyāya-Muktāvalī* has argued that in the *sūtra* 1.1.3 Gautama has not mentioned the names of four *pramāṇas* to show that there are actually four *pramāṇas*. Gautama actually wanted to show that *pramāṇas* are not five in number. There are philosophers who admit five *pramāṇas*. To negate their view or to show that *pramāṇas* cannot be five in number Gautama

mentioned the names in the *sūtra*. So the *sūtra* is to be understood in the negative sense (*niṣedhapara*). To say that *pramāṇa*s cannot be five is not to say that *pramāṇa*s must be four. It may as well be two or three or one in number. The *sūtra* only signifies *pramāṇa*s cannot be five. The number must be less than five. On the other hand Bhāsarvajña has his own reasons to admit that there are three *pramāṇa*s. So we are to accept Bhāsarvajña's view that *pramāṇa*s are three. And *upamāna* is reducible to other *pramāṇa*. To express the above view Aparārkadeva writes *catuṣṭābhidhānaṁsūtrepañcatvādinirākaraṇārthaṁ. na tritvapratiṣedhārthaṁ.*

We have only one argument against Bhāsarvajña's position. The charge of *sūtra-virodha* was brought against Bhāsarvajña. The charge is that his view about the number of *pramāṇa*s conflicts with the *pramāṇa vibhāga sūtra* of Gautama 1.1.3. In defence of Bhāsarvajña it was said that the import of *vibhāga sūtra* is not to fix strictly (*avadhāraṇa*) the number (*saṁkhyā*) of divisions or kinds of the things divided. The import of the *vibhāga sūtra* is to remove the doubt about the more (or less) number of the things divided. In support reference has been made to the *indriya vibhāga sūtra* 1.1.12 of Gautama. In this *sūtra* the names of five sense organs have been listed. But Gautama and his followers admit six sense organs. So, according to Bhuṣaṇakāra and Aparārkadeva, the right interpretation of the *sūtra* 1.1.12 is that in this *sūtra* Gautama has removed the doubt whether the number of *indriya*s is less (than five).[21] Similarly according to them the right interpretation of the *sūtra* 1.1.3 is that there cannot be more *pramāṇa*s (than four). But we would like to remark the following. If one mentions the names of four *pramāṇa*s then it does not follow that there are just these four *pramāṇa*s; that *pramāṇa*s cannot be more than four. If there are five *pramāṇa*s, one can say there are four

21. Bhāsarvajña, 1968, p. 81; and Aparārkadeva, 1961, part II, p. 44.

pramāṇas. And it will be true. For four is included in five. If one says that there are four *pramāṇas* then it also does not follow that all the four *pamāṇas* which have been named are not *pramāṇas*; that the *pramāṇas* are less than four. There must be at least four *pramāṇas*. If there were less *pramāṇas* then the utterance that the *pramāṇas* are four or the *sūtra* 1.1.3 could be false. Therefore *pramāṇas* cannot be less than four. Bhāsarvajña's position conflicts with the position of Gautama. Therefore Bhāsarvajña's defence cannot be accepted.

The real issue here is how the *sūtra* 1.1.3 should be interpreted. Bhāsarvajña has two points to make. (a) This *sūtra* should not be interpreted to signify that the number of *pramāṇas* is (just) four. Import of this is not *avadhāraṇa* of *saṁkhyā*. (b) This *sūtra* should be interpreted to deny that the number of *pramāṇas* is five (*pañcatva saṁkhyā niṣedhapara*). Now the question is, can we accept Bhāsarvajña's interpretation? We can accept the interpretation if the principle behind it is correct.

A correct principle of interpretation is the following. We can interpret a sentence S_1 so as to replace it by another sentence S_2, if S_2 contains more than what S_1 says. For then the truth of S_2 does not falsify S_1. Let us take an example.

S_1 The eyes, ears, nose, tongue and skin are sense organs.

S_2 The number of sense organs (including the five eyes, etc.) is six.

If we interpret S_1 and replace it by S_2 then S_1 is not falsified. This shows in interpreting S_1 by S_2, we have not reduced the scope of S_1. We have rather denied scope reduction (*nyūnatāsaṁkhyāniṣedha*).

The following will be on the other hand a false principle of interpretation. Interpret a sentence S_I and replace it by S_J where S_J says less than what S_I says. This is a false principle because to interpret a sentence in this way is to make the interpreted sentence false. Let us take an example.

S_I Perception, inference, analogy and testimony are *pramāṇas*.

S_J Number of *pramāṇas* is only three (perception, inference, and testimony).

If this principle of interpretation is correct then

(a) S_I or the *sūtra* 1.1.3 does not say that the number of *pramāṇas* is just four; the import is not *saṁkhyā avadhāraṇa*.

(b) S_J rather says that the number of *pramāṇas* is not five; the import is *pañcatva saṁkhyāniṣedha*.

We doubt whether Bhāsarvajña is right when he thinks like this. Bhāsarvajña also thinks that S_J is not incompatible with S_I and that his position does not conflict with Gautama's *sūtra*. But if S_J is true than S_I is false. For S_J has reduced the scope of S_i. If S_j alone is true, if the number of *pramāṇas* is only *three,* then S_i must be false. One of the names listed in S_i does not name a *pramāṇa.* If this is so then S_i is false. S_j is the position of Bhāsarvajña. and S_i is actually the *sūtra* 1.1.3 of Gautama. So Bhāsarvajña's position really involves *sūtra-virodha*. Moreover the principle of interpretation we followed is unacceptable.

8

Upamāna Serves no Purpose in Darśana

I

One cannot say that *upamāna* creates more problems than it solves. One cannot say that Nyāya scheme of *pramāṇa*s is anomalous because it includes *upamāna-pramāṇa*.[1] But still one can say that *upamāna* is useless. One can support this by three arguments: (1) *upamāna* is useless because *śakti* can be known by other *pramāṇa*s. (2a) *upamāna* is useless because it serves no purpose in Nyāya or for interpretation of texts. (2b) *upamāna* serves no purpose in Nyāya which is a system of *darśana.* (3) *upamāna* is useless in the sense that it has no value outside philosophy or in our life.

(1) According to the Naiyāyikas *upamāna* cannot prove the existence or non-existence of anything. Its only value is that it gives us knowledge of *śakti*. But *upamāna* is not the only source of knowledge of *śakti. Śakti* is the object of other *pramāṇa*s also. For example *anumāna* can give us knowledge of *śakti*. When a child knows word-meaning relation for the first time he learns it by inference (*vṛddha vyavahāra*) and not by analogy. So it is useless to admit *upamāna* for the knowledge of *śakti*. We can say against

---

1. For an elaborate discussion on the anomalous Nyāya scheme, see Uma Chattopadhyay, "Is the Order of Four Pramāṇas Justified in Nyāya system?" in Ujjala Jha & Arun Ranjan Mishra (eds.), Delhi, 2008, pp. 38-45.

this argument that the Naiyāyikas accept *pramāṇa-saṁplava*. According to this *pramāṇa-saṁplava* theory, different *pramāṇa*s can know the same thing. We cannot say that a *pramāṇa* is useless because what it knows is also known by another *pramāṇa*. This defence cannot save *upamāna*. For the opponent will say, if there are different *pramāṇas*, then the next question is: can any two of them know the same thing? Is *pramāṇa-saṁplava* the correct theory? But here the situation is different. *Upamāna* has not been proved to be a *pramāṇa*. It has not been proved that there is *upamāna-pramāṇa*. Against the opponent we can say that the situation is that *upamāna* knows *śakti*. Another *pramāṇa, anumāna* also knows *śakti*. If this shows that *upamāna* is useless, then it also shows *anumāna* is useless. For if *anumāna* knows the thing which *upamāna* knows then *upamāna* also knows what *anumāna* knows. The opponent can refute this defence of a Naiyāyika. He will say that *anumāna* does not know *śakti* alone. It has other objects. So for the knowledge of those objects *anumāna* must be admitted and admitted as a useful *pramāṇa*. Once *anumāna* is there it can know what *upamāna* knows. But the same cannot be said about *upamāna*. *Upamāna* knows only *śakti*. If already there is a *pramāṇa* to know this object then *upamāna* becomes useless. This is the point of the opponent. *Anumāna* is already there. *Anumāna* can know *śakti* also. It will be useless to admit *upamāna*. To say this is to say in another way that *upamāna* should not be admitted.

There are two ways in which a Naiyāyika can answer this objection. He can show that there is a type of *śakti-jñāna* which *upamāna* alone can give. A Naiyāyika can show in the second place that *upamāna* has other uses also. Let us explain. The opponent said that *upamāna* is useless. For it knows only the thing *śakti*. It gives us only one knowledge — knowledge of *śakti*. But *anumāna* also knows the very same object. *Anumāna* also gives us knowledge of *śakti*. So *upamāna* is unnecessary. In answer a Naiyāyika may say that about the same *śakti*, these two *pramāṇa*s give different types of knowledge. *Upamāna* gives us a distinct type of knowledge of *śakti*.

We can give an example. Suppose I am in the kitchen. Suddenly there is a power cut. The room becomes dark. Something falls on the floor. From the sound I can infer that one of the larger bowls has been dropped by the maid. But I do not know which particular bowl. I know this when power supply is resumed. From the sound I knew (inferentially) that a bowl was dropped. But I did not know which particular bowl. Now I know which bowl. Similarly we can get *śakti-jñāna* from different sources. And the knowledge of *śakti* we have from different sources is different. These sources do not give us exactly the same knowledge. They give us knowledge of the same object. But they give us different types of knowledge of the same object. So all of them are necessary. In our example the knowledge of the meaning of the word *gavaya* can be derived from *anumāna*, from *śabda* and from *upamāna*. If *upamāna* gives us the same knowledge of the meaning of the word *gavaya* which *anumāna* gives us, then *upamāna* would be useless. But let us see whether this is the case or not.

The author of *Nyāyakandalī* has shown that our knowledge of the meaning of the word may come from different sources. When it comes from *anumāna*, it is *sāmānya jñāna*.[2] But when it comes from *pratyakṣa* it is not so general. The standard Vaiśeṣika view about *upamāna* is that it is actually inference. The Vaiśeṣikas admit only two *pramāṇas*, *pratyakṣa* and *anumāna*. Now keeping in mind the *Vaiśeṣika-Sūtra* 2.1.18 one may think that according to Kaṇāda *upamāna* should be included in *pratyakṣa*. If one tries to reduce it to any other *pramāṇa* then he will go against the

2. Śrīdhara, 1963, pp. 533-34.

evidence of the *sūtra*.[3] In view of the *Vaiśeṣika-Sūtras* 9.2.3 and 9.2.5, Śaṅkara Miśra says *upamāna* is included in *anumāna*.[4] But Vyomaśivācārya says *upamāna* is included in *śabda*.[5] Following Jayanta we explained before that *śabda* (*atideśa vākya*) can give knowledge of the meaning of the word *gavaya*. But the type of the knowledge we have from *atideśa vākya* is inferior to the knowledge we get from *upamāna*. Let us again take the inference which gives us knowledge of *śakti* of the word *gavaya*. According to Śaṅkara Miśra the inference has the following form:

> *The word* gavaya *names (the thing)* gavaya,
> *Because the* śiṣṭas *use or apply*
> *The word to that thing, etc.*[6]

From *upamāna* we have different types of knowledge of *śakti*. From the above inference we can know the word *gavaya* names (the thing) *gavaya* or names the thing which has *gavayatva*. But from *upamāna* we know, *gosādṛśya-upalakṣita gavayatvaviśiṣṭa (prāṇī)-gavayapadavācya*. This means the word *gavaya* names which has *gavayatva* and which can be recognized by its cow-similarity. This is a different type of knowledge. About this type of knowledge Udayana said that *pratyakṣa*, etc. cannot be the source.[7] We explained earlier what this means. *Pratyakṣa*, *anumāna* or *śabda* cannot give this type of knowledge separately. Udayana gave the final and comprehensive definition of *upamāna-pramāṇa* in his *Nyāyakusumāñjaliḥ Vṛtti*. This has been explained by Vīrarāghavācārya. From all these it is clear that *upamāna* gives a

3. *na ca vyākyādeva saṁketapratipattiḥ, . . . pratyakṣam saṁjñākarmeti sūtra vyāghātātca.* — Vyomaśivācārya (1930), p. 589.
4. Śaṅkara Miśra, 1930.
5. *vākyarūpaṁ upamānam iṣṭameva. tasya ca āgame antarbhāvaḥ na doṣāyeti* — Vyomaśivācārya, 1930, p. 590.
6. Śaṅkara Miśra 1930, p. 226. The inference which gives knowledge of *śakti* may also be constructed differently.
7. *pratyakṣāderasādhyatvātupamānaphalaṁ viduḥ.*
   — *Nyāyakusumāñjaliḥ* 3.18.

special type of knowledge of *śakti*. For this type of knowledge *upamāna* is necessary. So if *upamāna* has only one object *śakti* then also it is necessary. We shall now show that *upamāna* not only knows *śakti*, but it knows other things also.

II

Vātsyāyana in his *Bhāṣya* left the hint that *upamāna* has other uses. But earlier we said that *upamāna* gives us knowledge of *śakti* alone. It does not give us knowledge of the nature of the things discussed in philosophy. Nor it proves the existence or non-existence of anything. This truth about *upamāna* has been stated by Uddyotakara[8] and defended by Vācaspati Miśra[9] and Udayana.[10] But Vātsyāyana said, *evam anya api upamānasya loke viṣaya bubhutsitavya.*[11] (i) *Upamāna* can give us information of other things also. It is not true to say that it only gives us knowledge of *śakti*. (ii) Examples are there to show that *upamāna* has been used for other purposes also and not for knowledge of *śakti* only. We shall give examples of both. (i) In his *Vṛtti* Viśvanātha has shown that from *atideśa vākya* sometimes we may get information about some property or nature of things. We know that utterance of *atideśa vākya* is a necessary step in the process of *upamāna*. In some cases we can know some special feature or property of the things involved. Suppose one already knows that the thing *B* has a special property; it neutralizes the effect of poison. Now some one tells him that *A* is similar to *B*. From an utterance of this sort one comes to know that *A* also has the same property. What we know here by analogy? We do not know that a certain thing is called *A*. We know that the thing *A* has a certain property.[12] Thus we find that

8. Uddyotakara, 1987, p. 6.
9. Vācaspati, 1987, p. 26.
10. Udayana, 1987, p. 85.
11. Vātsyāyana, 1985, p. 172.
12. Phanibhusan, 1989, vol. I, p. 189.

upamāna knows not only *śakti* but also other things. (ii) Some people have used *upamāna* to show that there is no such thing as God. Any atheist can use *upamāna* for this purpose. Udayanācārya has noted this use in his *Nyāyakusumāñjaliḥ*.[13] But he disapproves of such uses.[14] He thinks that *upamāna* cannot be used successfully for this purpose. His argument is this — *niyataviṣayatvādeva na tena* (*upamānena īśvarasya*) *bādhaḥ*. Udayanācārya means to say that *upamāna* has fixed object (*niyataviṣaya*). Its objects are only similarity and dissimilarity.[15] Let not Udayana approve this use of *upamāna*. But he himself has noted that one may use it in this way. Udayana, Vīrarāghavācārya or even Haridasa Bhattacharya has not shown in detail how one can use *upamāna* to prove that God does not exist. Viśveśvara Siddhāntaśiromaṇi[16] has shown this. *Upamāna* may be used in this way to prove non-existence of God. *Śaśaśṛṅgasadṛśa īśvaraḥ;* "God is like a hare's horn." One who is told this, understands that God and hare's horn are similar in respect of being imperceptible, etc. Just as imperceptible hare's horn is non-existent so also the imperceptible God is non-existent.

III

We now consider the second objection or objections (2a) and (2b). *Upamāna* may be useful (as shown above) for the knowledge of *śakti*. Or it may be useful for proving non-existence of God. But from a philosophical point of view these cannot be considered as usefulness. *Upamāna* is admitted by two schools of Indian philosophy. So the important question is: does *upamāna* serve any purpose in Nyāya or in Mīmāṁsā philosophy? The opponent holds that *upamāna* is useless because it serves no purpose in Nyāya or in Mīmāṁsā. If *upamāna* can be shown to be useful for

---

13. Udayanācārya, 1941, p. 193f.
14. Udayanācārya, 1941, pp. 193, 204.
15. Vīrarāghavācārya, 1941, p. 204.
16. *Viśveśara Siddhāntaśiromaṇi*, 1962, p. 114.

liberation, then we can say that it has use in philosophy like Nyāya and Mīmāṁsā.

This objection has been considered by Jayanta. Jayanta formulated the objection in this way: *nanu upamāna lakṣaṇam asmin mokṣa śāstre kvopayujayate*?[17] Nyāya is a *darśaṇa*. And the value of *darśana* consists in liberation. *Darśaṇa* is a system of knowledge which tells us about the nature of liberation and the means of attaining liberation. From this point of view only three *pramāṇa*s seem to be useful.[18] But *upamāna* does not in any way help us in achieving liberation. Thus *upamāna* has no use either in Nyāya or in Mīmāṁsā. For both are *darśana*; so both are *mokṣa śāstra*.

In reply we may say that we do not deny that Mīmāṁsā is a *darśana* and so a *mokṣa śāstra*. But Mīmāṁsā is primarily a theory of interpretation of the sentences of the Vedas. And *upamāna* has an important use in *Mīmāṁsā* considered as a theory of interpretation. Mīmāṁsā develops and uses its own nyāya or maxims of interpretation of Vedic sentences. Sometimes considerations of similarity become necessary to complete the sense of some Vedic *vākya*s. Let us explain. The first part (or the first six chapters) of *Mīmāṁsā Sūtra* of Jaimini examines a group of *Vedic* sentences which are called *upadeśa vidhi*. In the second part (or in the last six chapters) another group of *Vedic* sentences are examined. This group of sentences are called *atideśa vidhi*.[19] An *upadeśa* imperative is concerned with the rite (*yāga*) about which complete information is supplied. And the rite about which all the information are explicitly stated in the Veda is called *prakṛti karma*. A complete information includes three major points:

17. Jayanta, 1936, p. 132.

18. *āgamāt tāvat ātmajñānam mokṣasādhanam setikarttavyatākam avagamyate, anumānāt āgamaprāmāṇyaniścayaḥ, pratyakṣāt anumānasya vyāptiparicchedaḥ.* — Jayanta, 1936, p. 132.

19. Bhūtanātha, BS 1345, part II, p. 193.

what is to be done, *why* it is to be done, and *how* it is to be done. Of these the last is called *itikartavyatā*. In case of *upadeśa vidhi* it is explicit from the *veda vākya how* the rite in question is to be performed. So *upadeśa vidhi* takes the form "Do it in this way," *ittham kuryāt*.

But another group of rites are there. These rites are called *vikṛti*. Complete information about these rites are not stated explicitly in the Vedas. The missing information is to be found where the corresponding *prakṛti karma* was discussed. So *atideśa vidhi*s take the form *tatvat kuryāt* "Do like that." This means this rite is to be performed in the same way in which the corresponding *prakṛti yāga* is performed. Thus the consideration of similarity with some *prakṛti yāga* enables us to understand how a *vikṛti yāga* is to be performed. And this similarity enables *atideśa vidhi*s to transfer certain information about *prakṛti yāga* to *vikṛti yāga*.[20]

One such *vikṛti yāga* is *saura yāga*. And there this *vidhi*, *śauryaṁcaruṁ nirvapet brahmavarcasakāmaḥ*. By the process of *atideśa* is decided how this rite is to be performed.[21] Śabarasvāmī has discussed in the seventh chapter of his commentary this *śaurya vidhi*. According to him this *vidhi* tells us *śauryayāgena apūrvamkṛtvā brahmavarcasaṁ sādhayet brahmavarcasakāmaḥ*.[22] Any way, this *śaurya yāga* is *vikṛti yāga*. We can ascertain how it is to be performed by the process of *atideśa*. But we can do this if we can decide which is the corresponding (*tajjātīya*) *prakṛti yāga*. For, a *vikṛti yāga* should be performed in the way the corresponding *prakṛti yāga* is performed. According to Śabarasvāmī in fixing the *prakṛti* the help of similarity (in respect of *dravya, devatā*, etc.) or *upamāna* is taken. Pattabhiram Shastri has stated in simple and clear language, *sauryādivikṛtau dravyadevatādiśādṛśyena upamānāt āgneya-*

20. Bhūtnātha, BS 1345, Part II, p. 193.
21. Ibid., p. 238.
22. Śabarasvāmī, 1883, part II, p. 57.

dharmaprāptirdr̥ṣṭātaduktam bhāṣyādau saptame upamiti-lakṣaṇapramāṇena hi sauryādāvāgneyavidhyanta.[23] Pattabhiram Shastri has shown other examples where considerations of similarity become useful in interpreting some Vedic *vākyas*. Jayanatabhaṭṭa in his *Nyāyamañjarī* also stated this view of the Mīmāṁsakas with reference to *śaurya yāga*.[24]

Jayanta has criticized the above explanation of *upamāna* in Mīmāṁsā. He has shown that similarity of *upamāna* is useful, according to the Mīmāṁsakas, for it helps us to fix the *prakr̥ti* of *śaurya,* or it yields information about how *śaurya* is to be performed. But this explanation is not consistent with their account of *upamāna*. According to them *upamāna* is the process through which we know that a thing which is not present is similar to a thing which is present.[25] The details of this criticism is subtle and beautiful. We cannot go into that.

The Naiyāyikas have a different theory of *upamāna*. According to this theory, *upamāna* primarily gives us knowledge of *śakti*. Can we say *upamāna* in this sense is useful in the interepretation of the Veda? Jayanta seems to hold that we can. Suppose we are to interpret or understand a Vedic imperative (*codanā*). In it some act has been enjoined. To perform this act an animal called *gavaya* is to be sacrificed. One cannot perform this *yāga* if one does not know the meaning of the word *gavaya*. For if one does not know which animal is called *gavaya* then one does not know which animal is to be sacrificed. In this and in similar cases *upamāna* becomes useful. We may know by *atideśa* and *upamāna* that *gavaya* is an animal which has similarity with cow.

We have found that *upamāna* is useful in the interpretation of the Vedas. But the opponent will say that it is still useless; it

23. Pattabhiram, 1987, p. 74.

24. Jayanta, 1936, p. 135

25. Ibid., p. 136.

serves no purpose in *darśana.*. For *upamāna* is of no help in attaining liberation. And if something is not connected with liberation then strictly speaking it is useless in *darśana*. Why should *darśana*, a *mokṣa śāstra,* discuss *upamāna*?

IV

We may say that the interpretation and understanding of the Veda is useful for liberation. And for such interpretation *upamāna* is useful. Thus *upamāna* and discussion of *upamāna* are indirectly useful for liberation. If we cannot understand the *veda-vākya*s correctly then we cannot perform the duties correctly. We cannot even do our duties in a *niṣkāma* way. But if we cannot do that it is difficult to attain the purification of *citta* (*cittaśuddhi*). But without *cittaśuddhi* we cannot have correct knowledge, about ourselves (*ātmadarśana*). And without this knowledge liberation is impossible. In this way *upamāna* is indirectly useful for *darśana* and *Nyāyadarśana,* through its usefulness in Mīmāṁsā.

Following Jayanta we can show more direct connection between *upamāna* and *mokṣa*. For *mokṣa* we are to attain immediate knowledge about the true nature of self (*ātmatattva*). For we are now in a state of bondage. The cause of it is our direct and perceptual beliefs about self which are false. These false beliefs can be removed by the (correct) knowledge about the self. We falsely believe that the self and the body are the same. We perceive ourselves falsely as happy or sorry, as fair or dark, as *brāhmaṇa* or *śūdra,* as lame or blind, etc. For liberation we must acquire the correct and direct knowledge of self. We must know directly or perceptually that self is not the same as this body or sense organ and the like. We must know directly that self is different from or other than body, etc. (*dehādivyatirikta*). How can we have this knowledge? The Vedic sentences like *ātmā vā are śrotavya mantavya nididhyāsitavya,* tell us how this knowledge can be acquired. We therefore must first understand such sentences. In this sentence the word *ātmā* is there. How can we know the meaning of this word? Like *gavaya* in our example this *ātmā* is still not known to us. Again this Vedic sentence tells us that to know *ātmā* properly we must receive instructions of Veda from the preceptor. This is *śravaṇa*. We must hear those Vedic sentences where all about *ātmā* has been said. In these sentences again the word *ātmā* must be there. How can we understand these sentences, if we cannot first know the meaning of the word *ātmā*? *Upamāna* can give us the knowledge of the meaning of this word in terms of similarity or dissimilarity of *ātmā* with other things. Thus *upamāna* becomes more directly useful for liberation through causing the proper knowledge of self. For this knowledge comes from understanding the Vedic sentences in which the word *ātmā* occurs.

The opponent may find this explanation forced and artificial. He will not be convinced that *upamāna* is useful for liberation. Jayanta seems to be aware of this possibility. So he says finally that Gautama has discussed *upamāna* not because it is useful for liberation. Gautama has discussed in his *Nyāyadarśana* all sorts of useful things. Some are directly useful for liberation; some are indirectly useful for liberation. Some other things have been discussed which are useful but not useful for liberation. Jayanta says:

> *sarvānugrahabuddhyā ca karuṇārdramatirmuniḥ*
> *mokṣopayogābhāve 'pi tasya lakṣaṇamuktavān.*[26]

We have already shown that *upamāna* is useful for both *śakti-jñāna* and for the knowledge of nature of things. We know from *upamāna* that the plant called *mudgaparṇī* is a medicinal plant (*oṣadhi*). It has medicinal value. Vātsyāyana has said that *upamāna* has this and many other (such) uses.

---

26. Jayanta, 1936, p. 132.

Part Five

Positive Views of Two Naiyāyikas

9

Jayanatabhaṭṭa's Views on Upamāna

In the fifth chapter I have considered mainly the objections which were brought against the Nyāya theory of *upamāna* by the Bauddhas and the Vaiśeṣikas. In the previous chapter I have considered Nyāya answers to some of the objections against the classical version of Nyāya theory of *upamāna*. In this chapter my objective is to see how the Naiyāyikas can meet another objection which the Mīmāṁsakas brought against the Nyāya theory of *upamāna*. The major source to be discussed is Jayanatabhaṭṭa's *Nyāyamañjarī*.

The objection that was raised by the Mīmāṁsakas was this. The classical Nyāya theory of *upamāna* cannot keep the independence of *upamāna*. In this theory *upamāna* has been reduced to *śabda-pramāṇa*. This objection applies to the *jaḍannaiyāyikas*. These Naiyāyikas are believed to hold that the statement of analogy is *upamāna-pramāṇa*. Usually Jayanatabhaṭṭa is called *jaḍannaiyāyika*. This chapter is devoted to a detailed discussion of Jayanta's view about *upamāna*. We may note in advance that Jayanta himself has discussed the views of the *vṛddhanaiyāyika*. We shall see that he has also defended the independence of *upamāna-pramāṇa*. So Jayanta is not the *jaḍannaiyāyika* according to whom *upamāna* is a *śabda-pramāṇa*.

It has been shown before that according to the Naiyāyikas *upamāna* gives us the knowledge of word-meaning relation, say, the knowledge that a certain animal has the name *gavaya*.[1] It has

1. Śakti is a desire or *icchā* which has any one of these forms: *asmāt śabdāt ayam artho bodhyavyaḥ, idam padaṁ imaṁ arthaṁ bodhayatu iti vā* →

also been shown that perception or inference cannot give us this knowledge. Further it has also been shown that *śabda* alone cannot give us this knowledge. But the specific charge which the Mīmāṁsakas made against the Nyāya view was not discussed. According to the Mīmāṁsakas the Naiyāyikas hold that *atideśa vākya* is *upamāna*. But then the knowledge we get from *upamāna* is really *śabda*. It is therefore alleged that the Naiyāyikas cannot preserve the independence of *upamāna* as *pramāṇa*. But really speaking Naiyāyikas do not accept that *upamāna* is identical with *śabda-pramāṇa*. It may be seen that according to the Naiyāyikas *upamāna* on the other hand is an irreducible (*svatantra*) *pramāṇa* for the knowledge of meaning relation. To prove this they must prove either of the following two things: (a) Naiyāyikas do not say that statement of analogy is *upamāna-pramāṇa*. (b) Even if *upamāna* is *atideśa vākya* yet the knowledge of *śakti* or *upamiti* cannot be reduced to *śabda*, etc. So *upamāna* is also irreducible. I am to discuss (b) first.

II

Jayanatabhaṭṭa in his *Nyāyamañjarī* has nicely shown that if we consider carefully the process of *upamāna* we will realize that the objection in question against classical Nyāya is not acceptable.

For an authentic account of the Nyāya theory of *upamāna* we need to examine classical, modern, and contemporary Nyāya literature on the subject. After considering the views of the classical philosophers like Gautama, Vātsyāyana, Uddyotakara, and Vācaspati Miśra and before considering the views of the neo-Naiyāyikas like Gaṅgeśa we want to consider Jayanatabhaṭṭa's views. Jayanatabhaṭṭa is generally taken to belong to the classical period of Nyāya philosophy. Udayana came as a bridge between the classical (or old) and the modern (or new) Naiyāyikas. In various places of his work, *Nyāyamañjarī*,

→ *icchā saṁketa-rūpa vṛttiḥ* — Gadādhara, quoted in Madhusudan, 1980, p. 5.

Jayanatabhaṭṭa considered himself as *navya* or neo-Naiyāyika. He there considered his predecessors as *vṛddha* or old Naiyāyikas. But it is not standard practice to call Jayanta a Navya-Naiyāyika. In the standard sense Gaṅgeśa and his followers alone are neo-Naiyāyikas (though among them also there are some differences of opinion). I am to follow generally this practice. We all know that Jayanatabhaṭṭa came before Udayanācārya. In any case for our purpose the views of Jayanatabhaṭṭa are more important than the question about his exact date. It is not very significant in this context whether he was old or modern Naiyāyika. We consider his views for their inherent worth. Everyone accepts that he occupies a distinct position in the whole Nyāya tradition.

In his *Nyāyamañjarī* Jayanatabhaṭṭa considers *upamāna* after considering *anumāna-pramāṇa*. In this he follows his predecessors. (But he does not follow Bhāsarvajña here, though according to Gopinath Kaviraj, Bhāsarvajña precedes Jayanta.) Jayanta considers this *pramāṇa* from the Nyāya point of view. He does not consider the Vaiśeṣika view on this particular issue. But he considered what he called the views of the "old" as well as "modern" Naiyāyikas. First he described the view of the old Naiyāyikas and discussed some objections against their view. Then he considered the view of the neo-Naiyāyika, of course in his sense of the term neo-Naiyāyika. He raised and discussed some critical points. From his writings it appears that Jayanta is in favour of those neo-Naiyāyikas among whom he seems to include Uddyotakara or Vācaspati Miśra. Jayanta thinks that according to both the old and the neo-Naiyāyikas the result of *upamāna-pramāṇa* is the knowledge of the relation of the name to its object (*saṁjñā-saṁjñi or vācya-vācaka saṁbandha-viṣayaka-jñānam*). To express it more specifically we should say that *upamāna-pramāṇa* knows the relation between a particular word or name and its corresponding object. One may have some kind of knowledge of the word *gavaya* but may not know the relation the word has to its corresponding object. No *pramāṇa* other than *upamāna* is perhaps able to yield this knowledge. So a Naiyāyika admits *upamāna* as the third *pramāṇa*.

According to Jayanta therefore the old and the neo-Naiyāyikas do not differ with regard to the object of the knowledge which *upamāna* produces. But it is doubtful whether they agree about the *karaṇa* or instrumental cause of this knowledge. The old Naiyāyikas think that the statement (*vākya*) of analogy is the *karaṇa* of *upamiti*.[2] The neo-Naiyāyikas on the other hand consider perception of similarity as the *karaṇa* or instrumental cause of *upamiti*. Jayanta explains the process of *upamāna* in this way. A city dweller does not know *gavaya* but wants to know it. He asks an experienced forester the question "How (like which) is *gavaya?*". The forester tells the city dweller "*gavaya* is like *go,* i.e. cow." The city dweller understands the utterance; and for the moment his question is answered. (He knows that there are animals similar to cow, but does not yet know which is that animal. So he takes the *atideśa vākya* to mean that if and when an animal similar to cow is found, that animal can be known to have the name *gavaya*. But that animal is to be seen first. Afterwards on some occasion the city dweller goes to the forest. He sees an animal like a cow. He remembers the content of the *atideśa vākya* or he remembers what he was told by the speaker of *atideśa vākya* (which he heard before). And now he has a distinctive knowledge of the relation of the word *gavaya* to the object (animal) *gavaya*. This knowledge is *upamiti.* The instrumental cause of this knowledge is the statement of the forester. This statement is therefore regarded by some old Nyāya philosophers as *upamāna-pramāṇa,* i.e. special means of the knowledge *upamiti*.

But to this kind of explanation of *upamāna-pramāṇa* some objections have been raised. It has been said that one knows the relation of a word to the corresponding object when one

2. . . . *vṛddha naiyāyikāḥ tāvat . . . svārūpya pratipādakam atideśa vākyameva upamānam.* — Jayanta, 1936, p. 128.

understands *atideśa vākya*. Now since this knowledge is due to the authentic statement of similarity (*atideśa vākya*) we are to accept this knowledge, whatever the object of it may be, as *śabda* (verbal). So the critics' objection is that the Naiyāyikas have reduced *upamiti* to knowledge by testimony (*śabda*). The Naiyāyikas admit verbal testimony as the fourth *pramāṇa*. In the *sūtra* 1.1.7 Gautama has defined *śabda* as *āptopadeśa-śabdaḥ*, where *upadeśa,* roughly speaking, stands for sentence (or words in the plural). Accordingly the knowledge that results from sentence or words is *śābda-jñāna.* If according to the Naiyāyikas so-called *upamiti* comes from statement then we are to accept it as *śābda-jñāna* and not a distinct kind of knowledge. The Naiyāyikas then cannot preserve the independence of *upamāna.*

Jayanatabhaṭṭa says in answer to this objection that though the process of *upamāna* involves a kind of statement yet the resulting knowledge of *upamiti* does not come directly or only from the statement. In case of knowledge by testimony the knowledge of the object is "direct" result of the statement. It is true that the city dweller heard the utterance of the forester. But immediately after that the city dweller does not have *upamiti* or the knowledge of the relation of the word *gavaya* to its object. When the city dweller later goes to the forest and perceives some object which has the similarity with cow then he remembers the content of that previously heard utterance of the forester. After all these conditions he (the city dweller) realizes that this (the yonder animal) is the object which corresponds to the word *gavaya* (*ayam-gavaya-gavaya padavācyaḥ*). This knowledge of the relation between the name and the object is *upamiti.* Now from this analysis of the process of *upamiti* it is clear that the resulting knowledge is not directly caused by the statement of the authoritative person. In case of knowledge by testimony the resulting knowledge is more directly caused by the utterance. Jayanta noticed this kind of difference and he defended the old Naiyāyikas. He therefore said that even if the old Naiyāyikas held that *atideśa vākya* is the *upamāna-pramāṇa* the resulting knowledge will not become *śābda*. For *śābda buddhi* the necessary condition is *memory* of word-meaning or *padārtha smaraṇa*. For *upamiti* perception of similarity is also necessary.

Let us explain the matter a little. In *śābda buddhi* there are roughly four steps. The step (0) falls outside a given case of *śābda buddhi*. We can take an example. A man hears an appropriate sentence and obtains the knowledge "Rāmacandra was the king of Ayodhyā." The steps are the following:

Step 0. The hearer in the past learned the meaning of each of the words of the sentence, may be at different times.

Step 1. Hearing (perception) of the sentence "Rāmacandra was the king of Ayodhyā."

Step 2. Memory of the meaning of each of the words of the sentence (Rāmacandra, etc.).

Step 3. Verbal knowledge that Rāmacandra was the king of Ayodhyā.

Thus verbal knowledge (*śābda-jñāna*) is produced by a sentence (of an authoritative person) through the memory of word meaning.

In *upamiti* also there are four steps. The first step falls outside a given case of knowledge by analogy. The steps in the standard case are the following:

Step 0. Hearing or perception of the statement of analogy.

Step i. Perception of similarity.

Step ii. Memory of the content of *atideśa vākya*.

Step iii. *Upamiti* that the perceived object is called by the name *gavaya*.

Thus *upamiti* is produced by the perception of similarity through memory of the content of the statement of analogy. A sentence does play a role in *upamāna* but it is two steps removed.

In case of *śābda buddhi* it is only one step removed. If a factor is more than one step removed it cannot be a cause. If something cannot be a cause of a knowledge it cannot be a *pramāṇa*. Now let us return to Jayanta.

Jayanta has further said that we must distinguish between knowledge of an object and knowledge of the means (*upāya*) of the knowledge of that object. If we apply this principle we can answer the objection brought against the (old) Naiyāyikas. We can now admit that knowledge of *sādṛśya* comes from *śabda* (*atideśa vākya*). But it is not *upamiti*. This knowledge is at most the *upāya-jñāna* or knowledge of means. Let knowledge of means be *śabda*. The knowledge of *śakti* (*upeya*) is distinct. It is *upamiti*. Jayanta has illustrated the principle with the example of *parārthānumāna*.

In *parārthānumāna* the utterance of the five sentences, jointly called *nyāya* (*vākya*), gives the hearer the knowledge of the ground of inference. In case of *parārthānumāna* of fire from smoke, *nyāya vākya* tells us that the smoke has all the properties of a legitimate ground of inference. The legitimate *hetu* is capable of proving fire (or giving inferential knowledge). This knowledge of the ground (*hetu*) is the means (*upāya*) of the inferential knowledge of fire. We do not say that the (inferential) knowledge of fire is knowledge by testimony (or *śabda*) because the knowledge of the ground (smoke) comes from sentence (*nyāya vākya*). Similarly we cannot say that *upamiti* is *śabda* because the cause of *upamiti-sādṛśya-jñāna* comes from *śabda* (*atideśa vākya*). We may further add that the verbal knowledge of similarity is only one factor in the process of *upamiti* and this factor falls outside any given case of *upamāna*. Knowledge of similarity which functions as cause in *upamāna* comes from perception and not from *śabda*. Thus *upamiti* is a distinctive kind of knowledge of meaning relation.[3]

---

3. Jayanta, 1936, pp. 128-29.

Now the objector may bring another objection. He may say in the first place that the case of *upamāna* is different from *parārthānumāna*. In case of *parārthānumāna, nyāya vākya* gives knowledge of *hetu* or smoke. The resulting inferential knowledge is the knowledge of fire. In case of *upamāna,* the *atideśa vākya* gives us knowledge about *sādr̥śya. Upamiti* is also the knowledge of *sādr̥śya.* And for the knowledge of the same object it is unjustified to admit two *pramāṇa*s. In answer a Naiyāyika may say that the object of *upamiti* is not *sādr̥śya* but *śakti.* But now it may be said that one can get the knowledge of *śakti* from *atideśa vākya.* For *atideśa vākya* tells us *gavaya* is similar to cow. And one who wants to know what is *gavaya* (or what *gavaya* is like) (*kidr̥g gavayaḥ?*) will come to know from the statement of analogy that the animal which is similar to cow is called *gavaya.* Therefore for the same knowledge of *śakti* it is unjustified to admit two *pramāṇa*s. But if only one of the two — *śabda* and *upamāna* — is to be admitted, then which one should we admit? The *śabda-pramāṇa* has many other uses so it is to be admitted. *Upamāna* as a separate *pramāṇa* for the knowledge only of *śakti* should not be admitted.

The answer to this objection has already been given one paragraph back. Now a few more points may be added. It seems that the objector assumed that the *pramāṇa*s are different if the object of knowledge is different; and the *pramāṇa*s are the same if the objects of knowledge are the same. For the objection of the opponent was the following. The knowledge which *atideśa vākya* gives and the knowledge which *upamāna* gives are the same. According to them we cannot admit two distinct *pramāṇa*s here. The argument of the opponent is that here the knowledge (*phala*) produced is the same. Therefore the *pramāṇa* which causes the *phala* must also be the same. *Pramāṇa*s can be different only if the knowledges produced is different. But when can we say that two knowledges are different? Suppose we say, only when their objects are different. It now follows that there should be as many knowledges as things of the world. And there will be equal number of *pramāṇas*; this means there will be infinite number of *pramāṇas*.[4] The Naiyāyikas on the other hand admit *pramāṇa saṁplava,* i.e. the same thing can be known by more than one *pramāṇa*. But they admit that if the *pramāṇas* are different then the types of the resulting knowledge must be different even if the object is the same.

But the result we reached in the previous paragraph may go against the Naiyāyikas. Earlier we said that the knowledge which knows the *sādṛśya* the *upāya-jñāna* and knowledge which knows *śakti* the *upeya-jñāna* come from different *pramāṇas*. Apparently the reason may seem to be the following. The objects are different, so the *pramāṇas* are different.

But Jayanta does not think that two *pramāṇas* become different when they know things that are different. So even if the object of *upamiti* is different from the object of *śābda buddhi, upamiti* can still be a case of *śabda*. For like *śābda buddhi upamiti* is also caused by *śabda-pramāṇa*. The *śabda* which functions as *pramāṇa* in case of *upamiti* is the statement of analogy. In answer it may be said that the knowledge of *śakti* called *upamiti* does not come from *śabda;* it is not caused by *śabda*. It comes from the knowledge of similarity. This knowledge of similarity may come from *śabda*. This answer may not be sufficient. For the objector may accept this and still say that *upamiti* is *śābda*. For the answer only shows that *śabda* (*atideśa vākya*) gives the knowledge of *śakti* through the knowledge of *sādṛśya*. A sense organ (*indriya*) gives us knowledge of a thing through sense-object contact. But still the knowledge that is produced is *indriyaja* or sensuous. Similarly though *upamiti* is produced by *śabda* through the knowledge of similarity yet *upamiti* is *śābda*.

The answer to the objection considered so far is not fully satisfying. Perhaps thinking all these Jayanta has not given this

4. *phala vaicitryeṇa pramāṇānantaya prasaṅgāt* — Jayanta, 1963, p. 128.

easy answer. He has said instead that *śabda* (*atideśa vākya*) gives the knowledge of the means (*upāya*). The *phala* or the knowledge of the object (*śakti*) needs another *pramāṇa*. *Pramāṇa* need not differ if merely their objects differ. But if one *pramāṇa* knows the means and another gives knowledge of *phala*, then the two *pramāṇa*s must be different. *nāgarako na āraṇyakavākyāt eva taṁ prāṇinaṁ gavaya-śabdavācyatayā buddhyate . . . kim āraṇyaka vākyena na saṁpratyayo nāgarakasya, na brūmo na saṁpratyaya iti kintu sārūpyam upāyāntaraṁ tat . . . upadiṣṭavān iti tato avagatiḥ bhavantī . . . na śābdī sā pratītiḥ api tu aupamānikīti . . . upamānaṁ pramāṇāntaram iti yuktam.*[5]

III

So far the answer against the objector is given in one way. In this section the author will try to answer the objector in another way by following Jayanta. Here we shall say that the objector is wrong when he brought the objection. It is wrong to say that according to the Naiyāyikas statement of analogy is the *upamāna-pramāṇa* and knowledge of *śakti* is derived from this sentence. In the previous section we did not question whether the objector was right when he said that the Naiyāyikas (in the past) held the view that *atideśa vākya* is *upamāna-pramāṇa*. It is assumed (in the previous section) that the opponent was right. Assuming that it has been shown how even then a Naiyāyika could say that *upamāna* is a separate *pramāṇa*. In this section the task is to point out that the Naiyāyikas did not say that knowledge of *samākhyā sambandha* comes from *atideśa vākya*, or that *śabda* (*atideśa vākya*) is *upamāna*. Between the utterance of *atideśa vākya* and knowledge of *pada padārtha sambandha* there are many stages. As we have shown, first there is *śābda buddhi* of *sādṛśya*, then there is perception of *sādṛśya* (when the man goes to the forest), and then there is memory of the content of *atideśa vākya*. Thus the statement cannot be *karaṇa*. Relation between sense organ and

---

5. Jayanta, 1936, p. 129.

perceptual knowledge cannot be compared with *atideśa vākya* and *śakti-jñāna*. *Indriya* can be said to yield perception through *indriya sannikarṣa*. For between sense organ and *indriya sannikarṣa* or between *indriya sannikarṣa* and perception of jar there is no other condition. *Atideśa vākya* does not give knowledge of *śakti* through *sādṛśya jñāna*. For knowledge of *śakti* is not produced immediately after *sādṛśya jñāna* it cannot be said to be *śābda*. After perception (perceptual knowledge) of similarity there is another step. This is memory of the content of statement of similarity. This memory is *vyāpāra*. And the perceptual knowledge of *sādṛśya* is the *karaṇa* (instrumental cause) of *upamiti*.

Here two questions may be raised by the opponents. The first question is (1) "what is the need for both *śabda* and *pratyakṣa*?" The statement of analogy alone is sufficient. For either this statement tells us that the animal similar to cow is called *gavaya* or it does not say so. If the second alternative were true then we could say that perception of similarity (and not the *atideśa vākya*) enables us to know what is *gavaya*. But perception helps us to know the animal which is *gavaya;* yet it alone cannot enable us to know the animal *gavaya* as an animal which is *called gavaya*. In other words, as Jayanta would say, perception alone cannot give us *gavaya vācyatayā gavaya jñānam*. So we need the *atideśa vākya*. If this *atideśa vākya* tells us that the animal which resembles cow is called *gavaya* then one can have *gavaya vācyatayā gavaya jñānam* (knowledge of *gavaya* as the referent of the word *gavaya*), if the following conditions hold. One must perceive *gavaya* in the forest and remember the content of *atideśa vākya* (and before that one must have heard *atideśa vākya*, that the animal similar to cow is called *gavaya*).

Now the opponent would say, let *śabda* and not perception give us knowledge of *śakti*; or the knowledge that the animal similar to cow is called *gavaya*. There is no need for the perception of similarity. In that case it will be correct to say that the knowledge of *śakti* is *śabda*. Reductionist's position (Vaiśeṣika position) will be justified. The question which the Naiyāyikas must be able to answer is "what is the necessity of the perception of similarity over and above the *atideśa vākya*?" In short to answer the first question of the opponent the Naiyāyikas must be able to show that for knowledge of *śakti* both perception and statement of analogy are necessary.

The second question which may arise is this: (2) can we not say that knowledge of *śakti* results not from *upamāna*? If it does not result from *śabda* (or perception) it results from *anumāna*. Can we not say this? We shall try to answer this second question when we discuss Udayanācarya's views. Answer to the first question has been discussed in detail by Jayanta.

Following is the point of Jayanta. When one hears *atideśa vākya* one knows from the statement that *gavaya* is like *go*. But even then one does not know the relation of the word *gavaya* to the object *gavaya* in the form "this (animal *gavaya*) is called *gavaya*." But if a person hears the utterance of *atideśa vākya* and also perceives in the *gavaya* its similarity with *go* (cow) then he can have knowledge of that form. So this perceptual knowledge of similarity is important. Without this, one cannot have the knowledge of the relation which the word or the name bears to the object, in the form in which *upamāna* gives this knowledge. So the Naiyāyikas consider the perceptual knowledge of the similarity as the instrumental cause or *upamāna-pramāṇa*. Therefore *upamiti* or a certain kind of knowledge of *śakti* comes from (*sādṛśya*) *pratyakṣa* as well. It does not come from *śabda* alone. So it cannot be objected that the Naiyāyikas failed to keep *upamāna* distinct from *śabda* (*āgama bahirbhūta*).

The objector may say that all these may be true about the neo-Naiyāyikas who say *sādṛśya pratyakṣa* is *karaṇa*. But older Naiyāyikas failed to keep *upamāna* distinct from *śabda*. Jayanta says this also is not true. What Jayanta says in this connection has been, according to Jayanta, hinted at by Vātsyāyana.

Bhāṣyākṣṛāṇyapi caitatpakṣasākṣyacchāyāmiva badanti lakṣyante, tāni tu granthagauravabhayānna yojyanta ityalaṁ prasaṅgena.[6]

Now an opponent can grant this. But he can still say that it is better to consider this knowledge as perceptual than to admit another independent *pramāṇa* like *upamāna*. For the knowledge in question comes from perception. But this objection does not arise. One does not acquire from perception alone the knowledge of the relation of word and object. Other conditions are also necessary. Hearing the appropriate utterance, memory of the content of statement heard, etc. are some of these conditions. Very nicely Jayanta has explained this whole process when exactly the perception of similarity occurs and how the knowledge of *upamiti* results.[7]

So *upamiti* involves as cause the statement of similarity and perception of similarity; yet the resulting knowledge is neither knowledge by testimony nor it is perceptual, because this knowledge is not the result of just statement of analogy nor of mere sense object contact. It requires both. And the old and the neo-Naiyāyikas differ only on this point: which particular kind of knowledge of similarity will be considered as the *upamāna-pramāṇa*? About the nature of *upamiti* there is not much of difference between whom Jayanta describes as the old Naiyāyika and whom he describes as new Naiyāyikas. They do not even seem to differ about the definition of *karaṇa* or of *upamāna*. (Jayanta of course has his own view in the matter — *sāmagrīkaraṇatāvāda*.) According to this view, *karaṇa* of an effect is different from other causes of the effect. The difference is this. The effect is produced immediately after the *karaṇa*. Effect does not follow immediately after any other cause. According to Jayanta the effect does not immediately follow after this cause or that cause. It is produced only after all the causal conditions

6. Jayanta, 1936, p. 129.

7. . . . *tatdhī indriyajanitamapi . . . ucyate.* — Jayanta, 1936, p. 129.

are there. So the *karaṇa* of an effect is actually the totality (*sāmagrī*) of all causal conditions.

IV

The final view of Jayanta then is this. *Upamāna* is a separate and irreducible *pramāṇa*. The reason for its irreducibility is not that *upamiti* has different objects to know. To be different, *pramāṇa*s need not have different objects. For Jayanta has said before that if *pramāṇa*s were different when objects were different then there would be innumerable *pramāṇa*s. And secondly what we know in *upamiti* we also know (roughly the same) from *atideśa vākya*. But *upamiti* of *śakti* is still different from *śabda-jñāna* about *śakti*, because the cause of *upamiti* is different. The cause of *śābda buddhi* is hearing of sentence, etc. It may be thought that *upamiti* is caused by the utterance of sentence; by the utterance of *atideśa vākya*. But Jayanta says this is not true. Some knowledge of meaning relation is caused by *atideśa vākya*. But that knowledge is inferior to the knowledge of *śakti* which *upamiti* produces. Now the question is, why the knowledge from *atideśa vākya* is said to be inferior? Why the knowledge from *upamiti* is superior? What makes this knowledge superior? We shall see that perception of similarity (which comes after the hearing of *atideśa vākya*) helps the knowledge of *śakti* to become superior. But the superior knowledge of the relation between a word and the object it means, is not caused by perception (alone). This is the reason why *upamiti* is different from perception. *Upamiti* is different from memory also.[8] If thus *upamiti* is different from perception, inference, memory and *śabda* it is an irreducible different kind of knowledge. For the question of its being knowledge of any other kind does not arise.

Jayanta says that the role of perception in *upamiti* is confined to producing the knowledge of similarity. It does not give us

8. Jayanta, 1936, p. 134; Vātsyāyana, 1985, p. 169.

the knowledge of the object of *upamiti*. This is exactly what Vātsyāyana has clearly stated.[9] But from Vātsyāyana it is not very clear what this perceptual knowledge of similarity does to the knowledge of *śakti*. Jayanta says that it makes all the difference between the knowledge of *śakti* we have from *atideśa vākya* and knowledge of *śakti* we have from *upamiti*. If this difference is not there then there will be no need for *upamāna*. For before *upamāna* can give us knowledge of *śakti, atideśa vākya* gives it. Now Jayanta says that there is difference between the knowledge of *śakti* which *upamāna* gives and knowledge of *śakti* which *atideśa vākya* gives. The knowledge which *atideśa vākya* gives is inferior. Knowledge of the same object which *upamāna* gives is superior. And it becomes superior because there occurs perception of similarity in *gavaya* in between the two knowledges. According to Jayanta *atideśa vākya* which the forester utters (*atabikaratita vākya*)[10] to the city dweller cannot fully answer his query. It cannot produce fully satisfying (*nirākāṅkṣā* or *nirupaplava*) knowledge. Thus knowledge of *śakti* is produced by *atideśa vākya* but so long as perceptual knowledge of *gavaya* and of similarity in it is not there, fully satisfying knowledge of *śakti* is not produced. Therefore the superior or the fully satisfying knowledge of *śakti* comes after (or is caused by) both *atideśa vākya* and perception of similarity. This knowledge is not caused by *śabda* or by perception alone. It is not *śābda*, it is not *pratyakṣa*. It is a different kind of knowledge called *upamiti* which is caused by an independent source called *upamāna*. This is how Jayanta proves that *upamāna* is a separate *pramāṇa*. In his own words:

> *atrāhuḥ na atabikaratita vākyāt vispaṣṭaḥ saṁjñā-saṁjñi-sambandhapratyayo bhavitum arhati saṁjñinaḥ tadānīm apratyakṣatvāt, yadyapi go sārūpya viśiṣṭa-tayā tadavagama*

9. *kim punar . . . ityāha.* — Vātsyāyana, 1985, p. 169.

10. Jayanta, 1936, p. 130.

upapāditaḥ tathā api sopaplava iva bhavati tadānīṁ buddhiḥ.[11]

Now a question remains. What exactly is the nature of dissatisfaction or incompleteness or doubt or impediment (*upaplava*)? Why *atideśa vākya* fails to give *nirupaplava buddhi*? It may be noted that *atideśa vākya* tells us in a general way what is *gavaya* or what is called a *gavaya*. It tells us whatever thing has similarity with cow is called *gavaya*. But one may still wonder whether any such thing or animal is there. And if there is such an animal, which is it? But once one perceives a *gavaya* after hearing *atideśa vākya* one knows that *gavaya* (animal similar to cow) is *gavaya* or what is similar to cow is a *gavaya*. One also knows "this is *gavaya*." By the word "this" we are to understand the animal which the city dweller is seeing at the moment. Jayanta writes: . . . *atideśa-vacana-samaye go-sadṛśa mātropadeśe satyapi saṁjñini na nivarttate evopaplavaḥ pramāṇāntaraparicceheda-sāpekṣaka-saṁjñirūpopadeśāt. . . .*[12]

Jayanta here draws a comparison between knowledge by analogy and knowledge by inference. He says that in case of inference of fire one comes to know the fire before the inferential knowledge is produced. But what is then the need for inference? Jayanta says that when one has the knowledge of *vyāpti* one knows in a general way where there can be fire. One knows wherever smoke exists there fire also exists. But he does not know any particular place where fire is there. When he has inferential knowledge he knows fire as existing in a particular place. He has knowledge that this or that (hill) has fire; *atrāgnirīti*. This inferential knowledge of particular fire or of fire in a particular place cannot occur if there is no *pakṣadharmatā-jñāna*. *Pakṣadharmatā-jñāna* turns the general knowledge of *vyāpti* or fire to a particular case. It is like applying a general truth to a

11. Jayanta, 1936, p. 130.

12. Ibid., p. 131.

particular case. Similarly *atideśa vākya* tells us in a general way that whatever is similar to cow is called *gavaya*. Or anything that is similar to cow is called *gavaya*. This cannot answer the question whether a certain particular animal is *gavaya* or which particular thing which is similar to cow is called *gavaya*. *Upamāna* gives us just this knowledge. In the words of Jayanta the form of the knowledge by analogy or *upamiti* is *ayam sa gavayaśabdābhidheyaḥ*.[13] This is comparable to the form of *anumiti* shown above *atrāgnirīti*. *Upamiti* therefore is a knowledge which leaves nothing more to be said in the matter. It is *nirupaplava buddhi; (tathā atrāpi) anavagata vācya viśeṣāt vākyāt buddhiridānīṁ vācya viśeṣe dṛṣṭe nirupaplave jāyate ayaṁ sa gavaya śabdābhidheya iti*.[14]

Jayanta has also shown why this knowledge of a particular animal as the denotation of *gavaya* cannot be perception or inference. We are not going into the details here. I shall however note two points. The first point is this. According to Jayanta (and Naiyāyikas in general) *upamiti* results from perception of similarity. And he also says that the memory of the content of the statement of analogy which was heard before (*pūrvaśruta-āraṇyaka-vākyārtha-smaraṇam*), is the auxiliary condition (*sahakārī*). Therefore perception of similarity can be said to be the special means or cause of *upamiti*. Now this knowledge of similarity is *pratyakṣa;* it results from sense-object contact. And it is here *pramāṇa*. Therefore perception of similarity should be called *pratyakṣa* (*pramāṇa*) and not *upamāna* (*pramāṇa*). Jayanta has not only raised this question, he has also answered it. He says, *go svārūpya . . . darśanam adhyakṣa phalam api tadanavagatasaṁjñā-saṁjñi sambandha bodha vidhānāt upamānam ucyate*.[15] Or in other words the perception of similarity is called *upamāna* because it causes

---

13. Jayanta, 1936, p. 131.
14. Ibid.
15. Ibid.

upamiti. A question remains; though a neo-Naiyāyika may offer this argument how such *sāmagrī karaṇatāvādin* Jayanta can do that?

Another question which cannot be discussed here is this. How one can objectively decide whether a knowledge is satisfying or not? If one is satisfied when we tell him that a *gavaya* is like cow then there will be no need for *upamiti.* It may be said from the side of Jayanta that the knowledge that satisfies this man will not be *upamiti.* But if the man is not satisfied and wants to know what particular animal is *gavaya,* he will be satisfied if he has knowledge of the form *ayaṁ gavaya.* This knowledge will be *upamiti.* It seems that according to Jayanta the form of *upamiti* will always be *ayaṁ gavaya-padavācyaḥ* and not *gavayaḥ gavaya-padavācyaḥ.*

10

Udayanācārya's Views on Upamāna

I

In this chapter Udayanācārya's treatment of *upamāna,* which we find in his *Nyāyakusumāñjaliḥ* will be considered. In the earlier chapter his views in the matter were considered to some extent in the context of Prācīna Nyāya (old Nyāya) view. Udayana's *Nyāyapariśuddhi* is a (sub-sub) sub-commentary on Vātsyāyana's commentary on Gautama's *Nyāyasūtra*. Vātsyāyana in his commentary on *sūtra* 1.1.6 noted an objection offered by some opponents. They ask "what does *upamāna* do in *go-gavaya* case?" They suggest that perception here yields the result (i.e. so-called *upamiti*). While writing on this passage Uddyotakara formulated the relevant objection in this way: *pratyakṣāgamābhyāṁ nopamānaṁ bhidyate*. Jayanta noted the objection or suggestion that *upamāna* is reducible to *śabda* and *anumāna*. In his *Nyāyakusumāñjaliḥ* Udayana is mainly interested in showing that *samayo durgrahaḥ pūrvaṁ śabdenānumayāpi vā* (3.11). This means, what *upamāna* yields cannot be got either from *śabda* or from *anumāna*. Here Udayana does not discuss particularly the question whether *upamāna* can be reduced to *pratyakṣa;* we think there is reason. The reason is this. The frame of discussion in *Pariśuddhi* was determined by the preceding line of commentaries. But his *Nyāyakusumāñjaliḥ* is an independent work. Here he seems to have two groups of historical opponents, the Vaiśeṣikas and the Mīmāṁsakas. According to standard views early Vaiśeṣikas also believed that *upamāna* was reducible to *anumāna*. The Mīmāṁsā accept *upamāna* as an independent *pramāṇa*. But the early

Mīmāṁsakas thought that the way the Naiyāyikas define *pramāṇa* makes it reducible to *śabda* or testimony. This situation makes it necessary for Udayana to demonstrate that *upamāna* is not reducible to any of these two *pramāṇas*, viz. inference or verbal testimony. Exactly this has been done in *Nyāyakusumāñjaliḥ*. But in his *Pariśuddhi* he accepted the view of Vācaspati that word-meaning relation cannot be known from *śabda* or *pratyakṣa*. He writes there, *viśiṣṭasaivapratipattiḥ vākyādevāstu ityata āha —"na ceti." Pratyakṣamātrāt bhaviṣyati ityata āha "na ceti."*[1] In his *Pariśuddhi* Udayana argued further that word-meaning relation cannot be known from *śabda* and *pratyakṣa* jointly. He writes, *etenavākyo-pratyakṣosamāhāro 'pi nirastaḥ.*

The present discussion of the views of Udayana with special reference to the text *Nyāyakusumāñjaliḥ* will show how the theory of *upamāna* was developed in the syncretic school of Nyāya-Vaiśeṣika. Earlier the discussion is made separately on the views of the Naiyāyikas including Jayanta and the views of the Vaiśeṣikas including Vallabhācārya. Though Vallabhācārya came after Udayana he had a different view than Udayana. Unlike the thinkers of syncretic school he defended the earlier Vaiśeṣika view that *upamāna* is not an independent *pramāṇa*. This is the reason why we considered Vallabha's views before considering the views of Udayana and along with the views of the Vaiśeṣikas.

In this section we shall discuss the views of Udayana as the representative view of the syncretic school of Nyāya-Vaiśeṣika following his book *Nyāyakusumāñjaliḥ*. The founder of the Nyāyavaiśeṣika syncretic school is Udayana. Some exchange of views between the Naiyāyikas and Vaiśeṣikas must have began before. But an attempt of synthesis, of these two school, was made in the eleventh century by Udayana. "Here is no sign of it either in the *sūtras* or in the works written before Udayana."[2]

1. Udayana, 1967, p. 362. Passages of *Tātparyaṭīkā* to which references have been made here may be found in Vācaspati, 1985, p. 170.

2. Varadacari, 1987, p. 142.

Varadacari has remarked, "it is a secret as to how and why these two schools came together as sister systems." Varadacari discussed in detail the points of agreement and disagreement between these two schools. For our purpose here we shall discuss two great personalities of this syncretic tradition. In this chapter we shall discuss the views of the founder of this tradition Udayanācārya. Great scholar of this syncretic tradition Gaṅgeśa Upādhyāya came after Udayana and developed the theory of *upamāna*. Udayanācārya belonged to the middle age of the history of Nyāya and Vaiśeṣika. And Gaṅgeśa belonged to the modern period so a discussion of their views will enable us to see how the Nyāya theory of *upamāna* or knowledge by analogy was shaped in the middle and modern ages of Nyāya and in the schools of Udayana and Gaṅgeśa.

One may say, let Udayana be a syncretic philosopher. What his syncretism has to do with the theory of *upamāna?* So far as this theory is concerned, he is out and out a Naiyāyika. He accepts *upamāna* as a separate *pramāṇa*. So there is no difference between the school of Nyāya and the syncretic school so far as the theory of *upamāna* is concerned. In this chapter we will actually try to defend, following Udayanācārya, the Nyāya theory of *upamāna-pramāṇa*. Only a few Naiyāyikas are against this *upamāna*. Naiyāyikas from Gautama to Gaṅgeśa and even afterwards the syncretic philosophers of Nyāya and Vaiśeṣika are generally in favour of this *pramāṇa*. But other schools of Indian philosophy including Mīmāṁsā are against *upamāna* as such or against the Nyāya theory of *upamāna-pramāṇa*. Thus the Nyāya theory has both external and internal critics. Vaiśeṣikas are the internal critics and the Bauddhas are external critics. Mīmāṁsakas, from one point of view, may be taken as external critic and, from another point of view as internal critic.

Now, on the basis of the discussion so far we can say that regarding *upamāna* there are altogether three different views:

1. The strong rejectionist view is that *upamāna* is not a *pramāṇa;* it is not a form of valid cognition. The Cārvākas and the Buddhist philosophers are in favour of this view. They can be named as Rejectioninsts.
2. Some other groups of philosophers think that *upamāna* is a *pramāṇa* but it is not an independent *pramāṇa*. According to them what is called *upamāna* is a *pramāṇa* or knowledge; it has its own object. But this object, which the Naiyāyikas think to be known by *upamāna,* is actually known by some other familiar or accepted *pramāṇa.* Some like the Vaiśeṣikas think that it is known by a variety of inference; some other philosophers appear to think that it is known by perception and testimony jointly. These philosophers are the reductionists. The Vaiśeṣikas, the Jainas and the Sāṁkhyas belong to this group.
3. There is a third group of philosophers. They think *upamāna* is a valid cognition. They also think that this cognition comes from an independent source of knowledge. This is a distinct source called *upamāna* and the knowledge called (*upamāna* or) *upamiti* is also a distinct kind of knowledge. To these philosophers *upamāna* is neither devoid of object nor it is reducible to inference. The Nyāya and Mīmāṁsā systems of philosophies are in favour of this view. They are *svātantryavādins.* According to the Naiyāyikas *upamāna* is the third among the four *pramāṇas* they admit. The Mīmāṁsakas admit five or six *pramāṇas. Upamāna* is the fourth among these.

We find that among the three views stated above, the first two are the negative views of *upamāna.* The third view is the positive view of *upamāna.* Naiyāyikas and Mīmāṁsakas who uphold this positive view of *upamāna* think that *upamāna* is not reducible to some other *pramāṇa* and so the question of rejection also does not arise at all.

Before passing to a better understanding of the Nyāya theory of *upamāna* it is important to make the point clear why does a Buddhist philosophers say that *upamāna* is not a *pramāṇa* at all. How can they say that it is devoid of object? The Buddhist philosophers say that *upamāna* is devoid of object. What they mean is perhaps that *upamāna* does not know any of the things it is said to know. What is accepted as an object of *upamāna* by one school of philosophers is not accepted by the philosophers of other schools. For example, according to the Mīmāṁsakas object of *upamāna* is some kind of similarity. According to the Naiyāyikas *upamāna* does not have similarity for its object; it knows the relation between a particular kind[3] of word and its corresponding object. This particular relation is known as *vṛtti* or *samaya* (i.e. the meaning relation).[4] But if this is the situation then the philosophers are not unanimous about the object of *upamāna*.

When a Buddhist philosopher says that *upamāna* is devoid of object he, however, means to say that *upamāna* does not know similarity, or the meaning relation or any of the things it is said to know. According to them in every sense of the term, "object," *upamāna* is devoid of object. But the Mīmāṁsakas also admit that *upamāna* is devoid of object in the sense *upamāna* does not know the meaning relation;[5] the Naiyāyikas hold that *upamāna*

---

3. *Svārthaka śabda* (or *vācaka śabda)* as Jagadīśa said. Cf. Jagadisha Tarkalamkara, 1973, p. 29.

4. The word *vṛtti* is understood to mean *śakti* or *lakṣaṇā*. See Madhusudana, 1980, p. 73, fn. 1. But Ujjala Panse (Jha) in her article "Jayanta on the Relation between Word and Meaning" seems to have either excluded *śakti* from *vṛtti* or identified *śakti* with *vṛtti*. For she writes, *samaya* is . . . *saṁketa* and *lakṣaṇā* or *śakti* or *vṛtti*. Panse. 1992, p. 101. But see Madhusudana, 1980, p. 5. Madhusudana says that *śakti* and *lakṣaṇā* are divisions of *vṛtti*.

5. Actually the Naiyāyikas hold that *upamāna* knows some other object. But in any case they do not admit similarity as the object of *upamāna*.

does not have similarity as its object. So in different senses the first and the third view contend that *upamāna* is devoid of object.

So we come to this that if a philosopher is an absolute skeptic about *upamāna* or is a rejectionist as the Buddhists are then he will deny that there is any such thing as *upamāna*. And one of his arguments may be that *upamāna* has no object. And they may hold this on the ground that there is no such thing as similarity or *śakti* which is held to be the object of *upamāna*. When a Buddhist says that *upamāna* is devoid of any object he means to say that neither *śakti* nor *sādṛśya* nor any other thing is its object. When the Buddhist philosopher Ratnakīrti discarded *upamāna* he rejected the view that *upamāna* is the knowledge of similarity. He also rejected the view that *upamāna* is the knowledge of *śakti*.

But the picture becomes different when Udayanācarya in his *Nyāyakusumāñjaliḥ* discarded the Mīmāṁsā view of *upamāna*. As we have already said a Naiyāyika and so also Udayanācārya is only a partial skeptic or non-radical rejectionist. Udayanācārya does not, like the Buddhist philosopher, discard *upamāna* as such. The same is true about the Mīmāṁsakas. The Naiyāyika will reject *upamāna* if it means a distinct kind of knowledge of *similarity*. He will admit *upamiti*, if it means a distinct kind of knowledge of *śakti*. Similarly a Mīmāṁsaka will admit *upamāna* if it means a distinct kind of knowledge of similarity. But he will reject *upamāna* in the sense of a distinct kind of knowledge of *śakti*.

From the Nyāya point of view there are both radical rejectionists like the Bauddhas and non-radical rejectionists like the Mīmāṁsakas. So a Naiyāyika cannot prove his positive view unless he can disprove both the rival views — the radical rejectionism of the Bauddhas and the relative rejectionism of the Mīmāṁsakas. Similarly if a Mīmāṁsaka is to establish his own positive view about *upamāna* he must be able to reject the views of the Bauddhas and the Naiyāyikas.

In the old Nyāya tradition from Gautama to Jayanta the Bhāṭṭas and the Naiyāyikas tried to establish their own views by discarding mainly the views of the Buddhists and Vaiśeṣikas. From Udayanācārya we see that the Naiyāyikas began to discuss and criticize mainly and very seriously the views of the Mīmāṁsakas. Though the Mīmāṁsakas neither reject *upamāna* nor reduce it to some other *pramāṇa* yet there seem to be historical reasons why attention was shifted towards them. Anyway in his *Nyāyakusumāñjaliḥ* Udayanācārya has defended the Nyāya theory of *upamāna* against the Mīmāṁsakas as well. Udayanācārya's argument that similarity cannot be the object of *upamāna* is directed against the Mīmāṁsakas. According to Udayana similarity or *sādṛśya* cannot be said to be the object of knowledge by analogy; because, there cannot be a thing like *sādṛśya* which is distinct from all other things. If now one says like the Mīmāṁsakas that *sādṛśya* is the only object of *upamāna*, then *upamāna* will be impossible due to lack of object. Udayana thinks that the Nyāya view is correct. *Upamāna* knows not the *sādṛśya* but the relation between the word and its corresponding object. He has said even more. He said this relation of *śakti* cannot be known by other *pramāṇa*s but it can be known only by *upamāna*.[6]

It has already been stated in an earlier section that in the *sūtra* 1.1.6 of *Nyāyadarśanam* Gautama has defined *upamāna*. If one reads the relevant portions of commentaries and sub-commentaries written by Vātsyāyana, Uddyotakara, Vācaspati Miśra, Udayana and also Jayanta, one can see the development of Nyāya theory of *upamāna*. The picture that becomes clear is this that according to the Naiyāyikas the relation between word and its corresponding object is known by *upamāna*. Gautama in the aphorism has used the term *sādhya* for this relation. Different commentators have thrown light on the meaning of the word

6. *pratyakṣāderasādhyatvāt upamānaphalaṁ biduḥ* — *Kusumāñjaliḥ*, 3.10; Udayanācārya 1962, p. 120. This passage requires to be carefully understood.

sādhya.[7] To say that the *sādhya* is known by *upamāna* is to say that it is grasped by known similarity. And as *upamāna* (i.e. *upamiti*) is the knowledge from known similarity, we can say, on this ground, that *upamiti* is the knowledge by analogy. But what this knowledge by analogy knows? What is this *sādhya*, the *sādhana* of which is *upamiti*? According to the Naiyāyikas the knowledge by analogy knows the relation between word and its corresponding object. According to the Mīmāṁsakas, however, knowledge by similarity (*upamiti*) knows a kind of similarity.

In the old Nyāya tradition it has not been clearly stated why we cannot say that *upamāna* knows similarity. In *Nyāyakusumāñjaliḥ*, which was written in the middle age of the history of Nyāya we see that Udayanācārya has considered the view of the Mīmāṁsakas and answered that. And his analysis actually gives the complete shape to the Nyāya (or syncretic) position in the matter of *upamāna*. Udayana has considered the following major points:

1. Why similarity is not an independent category?
2. Even if we admit that there is a distinct type of knowledge, namely the knowledge of similarity, then that knowledge can be explained by some other *pramāṇa*. We do not need *upamāna* as a source of that knowledge.
3. We have the knowledge of certain particular kind of relation between a word and its object. *Pramāṇa*s other than *upamāna* cannot give this knowledge. So *upamāna* must be admitted in the system as an independent *pramāṇa*.
4. Finally Udayanācārya has shown that *upamāna* does not help one to prove the non-existence of God.

---

7. In his commentary Vātsyāyana stated, *samākhyāsambandha pratipattirūpamānārtha ityāha* — Vātsyāyana, 1985, p. 169.

It will be clear from the discussions of Udayana that Gautama and, following him, the other *prācīna* Naiyāyikas were right when they accepted *upamāna* as a *pramāṇa*. Now we shall try to understand how, after the old Naiyāyikas, Udayanācārya tackled various problems relating to this *upamāna*. Analysis of the four different points mentioned above will make Udayana's position clear. We will also understand whether Udayana could add something new to the discussion on *upamāna-pramāṇa* (from the side of the Naiyāyikas or as a syncretic philosopher).

For our purpose we shall discuss these points: (1) and (2) together; and similarly (3) and (4) may be taken together.

II

One cannot deny the fact that we have experience of similarity and also dissimilarity. Sometimes we have such knowledge as "a *gavaya* is like a *go*" or cats are like tigers. Again we have knowledge that a camel is different or dissimilar from cow. So we have knowledge of both similarity and dissimilarity. Now according to both the Naiyāyikas and Mīmāṁsakas knowledge is *svaviṣayaka*, i.e. must reveal some object. The knowledge of similarity or dissimilarity therefore cannot be devoid of object. It reveals similarity or dissimilarity as its object. Nobody can deny that we have knowledge of similarity or dissimilarity. But how do we know this similarity? It must be known by one *pramāṇa* or another. What is the harm if we admit perception as the source of knowledge of similarity? Similarity or dissimilarity obtains between pairs of things. There will be no difficulty in having perceptual knowledge of similarity if the sense organs are in contact with the objects between which the similarity holds. Let us take an example. Two (similar) jars are before our eyes and we perceive them. By perception we can say that the jars are similar. In the same way one can know similarity by inference if one knows the ground or *hetu* to infer. But the Mīmāṁsakas point out that in some cases similarity cannot be known by perception or inference or any other *pramāṇa*. So the Mīmāṁsakas admit another independent *pramāṇa* to explain the knowledge of similarity in such cases. Suppose a villager hears from a reliable person that a *gavaya* is like a cow or *go*; later he perceives an animal and perceives that it is similar to *go* or cow. He now remembers what he heard previously, namely that a *gavaya* is similar to cow. And finally he arrives at the knowledge that the cow (he saw in the village earlier) is like this animal which he is now perceiving. This is also a knowledge of similarity. The Mīmāṁsakas admit, *upamāna* is a distinct *pramāṇa* for this final knowledge of similarity or for the knowledge (*upamiti*) which knows this kind of similarity. This similarity exists in an object which is not in contact with our sense organ now[8] but it is known. We perceived this thing before, we are remembering it now. On the other hand there is some other object, i.e. the animal *gavaya* with which we now have contact of sense organ. We perceive this *gavaya*. And we also perceive in this *gavaya* cow-similarity.

In the system of Mīmāṁsā, *upamāna* therefore has distinct identity; it is a *svatantra pramāṇa*. And this distinct *pramāṇa* knows similarity as specified above. According to the Prabhākara Mīmāṁsakas this similarity is also a distinct category. The Bhāṭṭa Mīmāṁsakas do not accept any similarity as an independent category. But the Bhāṭṭas also think that a distinct *pramāṇa* must be admitted for the knowledge of similarity in question. So we can understand the Mīmāṁsā position in this way. A separate *pramāṇa* called *upamāna* should be admitted to account for the knowledge of a certain type of similarity. This view is common to both Bhāṭṭa and Prābhākara Mīmāṁsakas. But only the Prābhākaras hold that similarity is a distinct category of thing.

In his *Nyāyakusumāñjaliḥ* Udayanācārya has considered both the questions. Can *sādṛśya* be a distinctive kind of thing

8. *upamānamapi asannikṛṣṭe 'rthe buddhimutpādayati*. — *Śābara Bhāṣya*, 1.1.5.

(*padārthāntara*)? Do we need a separate *pramāṇa* (called *upamāna*) for the knowledge of similarity in a previously known thing (this similarity is with a thing which is being perceived at the moment)? To each of these two questions some Mīmāṁsakas offer affirmative answer. Udayana gave negative answer to each of these questions and he gave appropriate arguments also. After showing the untenability of the views of the Mīmāṁsā and some other schools Udayana gave positive argument for the Nyāya view of *upamāna*.

So our first task now is to show why the Mīmāṁsaka philosophers think that similarity is a distinct category and why the founder and member of the syncretic school of Nyāya-Vaiśeṣika, Udayanācārya cannot accept this. He cannot accept anything as real if it is not any one of the six (or seven) categories of things (*padārthas*) which the Vaiśeṣikas admit. He thinks that if a thing is real but is not (apparently) a *dravya*, *guṇa*, etc. it must be reducible to one or the other of these seven categories. So a philosopher of syncretic school may admit *sādṛśya* or (*pada*) *śakti*. But it should be possible to show that it falls within one or the other of these categories. It will be explained fully in the modern syncretic school of Navya-Nyāya that (*pada*) *śakti* belongs to the category of *guṇa*. According to Udayanācārya *sādṛśya* is a real thing but not irreducible thing. This point also will be fully developed in the school of Navya-Nyāya. Here we should note that neither *sādṛśya* nor *śakti* is admitted by Udayana as a distinct category. Yet he says *upamāna* is knowledge of *śakti* and not knowledge of *sādṛśya*. Udayana's rejection of the view that *sādṛśya* or *śakti* is additional entity is directed against the Prābhākara Mīmāṁsakas. Vīrarāghavācārya concluded his explanation of Udayana's argument (to show that *sādṛśya* is not an *atirikta padārtha*) with the comment, *tasmāt sādṛśyaṁ sarvātiriktam iti prābhākarābhimataḥ prathamaḥ kalpo na ghaṭate.*[9]

9. Vīrarāghavācārya, 1941, p. 194.

For our present purpose something is a distinct category if it is not reducible to any one of the seven categories of things which the Vaiśeṣikas admit. According to the Vaiśeṣikas there are six fundamental kinds of things (*padārtha*s) which are experienced as existing (*astibuddhi-viṣaya*). Sometimes we have belief of the form "x is not" (*nāsti buddhi*). In such belief we know the negative fact called *abhāva*. So the Vaiśeṣikas admit a seventh category (*padārtha*) known as *abhāva*. The belief "x is not" or "Here there is no jar" knows the absence (*abhāva*) of x or jar. Now to prove that similarity (*sādṛśya*) is a distinct category (or different ontological kind) the Prābhākaras must show that *sādṛśya* is none of the six *bhāva padārtha*s and also it is not included in *abhāva padārtha*. This they cannot show on the basis of perceptual evidence or perception. The Prābhākaras can however supply an inference to prove that similarity is the eighth category. The inference may take this form: similarity is none of the seven *padārtha*s because it resides in Absence or in Universal. The point of the argument is this. This argument shows that similarity is something other than the seven categories and so the Prābhākaras admit it as the eighth category. For the knowledge of this eighth category, similarity, the Prābhākara Mīmāṁsakas admit *upamāna* as a distinct *pramāṇa*.

If now we want to reject their theory of *upamāna* we should be able to discover the defects in the argument of the Prābhākaras which is sketched above. We can also reject their theory if we can prove on independent ground that *sādṛśya* is not a separate category or that knowledge of *sādṛśya* does not require a separate source of knowledge. Udayanācarya offers an independent argument here to prove that *sādṛśya* is not a distinct category. His argument is based on his acceptance of the Vaiśeṣika scheme of categories according to which there are only six positive and one negative categories. He argues thus. There are basically only two kinds of *padārtha*s, positive (*bhāva*) and negative (*abhāva*). Therefore for a thing there are only four possibilities. It is (i) positive or (ii) it is negative; or (iii) it is both positive and negative; or (iv) it is neither positive nor negative. Now (iii) cannot be true; similarity or any other thing cannot be both positive and negative. If a thing is both a positive fact (*bhāva*) and a negative fact (*abhāva*) then the thing will be self-contradictory in nature. Positive and negative (*bhāva* and *abhāva*) are exclusive of each other. It will be contradiction to say about anything (*sādṛśya*) that it is both positive and negative.[10] The last alternative or (iv) cannot also be true. We cannot say that *sādṛśya* is *neither* positive *nor* negative. The positive and negative — the *bhāva* and the *abhāva* are logically mutually opposed or exclusive and they are jointly exhaustive. So if something is not positive then it must be negative, and if it is not negative then it must be positive. We cannot say of a thing that it is neither positive nor negative. Because the positive and negative existents are mutually exclusive (jointly exhaustive and mutually exclusive) there cannot be a third possibility.[11] Two of the four possibilities must be rejected. Of the remaining two possibilities, similarity cannot be of the nature of absence. For we experience similarity in the way in which we experience positive facts like tables, chairs, etc. That is, similarity is experienced in the way positive entities are experienced. All these are acceptable to the Prābhākara Mīmāṁsakas. For the Prābhākaras also say that similarity is a positive kind of entity. But the Naiyāyikas think that *dravya, guṇa, karma, sāmānya, viśeṣa* and *samavāya* are the only (six) positive kinds of things. The Prābhākaras hold that similarity is an additional or seventh (from the Vaiśeṣika point of view) kind of positive entity. Udayana rejects this. He says if similarity is characterized by quality then it is nothing more than a substance (the first category). For only substance can have quality or *guṇa*.[12] If the

10. *naikatāpi birudhānāmuktimātra virodhataḥ.* — Udayanācārya, *Nyāyakusumāñjaliḥ*, 3.8.

11. *paraspara virodhe hi na prakārāntarasthitiḥ* — *Nyāyakusumāñjaliḥ*, 3.8.

12. Perhaps there is only one exception.

Prābhākaras want to say that *sādṛśya* is an additional eighth category, then they must say that it is other than substance also. But then they will have to say that similarity is not characterized by quality. But similarity has quality (*saguṇa*) or it does not have quality (*nirguṇa*). Suppose similarity is not the seat of quality (it is *nirguṇa*) and other than substance. It has then two possibilities. It is either the seat of *sāmānya* (*sāmānyādhikaraṇa*) or it is not the seat of *sāmānya*. If the first is true (and similarity is both different from substance and a seat of *sāmānya*) then there are two possibilities for similarity. It must be either *guṇa*, i.e. quality, or motion (*karma*). If similarity is neither the seat of quality nor the seat of *sāmānya* then it is other than the first three of the six positive categories. For the first three categories (substance, quality and motion) have either *guṇa* or *sāmānya*. Only *dravya* has *guṇa* and all the three have *sāmānya*. Similarity which is different from the first three categories is either a superstratum (*āśrita*) in some substratum (*āśraya*) or it is not *āśrita*. If it is not *āśrita* then it is included in the sixth positive category, i.e. *samavāya*. If on the other hand similarity is a superstratum (*āśrita*) then there are two possibilities. Its substratum is *only one* entity in which it inheres or it inheres in *more than one* substrata. If the first alternative is true then similarity is the same as *viśeṣa*. If the second is true then it is *sāmānya*. Thus Udayana shows that *sādṛśya* cannot be an additional (*atirikta*) *padārtha*. Anything which is a genuine entity must fall within one or the other of these seven categories. These seven categories fall into two groups, *bhāva* and *abhāva*. So if *sādṛśya* is to be admitted it must be either positive or negative fact. It cannot be something over and above these two. It is not negative so it must be positive. And as a positive entity it must belong to any one of the six categories. So it cannot be said to have some independent existence. Naiyāyikas or the Vaiśeṣikas are right when they do not admit similarity as an independent existent (*atirikta padārtha*).

The Bhāṭṭas also do not admit *sādṛśya* to be an additional entity. They have offered many other arguments to show why *sādr̥śya* cannot be admitted to be an additional *padārtha*. Gaṅgeśa has considered detailed discussion of this Bhāṭṭa view in his *Upamānacintāmaṇi* along with his own view.

We should also discuss another point. If *sādr̥śya* is one of the six (or seven), which one is it? Can it be *sāmānya*? Can it be *dravya*? And so on. Naiyāyikas and Bhāṭṭas have to answer these questions also.

Now if similarity is not an independent existent then we do not need to admit any independent *pramāṇa* like *upamāna* for the knowledge of it. At least the Prābhākara Mīmāṁsakas will not be in a position to say that because there is such an independent existent as similarity so for the knowledge of such similarity an independent *pramāṇa* like *upamāna* must be admitted.

Bhāṭṭa Mīmāṁsakas as well as Naiyāyikas admit *upamāna* as an independent source of knowledge. Bhāṭṭas do not believe that similarity is an independent category (*svatantra padārtha*). But they, like the Nyāya-Vaiśeṣika philosophers, admit that similarity is constituted by a number of properties which are common to many things (*bhūyo-sāmānya dharmatvam*). So from the objection that similarity is not an independent existent, it does not follow that *upamāna* need not be admitted. At least on this ground *upamāna* cannot be discarded.

Even a Naiyāyika does not say that we do not have experience of similarity. The Bhāṭṭas think that experience of similarity is a distinctive type of cognitive experience, though similarity is not a distinctive kind of entity. They say that we need to admit a *pramāṇa* like *upamāna*, to account for some knowledge of similarity. The Naiyāyikas also think that we need to admit *upamāna* as a separate *pramāṇa*. But this we need to account for the knowledge of the (meaning) relation which a word bears to the corresponding thing. So far the position of the four major schools of philosophers may be represented in the table shown here.

School	*Upamāna (upamiti)*	*Object of upamāna*	*Sādṛśya or Similarity*	*Knowledge of Similarity*
Prābhākara	Is an independent *pramāṇa*	Similarity (*sādṛśya*)	An independent category	Can be had in certain cases only by *upamāna*
Bhāṭṭa	Is an independent *pramāṇa*	*Sādṛśya*	Not an independent category	Can be had in certain cases only by *upamāna*
Naiyāyika	Is an independent *pramāṇa*	(Meaning) relation of word-object	Not an independent category	Does not require *upamāna* as a source of it
Vaiśeṣika	Is reducible to inference	(Meaning) relation of word-object	Not an independent category	Does not require *upamāna* as source of it.

Both the Prābhākaras and Bhāṭṭas hold that through *upamāna* we have knowledge of a kind of similarity. This kind of similarity exists in an object which was perceived before but which is now being remembered. A thing has this kind of similarity in relation to another object which is now being perceived.

Udayanācārya has critically examined and reflected on Mīmāṁsā view of *upamāna* in the third chapter (*tṛtīya stavaka*) of his *Nyāyakusumāñjaliḥ*. In this chapter he examined the views of those opponents who think that *pramāṇas* like *pratyakṣa*, *anumāna*, etc. can prove that God does not exist. Now the Mīmāṁsakas do not believe in the existence of God. But they accept *upamāna*. Can they take the help of *upamāna* to prove the non-existence of God? They cannot. For according to both Bhāṭṭas and Prābhākaras *upamāna* gives us knowledge of some *sādṛśya* or similarity. The Bhāṭṭas moreover think that non-existence or *abhāva* is known by means of a sixth *pramāṇa* called *anupalabdhi*. Thus *upamāna* does not know the existence or non-existence of anything. *Upamāna* cannot prove non-existence of God. Some other atheist philosopher may try to disprove God even with the help of *upamāna-pramāṇa*. Udayana has shown this in his *Kusumāñjaliḥ*.

The definition of *upamāna* Gautama has offered in the *sūtra* 1.1.6 tells us that knowledge by analogy (*upamiti*) is the knowledge from known similarity (*prasiddha sādharmya*). Following this definition an atheist may seek to conclude that God does not exist. Hare's horn does not exist; and God is like hare's horn in many respects, so we know the absence of the existence of God from the known similarity, which God has with hare's horn. Nobody has seen a hare's horn so also nobody has seen God. Therefore as there is absence of hare's horn, so also there is absence of God. Udayana objected against the use of *upamāna-pramāṇa* to prove the non-existence of God. The way *upamāna* has been used to disprove God is unconvincing and very weak. Hare's horn is something which is absolutely fictitious (*asat*); it cannot be taken into consideration in the context of *prasiddha sādharmya*. It cannot be said that *sādharmya* of God with hare's horn is known. For there cannot be similarity with a fictitious thing. Such similarity cannot be known also. So it is not a wise decision to make the similarity with hare's horn a consideration for the proof of non-existence of God.

An atheist may say that similarity may be more convincingly used to show that God does not exist. Hare's horn may be fictitious but empirical beings like *jīva*s or human individuals are not unreal. God is similar to *jīva* for both have consciousness. One can say that like empirical beings like ourselves, God has only limited knowledge and power. How otherwise there could be so much evils in the world and sufferings of human beings? But a God whose knowledge and power are limited is not God. To deny unlimited knowledge or power to God is to say that there is no God. So we find here an important use of *upamāna*, such use will be made by the philosophers who do not admit the existence of God.

Against such use of *upamāna* Udayanācārya writes in his *Nyāyakusumāñjaliḥ* — *upamānanam tu bādhakam anāśaṅkanīyam*. It means, one should not think that *upamāna-pramāṇa* stands in the way of admitting the existence of God. *Upamāna* cannot prove the existence of God; it cannot disprove the existence of God also.

Following the Nyāya tradition Udayanācārya also shows that *upamāna* is not a *pramāṇa* which gives us the knowledge of similarity. The Naiyāyikas admit it as a *pramāṇa* for the knowledge of the relation between a word and its corresponding object. So this *pramāṇa* cannot be used to disprove the existence of God. It may be said from the side of the Mīmāṁsakas that Udayanācārya cannot say that as *upamāna* knows the meaning relation, so it cannot know similarity. For a *pramāṇa* can know both. It is the other side of their *pramāṇa saṁplava* theory. According to this theory different *pramāṇa*s can know the same thing. Here we argue from the side of the Mīmāṁsakas that different things can be known by the same *pramāṇa*. A *pramāṇa* can know more than one kind of thing. For example, perception can know fire, it can know firehood and also the warmth of fire. Udayana offers independent argument why *upamāna* cannot be admitted as the *pramāṇa* for the knowledge of similarity. If for the knowledge of similarity one admits an independent *pramāṇa* as the Mīmāṁsakas do then for the knowledge of dissimilarity also one should admit another independent *pramāṇa*. But such a procedure will violate the requirement of parsimony or logical economy. Besides, the Mīmāṁsakas do not admit a separate *pramāṇa* for the knowledge of dissimilarity. If they can admit knowledge of dissimilarity without admitting a separate *pramāṇa* for it, then let them admit knowledge of similarity without admitting *upamāna* as a separate *pramāṇa*.

If a Mīmāṁsaka admits a separate *pramāṇa* for the knowledge of dissimilarity then the number of *pramāṇa*s according to the Prābhākara Mīmāṁsakas will become six and according to the

Bhāṭṭa Mīmāṁsakas the number will become seven. But that will be against the established Mīmāṁsā position. The Mīmāṁsakas have already admitted *arthāpatti pramāṇa*. They can say that the knowledge of similarity will be explained by *upamāna* and the knowledge of dissimilarity will be explained by *arthāpatti*. But against this the simple answer of the Naiyāyikas will be that if *arthāpatti* can give us knowledge of dissimilarity let it give us the knowledge of similarity also. No need for *upamāna*. So why then a Mīmāṁsā philosopher admits a separate *pramāṇa* for the knowledge of similarity. So *upamāna* in the Mīmāṁsaka sense of the term creates much difficulty in the system. According to the Naiyāyikas knowledge of similarity can be explained by *pramāṇa*s like perception, etc. But *upamāna* should be admitted as a separate *pramāṇa* for the knowledge of *śakti*.

III

But how does Udayanācārya or any other Naiyāyika propounds the view that for the knowledge of *śakti* one needs an independent *pramāṇa* called *upamāna*? Udayanācārya did not simply say that *upamāna* knows *śakti*. He has made a stronger statement. Perception, etc. are unable to give us the knowledge of the relation of *śakti* which *upamāna* gives. So *upamāna* must be admitted. According to him inability of perception, etc. justifies the acceptance of an independent *pramāṇa*; and this is *upamāna*.[13]

It has already been considered with reference to Gautama, Vātsyāyana, Uddyotakara and Vācaspati Miśra what is *upamāna*. It has also been discussed whether the knowledge by *upamāna* is a different kind of knowledge. Udayanācārya shows explicitly and in detail that the relation of *śakti* cannot be known by verbal

13. *pratyakṣāderasādhyatvāt upamānaphalaṁ biduḥ* — *Nyāyakusumāñjaliḥ*. 3.10. We shall later examine how strong really is this formulation. Can Udayana really mean that *śakti* cannot be known by any other means?

testimony (*śabda-pramāṇa*), etc. So *upamāna* is to be admitted for the knowledge of *śakti*. Udayanācārya categorically stated that for the knowledge of *śakti* other *pramāṇa*s are of no use and so *upamāna* becomes indispensable. Udayana's statement is bold and explicit. But it creates a problem. For a part of what he says goes against the views of the Naiyāyikas themselves. According to the standard Nyāya view there are at least eight sources for the knowledge of *śakti*.[14] These eight sources are grammar, *upamāna*, dictionary, statement of reliable persons, established usages, *vākyaśeṣa*, descriptive account and use in the context of familiar words. Among these sources *upamāna* is only one. How then being a Naiyāyika Udayanācārya propounds such a view that *śabda*, *anumāna*, etc. are not able to know the *śakti* relation. This part of what he says is difficult to accept. What he says in the other part, that *upamāna* is a source of knowledge of *śakti*, can be easily accepted.

But this problem can be resolved if we try to understand the real import of Udayanācārya's view. Udayanācārya's view is not that the other sources cannot give us the knowledge of *śakti*; *upamāna* alone is the *pramāṇa* for the knowledge of *śakti*. His view seems to be this: there are cases where knowledge of *śakti* is accountable only by *upamāna-pramāṇa*. *Upamāna* gives us knowledge of *śakti* in this case. Secondly *upamāna* gives us knowledge of no other thing. For example, a person is there who does not know which animal is called *gavaya*. He hears from a person P that *gavaya* is like cow. After some days he goes to a forest or similar place. He there perceives an animal which is similar to cow. He remembers what he heard previously. In other words he remembers the meaning of the sentence (*vākyārtha*). This is the *vākya* he heard before from P. It is called *atideśa vākya*. After he remembers the meaning of the *atideśa vākya*

---

14. *Śaktigrahaṁ vyākaraṇopamānakoṣāptavākyād vyāvahārataśca, vākyasya śeṣāt vivṛtervadanti sānnidhyataḥ siddha-padasya vṛddhāḥ* — quoted in Vishvanatha Panchanan, 1989, p. 266.

(or *atideśa vākyārtha*) he comes to know a particular relation of the word *gavaya* to the animal he is now perceiving. The knowledge he has is of the form "This (animal) is the denotation of the word *gavaya*." *Ayam gavaya padavācya*.[15] This knowledge cannot be the result of perception of similarity or memory of the meaning of the *atideśa vākya*. Udayanācārya even says that the knowledge of *śakti* in this case cannot be produced by *atideśa vākya* and *pratyakṣa* together (*samāhāra*). What is his argument against *samāhāra*? This has been stated in Note 16.

Both *atideśa vākya* and *sādṛśya* give us knowledge of similarity. This knowledge is necessary in this case for the knowledge of *śakti*. The ultimate resulting knowledge is knowledge by analogy or *upamiti*. Both perceptual and verbal knowledge *of similarity* are important conditions of *upamiti*. But these knowledges of similarity know *similarity*. They do not know *śakti*. *Upamiti* knows *śakti*. This knowledge of the relation of *śakti* which is produced jointly by so many conditions is regarded as a distinct kind of knowledge by the Naiyāyikas.

So the point of the Naiyāyikas or Udayanācārya is not that for the knowledge of *śakti* as such one needs *upamāna*. The point is, there are cases of knowledge of *śakti* (as we have just shown) where a distinct *pramāṇa* called *upamāna* is necessarily involved. Technically speaking, when after hearing *atideśa vākya* and perception of similarity one knows the relation of *śakti* one has the knowledge by analogy or by *upamāna-pramāṇa*. This *upamāna-pramāṇa* should also be taken as a distinct means. It is not perception and utterance put together. For Udayanācārya says, the utterance and the perception occur at different times.[16] The

---

15. *yathā goustathā gavaya iti śrutātideśa-vākyasya, go sadṛśam piṇḍam anubhavataḥ, smarataśca vākyārthaṁ ayam asau gavaya śabda vācya iti bhavati matiḥ.* — Udayana, 1941, p. 197.

16. *nāpi samāhāraphalam, vākyapratyakṣayorbhinnakālatvāt.* — Udayana, 1941, p. 197.

point of Udayanācārya then is that the knowledge of *śakti* in these cases cannot be explained by any other *pramāṇas*[17] like perception, inference or verbal testimony. So *upamāna-pramāṇa* must be admitted in the system as a separate means of knowledge.

We shall see presently why *śakti* in this case cannot be said to be knowable by perception. We shall soon examine, following Udayana, the claim of the opponent that *śakti* can be known by other *pramāṇas* like *anumāna, śabda* and the like. But before that we would like to consider also the views of the more radical opponent. These opponents would say the question whether *śakti* is known by *upamāna* or by some other *pramāṇa* does not arise. For there is no such thing or relation as *śakti*. To deny the need for *upamāna* in the case in question an opponent can say that there is no relation at all between the word *gavaya* and the animal *gavaya*. Or the opponent can say that the relation is there but its knowledge can be given by perception (particularly recognition), language (*śabda*) or inference.

Most of the philosophers belonging to different traditions believe that there is some kind of relation between words and the things which correspond them. So they will not adopt the first alternative to reject *upamāna* as a *pramāṇa*. Against those who will deny word-object relation we may offer the following argument. If words have no relation to things and yet they mean things then any word can mean anything.[18] But nobody will say "fire" if he wants to mean water. Here the author is not to consider the view of those who may hold that words bear no relation to things and they also do not mean things. For this view is paradoxical and against common sense and intuition.

---

17. One can say this because *vyākaraṇa, koṣa,* etc. all are reducible to the respective *pramāṇas* like (perception), inference or testimony, etc.
18. *asambaddhasya gamakatve ca atiprasaṅgāt.* — Śrīdhara Bhaṭṭa, 1963, p. 516.

Ratnakīrti brought almost this kind of objection which has already been discussed.

Now *śakti* is to be admitted as a relation which holds between words and the things they mean. Do we need to admit knowledge of this *śakti*? Let us take an example. Suppose there is a hot plate. It will burn my finger if I touch it. And it will burn whether we know it to be hot or do not know it to be hot. Similarly one may say that if there is the relation of *śakti* between a word w_1 and a thing t_1 then w_1 will mean t_1. It is not necessary that we should know the relation. If knowledge of *śakti* is not necessary then no *pramāṇa* for this knowledge is necessary. We shall not discuss this point here. But we shall state the Nyāya position. Naiyāyikas say that *knowledge* of *śakti* is necessary. They also hold that we have knowledge of *śakti*. Now there arises the question what is the source of this knowledge? If one takes the first alternative and states that one can have the knowledge without *upamāna* one must also explain what does then *upamāna* do. The point is this. Suppose one holds that the villager in our example comes to learn the meaning of the word *gavaya*, but he does not learn it from *upamāna*. If he does not know from *upamāna* then for the knowledge of *śakti* he does not need to hear the statement of analogy (*atideśa vākya śravaṇa*) or perceive similarity with cow in certain animal in the forest (*piṇḍa*). He also does not need to remember the meaning of the sentence heard. Are all these then useless?

The opponent perhaps means to say that *upamāna* is not necessary. Knowledge of *śakti* can be derived from either (a) sentence (*śabda*) or (b) *anumāna*. When the city dweller hears the *atideśa vākya* he derives knowledge of *śakti*. For this knowledge it is not necessary for him to go to forest and perceive either *gavaya* or cow-similarity. But if he goes to the forest and has that perception then he has a recognitive awareness of *śakti* which he already knows from *śabda*. Vardhamānopādhyāya in his *Prakāśa-Ṭīkā* on *Nyāyakusumāñjaliḥ* has this point following

Udayana.[19] We can explain this quoted sentence. The knowledge of *śakti* of the form "This animal is the meaning of the word *gavaya*" is *śābda*; it is derived from the utterance of the statement of analogy (*atideśa vākya*). The hearer actually had this knowledge when he first heard that sentence. Later when he saw an animal which resembles cow and remembers what he heard when he heard the *atideśa vākya* he had another knowledge: that cow-resembling thing (which I see now is what) I knew (from the utterance of *atideśa vākya*) to be the meaning of the word *gavaya*. This piece of knowledge is nothing but recognition (*pratyabhijñā*). It is a variety of perception. So in the Nyāya account of *upamāna* when the knower knows the *gavaya* as the meaning of the word *gavaya* after perception of *gavaya* and its similarity to cow he actually recognizes a certain animal to be the same as what he knew to be the meaning of the word. Thus he knows *śakti* from *śabda*. Then he has perception. Lastly he has recognition. He has no *upamiti*.

According to Varadarāja very old (*jaḍat*) Naiyāyikas held this view that *śakti* or *samaya* is known (in the cases in question) from *śabda* or language. To be more particular, in such cases one knows *samaya* form the statement of analogy *atideśa vākya* itself. Later on when the man is said to have awareness of the form this is the meaning of the word *gavaya* he actually has a recognitive awareness which really has the form *ayam asau*.[20] Udayana will criticize and reject this view later. But before that he has noted the view of another section of the opponents who hold that the knowledge of meaning relation, in the case in question, is actually a case of inference. One infers that the animal which resembles a cow is called *gavaya* from the fact that people

---

19. *yo go sadṛśa dharmī gavaya śabda vācyatayā avagataḥ taṁ sākṣāt karomī iti pratyabhijānāti ityarthaḥ* — Vardhamānopādhyāya, 1957, p. 378.

20. *nanu ca vākyādeva anena samayaḥ paricchinnaḥ . . . kevalamidānīm pratyabhijānātyayamasāviti.* — Udayanācārya, see also *Prakāśa*, 1957, p. 378.

use or apply (*prajujyate*) the word *gavaya* to this sort of animal. Varadarāja credits the *ādhunika* or modern thinkers with this view. He credited *jaḍat*-Naiyāyika with the other view.[21] This other view — that *śakti* is known from *vākya* — he referred not just to his old predecessors but to old Naiyāyika (*jaḍannaiyāyika*). This view, that *śakti* is known through inference, he refers to the modern or later (*ādhunika*). Who he has in mind is not very clear.

Since Udayana has noted this view, as one of the views of the opponents, it was surely older then Udayana. The *ādhunika* must be later then *jaḍannaiyāyika*. He may be Udayana himself or someone later than him or slightly older than him. Bhāsarvajña was a Naiyāyika (i) who was not very old (*jaḍat*), but (ii) he preceded Udayana.[22] He also (iii) held that there was no fourth *pramāṇa* called *upamāna*. Did he also (iv) believe that even in case of the meaning of the word *gavaya*, which we are considering here, the meaning is not known by *upamāna* but from inference? But Bhāsarvajña held that there are only three *pramāṇas*. *Evam etāni trīṇyeva pramāṇāni*.[23] He held *upamāna* in question is actually *śabda*. He also held that Gautama rejected the reduction of *upamāna* to *anumāna* but not to *śabda*.[24] Even if nobody actually held that *upamāna* is *anumāna* one could hold this view. One could believe that in the case under consideration, the knowledge of the meaning of the word *gavaya* is a case of inference. One infers this relation from the linguistic practice (*prayoga*).

Now the inference which is involved here may be formulated in the following way. What has the generic property *gavayatva* is the meaning of the word *gavaya*; because it has similarity with

---

21. Varadarāja, 1957, p. 378.
22. Gopinath Kaviraj, 1982, pp. 3-4, 116.
23. Bhāsarvajña, 1968, p. 417.
24. Ibid, p. 425.

cow, *gavayatva viśiṣṭo dharmī gavaya-pada vācya, go sadr̥śatvāt*. The inferential relation of *vyāpti* involved in this inference is wherever there is the similarity with *go* (*go sādr̥śya*) there is *gavaya padavācyatva* (or the property of being the meaning of the word *gavaya*). The inference appears to be correct. So it is thought that there is no need for *upamāna* for knowledge of *śakti*. We can discard *upamāna*.

Following Udayana two views of the opponents are discussed. The first group of opponents think that meaning of *gavaya* can be known from *atideśa vākya*, so we do not need *upamāna* as a separate *pramāṇa* for that. The second group of thinkers maintain that the meaning of *gavaya* can be known from inference. So we do not need *upamāna*. Udayana now shows that both *atideśa vākya* and inference can enable us to have the knowledge of *śakti*. But the form of this knowledge is the word *gavaya* refers to an animal which has *similarity* with cow and because it has *similarity* with cow. But the inference or *vākya* (*śabda*) does not know as the meaning of *gavaya* something which has the property of *gavayatva*. It knows as the meaning of *gavaya* something which is qualified by the property of being similar to cow (*go sadr̥śatva*). But to know the meaning of a word *gavaya* is to know as meaning a thing which has that property which is especially associated with the word *gavaya*. Such a property functions as a criterion of application (*pravr̥tti* or *prayoga nimitta*). Now the question is which of the two properties, viz. *gavayatva* or *go sadr̥śatva* may be taken as the criterion for the application of the word *gavaya*? The property which functions as criterion for the right application of a word is known as *pravr̥tti nimitta*. If *upamāna* is reduced to inference of meaning (*tat padavācyatva*) form similarity, then here *go sadr̥śatva* will be the *pravr̥tti nimitta*. But will it be right to take *go sādr̥śya* as the *pravr̥tti nimitta* or criterion of use of the word *gavaya*?

According to the Naiyāyikas the simpler property should be admitted as determinant (*avacchedaka*) of *śakyatā*. *Jāti* or universal property is simple because it is unanalysable. And where *jāti* can be found there the *jāti* will be the criterion of use of the relevant word. But *go sādṛśya* is an *upādhi* and not a *jāti*, so it cannot be the criterion. In the present case if one has the knowledge of *śakti* by *śabda* or *anumāna* then the criterion for use becomes *go sādṛśya* and not the *jāti gavayatva*. So according to Udayana inference of meaning from similarity cannot replace *upamāna*. It is also to add that the word *gavaya* refers to all the *gavaya*s and not to this *gavaya* only. *Gavayatva* is a property which all and only the *gavaya*s have. But animals other than *gavaya* can have *go sādṛśya*. So it will be wrong to take as *gavaya* anything which has *go sādṛśya*. But *śabda* or *anumāna*, i.e. testimony or inference cannot give us the thing, which has *gavayatva*, as the referent of the word *gavaya*. So such inference or *śabda* cannot be the substitute of *upamāna*. When *upamāna* knows the *gavaya* as the meaning or referent of the word *gavaya*, it knows as referent the *gavaya* insofar as it is qualified by the generic property *gavayatva*. The right mode of referring to *gavaya*s is to refer to them as animals having *gavayatva*. When one learns the meaning of the word by analogy one uses this word to refer to the animals having *gavayatva*. These animals may be easily recognized by their similarity with cow. In this case *upamāna* and no other *pramāṇa* can know as referent of the word *gavaya* what is qualified by *gavayatva*. And this *gavayatva* is the determining property (*avacchedaka dharma*) which determines the *gavaya* to be the referent (*vācya*) of the word *gavaya*.

The Naiyāyikas can also say that there are cases where *śabda* or *anumāna* presupposes *upamāna*. This shows that *upamāna* does not necessarily presuppose or involve *śabda* or *anumāna*. So *upamāna* must be admitted in the system. It cannot be reduced to anyone of the other three *pramāṇa*s. None of these three can replace *upamāna*.

Udayanācārya anticipates some replies. The reductionists may try to defend their position in the following way. Language (*atideśa vākya*) can do the job of *upamāna*. After hearing the sentence "*gavaya* is similar to cow" one can have the knowledge the animal (*gavaya*) which has *gavayatva* is the referent of the word *gavaya* or *gavayatvaviśiṣṭa* (*prāṇī*) *gavaya padavācya*. One can have this knowledge because the expression "similar to cow" directly signifies (through *śakti*) the property of resembling a cow; but it indirectly signifies (through *lakṣaṇa*) *gavayatva*. There is a standard example. One hears the utterance "Ghoṣa families reside or live on the Ganges" (*gaṅgāyām ghoṣā*). The listener here does not take the word Ganges in its literal and direct sense. In the literal sense the word means certain stream of flowing water. On a flowing stream a family cannot live. The listener therefore takes the word to mean "by the side of the Ganges," i.e. on the bank of the river Ganges. On this bank the Ghoṣa families live according to the speaker. In the same way the defender of the view that *śabda-pramāṇa* can do the job of *upamāna*, can say that from *śabda*, i.e. *atideśa vākya* one can know indirectly that the word *gavaya* means the animal which has *gavayatva*. This *gavayatva* then is the *vācyatāvacchedaka*. In short *atideśa vākya* contains the word *gosadṛśa* or the like. This literally and primarily means "similar to cow." But indirectly this expression means *gavayatvaviśiṣṭa* or the thing which has *gavayatva*.

Udayana cannot accept this defence. We cannot understand an expression in its extended or indirect sense unless there is a reason for that. We want to understand a word in its indirect meaning when there is reason why we cannot take it in its direct meaning. The reason is that if the expression is taken in its primary and direct meaning then the sentence in which it occurs cannot make any consistent sense. In such case we preserve the meaningfulness of the sentence by taking the expression in the secondary sense. In the example of the sentence "the Ghoṣas live on the Ganges" there is reason for taking the word "Ganges" in the indirect meaning. But such reason is not there in case of the word *gosadṛśa* in the sentence *gavaya* is *go sadṛśa* or *go sadṛśa gavaya*.[25]

Udayana concludes that neither testimony nor inference can know the meaning relation. More accurately they cannot give the knowledge of the meaning of the word like *gavaya* which *upamāna* gives. Perception also cannot know it. A city deweller, however, learns the meaning of the word *gavaya* if he is told that "*gavaya* is like cow" and if he later perceives *gavaya*. If perception, etc. cannot give this knowledge (*pratyakṣāderasādhyatvāt*) we should admit *upamāna* as source. As a consequence *upamāna* cannot be discarded. On the other hand *upamāna* reveals the meaning of *gavaya* as qualified by *gavayatva* which is needed as the criterion of use of the word. And so *upamāna* must be admitted.

We may summarize the ground for rejecting the view that *upamāna* can be reduced to *anumāna*. The inference as formulated above cannot enable us to know as referent of *gavaya* what has *gavayatva*. But we have this knowledge. So this knowledge must have been derived from some other source. This other source is *upamāna*.

The Vaiśeṣika philosophers may say that the previous *anumāna* failed to reveal the generic property *gavayatva* as *vācyatāvacchedaka* but they can offer another inference. It is an inference of the type called *sāmānyataḥ dṛṣṭa anumāna*. The inference can be formulated in the following way.

Gavayapadam sapravṛtti-nimittakaṁ, sādhupadatvāt. This means that the word *gavaya* has criterion of correct use (associated with it), as it has the property of being a well-formed and genuine word.

This inference also does not reveal the property *gavayatva* because *gavayatva* is not the *vyāpakatāvacchedaka dharma*, or the property as possessing which a thing is inferred. This inference

25. Udayanācārya, 1941, p. 199, verse 3.12.

reveals only *sapravr̥tti nimittakatva;* for that is the *vyāpakatāvacchedaka*. How can one say that one is able to know from the present inference something which is qualified by the generic property *gavayatva* is (the referent of) *gavaya?* Like the previous one this inference also fails to give us the sort of knowledge which *upamāna* gives us.

To revive the position the opponent may offer another inference that can be this:

> *gavaya padaṁ gavayatva pravr̥ttinimittakaṁ*
> *itarāpravr̥ttinimittakatve sati sapravr̥ttinimittakatvāt.*[26]

In this inference *gavayatva* figures as part of *sādhya*. So this inference may be accepted as capable of replacing *upamāna*. For, this inference yields the knowledge which *upamāna* is believed to yield. It yields the knowledge of the relation of *gavaya* to the animal *gavaya* as qualified by the property *gavayatva*.

But if we examine the inference very closely we find that this *vyatirekī* inference is defective. It involves the defect of *sādhyāprasiddhi*, because the *sādhya* involves *gavayatva* as *pravr̥tti nimitta*. But this has not been known earlier. We are examining how it may be known. So it cannot be made the *sādhya*. So the inference is defective or fallacious. We therefore come to this conclusion that *upamāna* cannot be reduced to inference.

When *anumāna* wants to do the job of so-called *upamāna* it is not able to reveal the *gavaya* which is qualified by *gavayatva* to be the referent of the word *gavaya*. If we carefully examine we will also find that the knowledge of the reference of names like *karabha* is obtained not from *śabda* but from *upamāna*. Haridasa Bhattacharya does not deny that in such cases statement of analogy or similarity is there. But the knowledge which is finally obtained is *upamiti* about the meaning relation which the name in question bears to the appropriate thing.

---

26. Haridasa Bhattacharya, 1962, p. 123.

Knowledge by disanalogy or *vaidharmya* may also be admitted as a special case of *upamāna*. We find Udayana's views about other use of *upamāna* also in his *Nyāyakusumāñjaliḥ*. One may be convinced that *upamāna* is a distinct *pramāṇa* and can yet say it is useless if one wants to prove the non-existence of God. We have shown earlier that some thinkers sought to deny the existence of God on the basis of God's analogy to those who are non-omniscient or non-omnipotent. For what resembled someone in respect of non-omniscience cannot be God.

In this connection Udayanācārya has said in his *Nyāyakusumāñjaliḥ* that the function of *upamāna-pramāṇa* is only to give the knowledge of the relation between word and its corresponding object, i.e. *saṁjñā-saṁjñi sambandha jñānam upamānasya phalam*. It is beyond the power and scope of *upamāna-pramāṇa* to tell us anything about the existence or non-existence of a thing. Of course, some philosophers think that *upamāna* can inform us of things other than meaning relation also. But still it may be held that it cannot yield knowledge of existence or non-existence.

Conclusion
Dishonoured by Philosophers?

I WISH to re-open the moot question in this concluding chapter: How, why and to what extent do philosophers really dishonour the notion of *upamāna* in Indian epistemology? We know that the theory of *upamāna* has a unique position in Indian epistemology. Most of the philosophical systems are very much negative regarding the acceptance of *upamāna*. Either they have reduced this to other *pramāṇa* or they have discarded this altogether. But this rejection, hesitation and partial acceptance also make us to think and re-think on the point that this is a very unique *pramāṇa* in the sense that it is accepted by both the more prominent realistic schools, viz. Nyāya and Mīmāṁsā. Of course, from within the system also, the theory of *upamāna* had to face many criticisms. The negative attitude of Bhāsarvajña of Nyāya tradition is an example. So the theory is accepted but also is disregarded and dishonourned in many ways. But do we have really the right to dishonour the theory when it is accepted by some philosophers who are very much honoured by the systems? In the Nyāya tradition, both Gautama and Gaṅgeśa are very much positive regarding this *upamāna*. Gautama clearly mentions *upamāna* with the other *pramāṇa*s in the *sūtra* 1.1.3 and gives the definition which is primarily required for the admission of any object (*padārtha*) in the *sūtra* 1.1.6. Gaṅgeśa in the same way has shown his positive support by writing *Upamānacintāmaṇi* which is a part of his monumental work *Tattvacintāmaṇi*. In the recent times, even the famous scholar Badrinath Shukla has written a detailed essay on *upamāna* and there he has supported the Nyāya view. Of course, the paper is unpublished as he presented the paper in a seminar before his death.[1] These are all very positive arguments regarding *upamāna*. And the moot question now becomes: do we really have the right to dishonour this unique source of the knowledge *upamāna*?

In this book, I have finally supported the theory of *upamāna* given by the different Naiyāyikas. I have extended the Nyāya view up to Udayana, the beginner of a new tradition of Nyāya. I have not dwelt here on the detailed analysis on the subject by Gaṅgeśa, our stalwart philosopher in the Navya-Nyāya tradition. However, even to Udayana, it becomes very clear how far *upamāna* is important, how it functions and what is the status of *upamāna*. I have made also the point clear that even when *upamāna* is not a *vastusādhaka pramāṇa*, it is indispensable in some use as *śakti-grāhaka* (to know the meaning relation). In such cases knowledge of the meaning relation without *upamāna* is impossible and all the other sources fail to give the knowledge of such meaning relation.

In this chapter I also wish to mention that finally I have supported the Nyāya theory of *upamāna* (NTU) but not the Mīmāṁsā theory of *upamāna* (MTU). I have not rejected the Mīmāṁsā theory unconditionally. It is normally expected that, before I reject the MTU, I should make a comparative study of NTU and MTU and then I should show that NTU is better than MTU. But, as stated earlier, in this case comparison of MTU and NTU is not possible. Because the use of the term *upamāna* is also deceptive. The two schools have introduced *upamāna* in two different senses. So the debate or controversy regarding *upamāna* is absolutely different from many other familiar philosophical disputes. Take, for example, the following case. When there is a controversy about the seat (*āśraya*) of *śakti*, the

1. Badrinath Shukla 1986.

Mīmāṁsakas take the position that universals like cowness *alone* are the seat of word meaning or *pada-śakti*. A part of the Nyāya position accepts that universals alone are not the seat of *śakti*.

Similarly, the Prābhākaras hold that *sādṛśya* is an independent category (of being); the Naiyāyikas, on the other hand, categorically deny this. These are some examples of straightforward controversies. The groups of philosophers in these cases are directly opposed to each other and their views are mutually exclusive. So both their views cannot be true.

Primarily I think that the controversy about *upamāna* is of the same nature, where a point is accepted by both the partners but differences occur. But when I enter into the debate or controversy relating to *upamāna*, I realize that the controversy between these two groups of philosophers is uniquely different. NTU and MTU are not two different and incompatible versions of a single theory of *upamāna*. For MTU is not a theory about how we learn word meaning. Similarly, NTU is not about how we know the similarity in imperceptible objects by the perceptible similarity. They are actually two different theories about two different things. NTU is a theory of how we learn the meaning of words in certain cases, e.g. *go-gavaya* case. MTU is a theory of how we know in certain cases, e.g. *go-gavaya* case, that the cow is similar to *gavaya*. How can we compare theories that are so different? There seems to be no common point. How can we make any comparative assessment?

We have considered some objections of the Mīmāṁsakas when we developed the Nyāya theory. Gaṅgeśa has considered the Mīmāṁsā position in minute details but finally criticized the MTU. Here as we are not considering the detailed discussion from Gaṅgeśa, I do not want to reject MTU altogether. I believe that MTU has also some good points. I have only tried to give some answer to the objections that were raised by the Mīmāṁsakas. And maybe my answer is partial as I am not considering here the position of Gaṅgeśa in detail.

Here this is also to note that the Mīmāṁsakas may not deny that sometimes similarity is used to teach word-meaning. They may also accept the Nyāya description of the process of knowledge of word-meaning by analogy. But they will say that if the knowledge of word-meaning by analogy is a process as described by the Naiyāyikas, then it is not different from the process of knowing from words or *śabda-pramāṇa*. But we would like to say first that according to NTU the process of *śakti-jñāna* involves the knowledge of the "go." For the process involves a statement (*atideśa vākya*) which involves reference to "go." Again the process involves a perception of similarity of "go" or the *upamāna*. So far the process of desiring the knowledge of *śakti* according to NTU may be called *upamāna-pramāṇa*.

But here is also some doubt. The Naiyāyikas themselves have raised a question. Is statement or verbal knowledge of analogy (similarity) necessary for *upamāna*? In his commentary on (*śabda*) *Cintāmaṇi* of Gaṅgeśa, Mathurānātha, while discussing the point why *śabda* is considered after *upamāna* has discussed the point. One can say that *śabda* should be discussed before *upamāna* because in order to know word-meaning by analogy there must first be *śabda-pramāṇa*, namely, *atideśa vākya*. Mathurānātha here answers this objection and defends Gaṅgeśa (and generally the Nyāya position) way of ordering the *pramāṇas*. He says that it is possible that in answer to the question "what is like *gavaya*?" (*kidṛk gavaya*), nobody utters a statement of analogy. Instead, a picture of *gavaya* is shown to the inquirer. Here *upamiti* or *upamāna* (perception of similarity) is not preceded by *vākya* or *atideśa vākya*.[2] If this defence of Mathurānātha is accepted, then there are cases where *atideśa vākya* is not employed. So it makes the point clear that in some cases knowledge of *śakti* is not preceded by *atideśa vākya* or the

2. Mathurānātha, 1990, vol. IV, part I, p. 4. There is a long and interesting discussion on this point. See also Rucidatta, 1991, p. 1.

knowledge of *atideśa vākya*. Here the process of *śakti-jñāna* does not involve *upamāna*. So the process of *śakti-jñāna* cannot rightly be described as *upamāna*. If *atideśa vākya* is a necessary part of knowing *śakti* in *go-gavaya* case, then we can say that the process is *upamāna*.

It seems on the other hand that the Mīmāṁsakas use the word *upamāna* in the sense of the opposite of *upameya*. Secondly, they use the word *upamāna* as the act of knowledge of comparison. Both these senses are supported by dictionary. Accordingly, it can be said that Mīmāṁsā theory of *upamāna* is primarily a theory of comparison. It aims at explaining how we can know the *upamāna* in cases like *go-gavaya* or *āgneya-saurya*. In an act of comparison, the *upameya* is the thing which is compared. The *upamāna* is the thing with which some other thing is compared. Now a theory about the thing which is *upamāna* may legitimately be called a theory of *upamāna*. Therefore the Mīmāṁsā sense of *upamāna-pramāṇa* is quite legitimate. Accordingly, in *go-gavaya* case *go* is *upamāna*. This *go* is not perceived. The knower in this case is perceiving the *gavaya* and the *go* is in the city. There is no condition of inferential knowledge here and the Mīmāṁsakas do not take *atideśa vākya* to be a necessary condition. Parthasarathi Mishra does not even mention *atideśa vākya* in his statement of Mīmāṁsā view of *upamāna*.[3] In addition to this, the Mīmāṁsakas accept *upamāna* as the act or knowledge of comparison. So it is now clear that Mīmāṁsā theory of *upamāna* is primarily a theory of comparison. And so it is called the theory of *upamāna*. Using the language and technique of Navya-Nyāya we may show the *ākāra* (form) of this knowledge of *upamāna*. It is *upamāna viṣayaka, upameya pratiyogikasādṛśya prakāraka jñānam*. Or the *ākāra* is *gavaya sadṛśī gauḥ*. Further this knowledge is caused by another knowledge. This knowledge has three features: (1) It is perceptual, (2) it has

3. Parthasarathi Mishra, 1913, p. 208.

a *upameya* (*gavaya*) for its subject, and (3) it has *upamāna*, i.e. (*go*) *pratiyogika sādr̥śya* as predicate.

A Naiyāyika may not reject MTU as described above. They may agree that sometimes we may have *upamāna viśeṣyaka jñānam* caused by *upameya viśeṣyaka jñānam*. But they themselves are not interested in the question how in cases like *go-gavaya*, we may know the *upamāna*. The Naiyāyikas are more interested in the question how the knowledge of similarity with the *upamāna* helps us in knowing the reference of the name of the *upameya padārtha*. From the philosophical point of view the semantic question "How the reference of a certain term is determined (in certain context)?" is more important. But why is the theory which deals with the semantic called a theory of *upamāna*? The reason is this. What distinguishes a pair of things as the pair which comprises *upamāna* and *upameya* is that the things resemble each other. Utilizing one's knowledge of similarity between a pair of resembling things, one may teach word-meaning to another man. This other man is one who knows one of the things of the pair (*go-gavaya*) and its name (go) but he does not know what is the meaning of the name of the other thing in the pair, viz. the *gavaya* (bison).

But are we really justified in calling the Nyāya theory of knowledge of *śakti* as the theory of *upamāna*? Here the resulting knowledge is the knowledge of the reference of the name of the *upameya padārtha*; it is the knowledge of *gavaya pada vācyatva*. And this knowledge, as we have mentioned earlier, results from a perception and memory. The perception has the following form. It is *upameya* (*gavaya*) *viśeṣyaka upamāna* (*go*) *pratiyogika-sādr̥śya prakāraka jñānaṁ*. This is the same as in MTU. For there also perception of *sādr̥śya* is admitted. The form of the memory causing the *śakti-jñāna* here is determined by the form of the *atideśa vākya*. For, this memory is the memory of the content of the *atideśa vākya*. This *atideśa vākya* again involves the names of both *upamāna* and *upameya*. Therefore *upamāna-upameya* and their knowledge are all through present in the Nyāya theory of *padaśakti-jñāna* in the *go-gavaya* case. Hence we find justification in describing this theory as the theory of *upamāna*.

And finally, it can be stated now that the knowledge of *śakti* (word-meaning relation) in some cases is so different that it cannot be explained neither by the admitted *śakti-grāhaka*s nor by the different *pramāṇa*s. So *upamāna* as a *pramāṇa* for *śaktigraha* (knowledge of meaning relation) makes its unique position in the scheme of *pramāṇa*s admitted by the Naiyāyikas and in Indian epistemology.

Now, therefore, it is clear how, i.e. in which way NTU is dishonourned by the internal and external critics and also why the critics are so much negative regarding NTU. But finally we come to the end by saying that the uniqueness of *upamāna* was realized by both Gautama and Gaṅgeśa and also many others; so the *upamāna* as a *pramāṇa* is admitted with all other *pramāṇa*s and cannot be dishonourned. Rather the scholars need to provide much concentration on this source and should honour the dishonoured.

Bibliography

Annaṁbhaṭṭa or Annaṁbhaṭṭopādhyāya, *Tarkasaṁgrahah* with *Dīpikā*, ed. with his own translation and elucidation in English by Gopinath Bhattacharya, Kolkata: Progressive Publishers, 1976.

Aparārkadeva, *Nyāyamuktāvalī* on *Nyāyasāraḥ* of Bhāsarvajña. See Bhāsarvajña, 1961.

Bhāsarvajña, *Nyāyasāraḥ*, ed. Subrahmanya Śāstrī with the commentaries of *Nyāyamuktāvalī* by Aparārkadeva and *Nyāyakalānidhi* by Ānandānubhavācārya, Chennai, 1961.

———, *Nyāyasāraḥ*, with the author's own commentary *Nyāyabhūṣaṇam*, ed. Swami Yogindrananda, Varanasi: Chowkhamba Vidya Bhavan, 1968.

———, *Tarkasaṁgraha* with *Dīpikā*, ed. with *Adhyāpanā Ṭīkā* (in Bengali) by Narayan Chandra Goswami, Calcutta: Sanskrit Pustak Bhandar, 1390 (Baṅgābda).

Bhattacharya, Gopinath, *Translation and Elucidation of Tarkasaṁgraha*, see Annaṁbhaṭṭa, 1976.

Bhattacharya, Haridasa, *Vivṛtti* (*vyākhyā*) in Sanskrit on *Nyāyakusumāñjaliḥ* (*kārikā*) by Udayanācārya, ed. with Hindi elucidation by Pandit Vishveshwar Siddhanta Siromani, Chowkhamba, 1962.

Bhaṭṭācārya, Jīvānanda Vidyāsāgara (ed.), *Mīmāṁsā Darśanam*, Calcutta, 1883.

Bhatta, Jaypuri Narayan, *Nyāyasiddhi* on *Prakaraṇapañcikā* in Śālikanātha, 1961.

Kumārila Bhaṭṭa, *Ślokavārttikam* with *Nyāyaratnākara* by Parthasarathi Mishra, ed. Svami Dvarikdas Shastri, Varanasi: Tara Publicaitons, 1978.

Umbeka Bhaṭṭa, (Bhaṭṭombeka), *Tātparyaṭīkā* on Kumārila's *Ślokavārttika*, ed. S.K. Ramanath Shastri, University of Madras, 1940.

Chandra, Prabha, *Prameya Kamala Mārtaṇḍa*, ed. Mahendra Kumar Shastri, Published by Satyabhamabai Pandurang, Mumbai: Nirnaya Sagar Press, 2nd edn., 1941.

Chandrakānta Tarkālaṁkāra, *Vaiśeṣikadarśanaṁ* (or *Vaiśeṣika bhāṣya*), Calcutta, 1869.

Chattopadhyay, Uma, "Is the Order of Four Pramāṇas justified in Nyāya System," in *Dimensions of Contemporary Sanskrit Research*, ed. Ujjala Jha and Arun Mishra, Delhi: New Bharatiya Book Corporation, 2008.

Dharmakīrti, *Pramāṇavārttikam*, ed. Svami Dvarikdas Shastri with the commentary *Vṛtti* of Manorath Nandin, Varanasi: Bauddha Bharati, 1968.

———, *Nyāyabindu*, ed. with Dharmottara's commentary *Nyāyabindu Ṭīkā* and Durveka's sub-commentary *Dharmottarapradīpa* by Pandit Dalsukhbhai Malvania, Patna: Kasi Prasad Jayaswal Research Institute, 1955.

———, *Pramāṇavārttikam*, ed. Rāhul Sāṅkṛtyāyana with Prajñākaragupta's *Pramāṇavārttikabhāṣyam* or *Vārttikālaṁkāraḥ*, Patna: Kasi Prasad Jayaswal Research Institute, 1953.

Dharmottara, *Nyāyabindu Ṭīkā* in Dharmakīrti, 1955.

Dvivedin, Vindheshwari Prasad (ed.), *Praśastapāda Bhāṣya Ṭīkā Saṁgraha* (This collection of commentaries of *Praśastapāda Bhāṣya* includes *Kaṇāda Rahasya* and *Tarkālaṁkāra Bhāṣya Parīkṣā*), Benares: Chowkhamba Sanskrit Series, 1971.

Edwards, P. (ed.), *The Encyclopedia of Philosophy* (in 8 volumes), Macmillan Publishing Co., Reprint edition, 1972.

Guṇaratna, *Tarkarahasya Dīpikā* (a commentary on *Saḍdarśana Samuccaya* by Haribhadra), ed. L. Suali, Kolkata: The Asiatic Society, Reprint, 1986.

Gāgābhaṭṭa, *Bhāṭṭacintāmaṇi* (*Tarkapādaḥ*), ed. Pt. Surya Narayan Shukla, Benares: Chowkhamba Sanskrit Series Office, 1933.

Gaṅgeśopādhyāya, *Tattvacintāmaṇi* (Upamāna-Khaṇḍa), with the commentary *Prāgalbhī* by Pragalbhācārya, ed. Gourinath Shastri, Varanasi: Sampurnananda Sanskrit Visvavidyalaya, 1983.

———, *Tattvacintāmaṇi* (vols. I-IV), ed. Kamakhyanatha Tarkavagisa, with the commentaries *Māthurī, Kṛṣṇakāntī* (*Dipanī*), etc. Kolkata: Chowkhamba Sanskrit Pratisthan, Reprint, 1990.

———, *Tattvacintāmaṇi* (Upamāna-Khaṇḍa) with the commentary *Raśmicakra* by Gokulnatha Upadhyaya, ed. Pandit Ramsevaka Jha, Darbhanga: Kamesvarsimha Darbhanga Sanskrit Visvavidyalaya, 1983.

Gautama, *Nyāyadarśanam*, with *Bhāṣya, Vārttika, Tātparyaṭīkā* and *Vṛtti*, ed. Taranath Tarkatirtha, New Delhi: Munshiram Manoharlal Publishers Pvt. Ltd., 1985.

———, *Nyāyadarśanam*, ed. Anantalal Thakur with *Bhāṣya, Vārttika, Tātparyaṭīkā,* and *Pariśuddhi*, Darbhanga: Mithila Institute, 1967.

Gaurinath Shastri (ed.), *Kiranāvalī* (edited with his own elucidation in Bengali), Calcutta: Sanskrit Pustak Bhandar, vol. I 1935 and vol. II 1957.

Gopinath Kaviraja, *The History and Bibliography of Nyāya-Vaiśeṣika Literature*, Sampurnananda Sanskrit University, Varanasi, 1982.

Hemacandrācārya, *Pramāṇamīmāṁsā*, ed. Sukhlalji Sanghavi, Kolkata, 1939.

Jaimini, *Mīmāṁsāsūtra*, ed. with *Śabarabhāṣya* by Jīvānanda Vidyāsāgara, Kolkata, 1883.

Jayantabhaṭṭa, *Nyāyamañjarī*, ed. Pandit Surya Narayan Shukla, Varanasi: Chowkhamba Sanskrit Series Office, 1936 (Reprint 1971).

Jha, Durgadhar, Hindi translation of *Nyāyakandalī Ṭīkā* by Śrīdhara Bhaṭṭa. See Śrīdhara (Praśastapāda), 1963.

Jhalkikar, Bhimacharya, *Nyāyakosaḥ*, Poona: The Bhandarkar Oriental Research Institute, 1978.

Jñānaśrīmitra, *Jñānaśrīmitranibandhāvalī*, ed. Professor Anantalal Thakur, Patna: Kasi Prasad Jayaswal Research Institute, 1959.

Kālidāsa, *Raghuvaṁśam*.

Kamalākarbhaṭṭa, *Mīmāṁsā Kutuhalaṁ*, ed. with notes by Pattabhiram Shastri, Varanasi: Sampurnananda Sanskrit University, 1987.

Kamalaśīla, *Pañjikā*. See Śāntarakṣita, 1968.

Kaṇāda, *Vaiśeṣikasūtra* ed. with *Upaṣkāra* by Jibananda, Benares, 1889.

Kaviraja, Gopinath *The History and Bibliography of Nyāya-Vaiśeṣika Literature*, Varanasi: Sampurnananda Sanskrit University, 1982.

Krishnakanta Vidyavagisha, Dīpanī on *Upamānacintāmaṇi* ed., Kamakhyanath Tarkavagisha, Calcutta, 1987; reprinted by Delhi: Chowkhamba Sanskrit Pratisthan, 1990.

Kumar, Shiv, *Upamāna in Indian Philosophy*, Delhi: Eastern Book Linkers, 1980.

Matilal, Bimal Krishna, *Perception — An Essay on Classical Indian Theories of Knowledge*, Oxford: Clarendon Press, 1986.

Manorathanandin, *Vṛtti*, in Dharmakīrti, 1968.

Mishra, Durveka, *Dharmottarapradīpa* in Dharmakīrti, 1955.

Miśra, Prabhākara, *Bṛhatī* in Śabarasvāmī, 1934.

Mishra, Parthasarthi, *Nyāyaratnākara*, a commentary on Ślokavārttika of Kumārila. See Kumārila, 1978.

———, *Śāstradīpikā*, with Ramakrishna's commentary *Yuktisnehaprapūraṇī* and also with *Mayūkha Mālikā Ṭīkā*, ed. Pandit Lakshman Shastri Dravida, Varanasi: Chowkhamba Sanskrit Series, 1913.

Mishra, Ramakrishna, *Yuktisnehaprapūraṇī* in Parthasarathi, 1913.

Mishra, Śālikanātha, *Ṛjuvimalā Pañcikā* in Śabarasvāmī, 1934.

Miśra, Saṅkara, *Kaṇādarahasya* in Vindheswari Prasad Dvivedi, 1917.

———, *Kaṇṭhābharaṇam* on *Nyāyalīlāvatī* by Vallabhācārya, Varanasi: Chowkhamba Sanskrit Series, 1934.

———, *Upaskāra* on *Vaiśeṣikasūtra* in Praśastapāda 1930 (in this edition the copy of *Upaskāra* consulted by author was appended).

Miśra, Śālikanātha, *Prakaraṇapañeikā* with *Nyāyasiddhi* by Jaipuri Narayan Bhaṭṭa, ed. Subrahmanya Shastri, Benaras: Hindu University Varanasi, 1961.

Mishra, Sucharita, *Kāśikā*, a commentary on *Ślokavārttika* of Kumārila, ed. B.A. Ramaswami Shastri, Thiruvananthapuram: Anantasayan Visvavidyalaya, 1943.

Miśra, Vācaspati, *Sāṁkhyatattvakaumudī* with the commentary *Adhyāpanā* by Narayana Chandra Goswami, Kolkata, 1982.

———, *Tātparyaṭīkā* on *Nyāya Vārttika* of Uddyotkara, See Gautama, 1985.

Mukhopadhyay, P.K., "Cognitive Act", in *Journal of Indian Philosophy* 2 (1973), pp. 115-37 (ed. Bimal Krishna Matilal), Boston, USA: D. Reidel Publishing Company, 1973.

———, *Indian Realism — A Rigorous Descriptive Metaphysics*, Kolkata: K.P. Bagchi & Company, 1984.

Musahi, Tachikawa, *The Structure of the World in Udayana's Realism — A Study of Lakṣanāvalī and Kiraṇāvalī*, Boston, USA: D. Reidel Publishing Company, 1981.

———, *Tattvacintāmaṇi* (*Upamāna Khaṇḍa*) with the commentary *Prāgalbhī* by Pragalbhācārya, ed. Gourinath Shastri, Varanasi: Sampurnananda Sanskrit Visvavidyalaya, 1983.

Nārāyaṇa Bhaṭṭa or Nārāyana Paṇḍita, Mānameyodaya, Madras: Theosophical Publishing House, 1933 (edited with an English translation by Kumar Raja).

Nyayacharya, Madhusudan (ed.), Translation and exposition of *Sabdaśaktiprakāśikā* by Jagadiśa Tarkālaṁkāra, vol. I to vol. II, Kolkata: Sanskrit College, 1980.

Pañcānan, Viśvanātha Nyāya, *Bhāṣā-pariccheda*, with *Nyāyasiddhānta Muktāvalī*, ed. Pt. Panchanan Bhattacharya Shastri with *Muktāvalī Saṁgraha Ṭīkā*, 1377 (Baṅgābda).

———, *Nyāyasiddhānta-Muktāvalī*, ed. Hariram Shukla Shastri, Varanasi: Chowkhamba Sanskrit Sansthan, 1989.

Panse (Jha), Ujjala, "Jayanta on the Relation between Word and Meaning," *Relations in Indian Philosophy*, ed. V.N. Jha, Delhi: Sri Satguru Publications, 1992.

Potter, Karl (ed.), *Encyclopedia of Indian Philosophy*, Delhi: Motilal Banarsidass.

Pragalbhācārya, *Prāgalbhī*, a commentary on *Tattvacintāmaṇi* of Gaṅgeśa (Upamāna Khaṇḍa), ed. Gourinath Shastri, Varanasi: Sampurnananda Sanskrit Visvavidyalaya, 1983.

Prajñākaragupta, *Vārtikalaṁkāra* on *Pramāṇavārttika* in Dharmakīrti, 1953.

Prakasha, Rucidatta (on *Śabdacintāmaṇi* by Gaṅgeśa), ed. Prof. Sukharanjan Saha and Prof. P.K. Mukhopadhyay, Kolkata: K.P. Bagchi and Company, 1991.

Praśastapāda (Praśastadeva), *Padārtha-dharmasaṁgrahaḥ* (*Praśastapāda Bhāṣya*), ed. with *Nyāyakandalī* and Hindi translation by Durgadhar Jha, Varanasi: Varanaseya Samskrita Visvavidyalaya, 1963.

———, *Praśastapādabhāṣyam* ed. with *Sūkti-Setu* and *Vyomavatī* by Gopinath Kaviraj and Dhundiraj Shastri, Benares: Chowkhamba Sanskrit Series, 1930.

Mishra, Parthasarathi, *Nyāyaratnākara* on Ślokavārttikam, Varanasi: Tara Publications, 1978.

Rāmānujācārya, *Tantrarahasya,* ed. Shama Shastri and K.S. Ramaswami Shastri with English Introduction, Baroda Oriental Institute, 1956.

Ratnakīrti, *Ratnakīrtinibandhāvalī,* Tibetan Sanskrit Works Series, vol. III, ed. Professor Anantalal Thakur, Patna: Jayaswal Research Institute, 1957.

Rueidatta, *Prakāśa* (on Śabdaeintāmaṇi by Gaṅgeśa), (ed.) Professor Sukhoranjan Sahe and Professor P.K. Mukhopadhyay, Calcutta, K.P. Bagehi and Company, 1991.

Saptatīrtha, Bhutanatha, *Mīmāṁsā Darśanam* (in Bengali), Part I, Kolkata: Basumati Sahitya Mandir, 1345 (Baṅgābda).

Śabarasvāmī, *Bhāṣya* on *Jaiminisūtra,* ed. with Prabhākara Miśra's *Bṛhatī* and Śālikanātha Miśra's *Ṛjuvimalā Pañcikā* by S.K. Ramanath Shastri, University of Madras, 1934.

———, *Mīmāṁsā Bhāṣya*, ed. and published by Jivananda Vidyasagar Bhattacharya, Kolkata, 1883.

———, *Prakaraṇapañcikā* with *Nyāyasiddhi* by Jaipuri Narayan Bhatta, ed. A.

Subrahmanya Shastri, Varanasi: Banaras Hindu University, 1961.

Śāntarakṣita, *Tattvasaṁgrahaḥ*, ed. with the commentary, *Pañjikā* of Kamalaśīla by Swami Dwarikdas Shastri, Varanasi: Bauddha Bharati, 1968.

Shastri, Panchanan Bhattacharya, *Muktāvalīsaṁgraha* in Viśvanātha Nyāya Pañcānan, 1377 (Baṅgābda).

———, Translation and elucidation in Bengali of *Tarkasaṁgraha* by Annaṁ Bhaṭṭopādhyāya, Nababharat Publishers, 1393 (Baṅgābda).

———, *Nyāyaratnākara*, a commentary on *Ślokavārttika* of Kumārila Bhaṭṭa. See Kumārila Bhaṭṭa, 1978.

Shastri, Dvarikadas (Svami), ed., *Saḍdarśana-Sūtrasaṁgrahaḥ*, Sudhi Series, 5, Varanasi: Sudhi Prakashan, 1984.

Shastri, Pattabhiram, *Mīmāṁsānyāyamañjarī* with *Pariśiṣṭam*, Varanasi: Sampurnananda University, 1984.

Shastri, Ramaswami, ed. with his own introduction, *Kāśikā* by Sucharita Mishra, Trivandrum: Anantasayan Visvavidyalaya, 1943.

Shastri, Subrahmanya, Introduction to *Prakaraṇa Pañcikā* of Śālikanātha. See Śālikanātha, 1961.

Singh, B.N., *Indian Logic*, Varanasi: Asha Prakashan, 1986.

Shukla, Badrinath, "Navya-Nyāya mein upamāna-pramāṇa" (unpublished paper) presented in the seminar "Enterprise of Navya-Nyāya : A Tradition of Medieval and Modern Indian Logic", New Delhi: NISTADS, 1986.

Siromani, Raghunatha, *Avacchedakatva Nirukti*, ed. with his own commentary by Dattatreya Shastri, Varanasi, 1968.

Śrīdharācārya (Śrīdhara Bhaṭṭācārya), *Nyāyakandalī*, a commentary on *Padārthadharmasaṁgrahaḥ*. See Praśastapāda, 1963.

Śāstrī, Gourinath, (ed.), *Tattvacintamaṇi* (*Upamānakhanda*) with the commentary *Prāgalvī* by Pragalbhācārya, Varanasi, Sampurnananda Sanskrit Visvavidyalaya, 1983.

Tarkālaṁkara, Jagadīśa, *Śabdaśakti Prakāśikā* with *Kṛṣṇakānti* and *Prabodhinī*, ed. Pandit Dhundiraj Shastri, Varanasi: Chowkhamba Sanskrit Series Office, 1973.

———, *Sūkti* (a commentary on *Praśastapāda Bhāṣya*). See Praśastapāda, 1390.

Tarkatīrtha, Ananta, *Vaibhāṣika Darśana* (in Bengali), Calcutta.

Tarkavagisa, Mathuranatha, *Rahasya* (*ṭīkā*) on *Tattvacintāmaṇi*, in Gaṅgeśa, vol. IV, part I, 1990.

Tarkavagisa, Phanibhusan, *Nyāyadarśana*, containing translation and elucidation in Bengali of *Nyāyasūtra* and *Vātsyāyanabhāṣya*, Kolkata: West Bengal Book Board, 1981-1989.

Tarkavagisa, Phanibhusan, *Nyāya Paricaya* (in Bengali), Kolkata: West Bengal Book Board, 1978.

Udayanācārya, *Nyāyakusumāñjaliḥ*, ed. with two commentaries by Dharmadatta Jha, Varanasi: Chowkhamba Sanskrit Series Office, 1957.

———, *Nyāyakusumāñjaliḥ* (*Karikā* and *Vṛtti*), ed. with his own commentary *Vistāra* by T. Vīrarāghavācārya Śiromaṇi, Tiruvadi, 1941.

———, *Nyāyakusumāñjaliḥ* (*Kārikā*), ed. with Haridāsa Bhaṭṭācārya's Sanskrit commentaries and his own Hindi commentary by Vishveshvar Siddhanta Shiromani, Varanasi: Chowkhamba Vidya Bhavan, 1962.

———, *Nyāyakusumāñjaliḥ*, ed. with two commentaries by Sri Dharmadatta Jha, Varanasi: Chowkhamba Sanskrit Series Office, 1957.

———, *Tātparyaṭīkā* on *Nyāya-Vārttika* of Uddyotakara. See Gautama, 1985.

Uddyotakara, *Vārttika* on *Vātsyāyana Bhāṣya* in Gautama 1967 and 1985.

Vallabhācārya, *Nyāyalīlāvatī*, ed. with the commentaries of Vardhamānopādhyāy, Śaṅkara Miśra and Bhagīratha Ṭhakkura (and with his own notes, etc. by Harihara Shastri) by Dhundiraja Shastri, Benares: Chowkhamba, 1934.

Varadācāri, V., "Nyāya-Vaiśeṣika Tradition," in *Philosophical Essays — Prof. Anantalal Thakur Felicitation Volume*, ed. Ramaranjan Mukhopadhyay, Kolkata: Sanskrit Pustak Bhandar, 1987.

Varadarāja, "Bodhini" in Padmaprasada Upadhyaya and Dhundiraj Shastri (eds.), *The Nyāya Kusumāñjaliḥ*, Varanasi, Chowkhamba Sanskrit Series, Chowkhamba, Kashi: Kashi Sanskrit Series, no. 30, 1957.

Vardhomānopādhyāya, *Prakāśa*, a commentary on Udayana's *Savṛtti Nyāyakusumāñjaliḥ*. See Udayana, 1957.

Vātsyāyana, *Bhāṣya* on *Nyāyasūtra*. See Gautama 1967, 1985.

Vidyabhushan, Satischandra, *A History of Indian Logic*, Delhi: Motilal Banarsidass, rpt., 1978.

Vīrarāghavācārya, T., *Kusumāñjaliḥ Vistāra*. See Udayana, 1941.

Viśvanātha, *Vṛtti* on *Nyāyasūtra*. See Gautama, 1985.

Vyomaśivācārya, *Vyomabatī* in Praśastapāda, 1930.

Index